ADVANCE PRAISE FOR
ONE BREAD, ONE BODY

Vital
Worship,
Healthy
Congregations

One Bread,
One Body

EXPLORING
CULTURAL DIVERSITY
IN WORSHIP

C. Michael Hawn

Foreword by
Justo L. González

An Alban Institute Book
ROWMAN & LITTLEFIELD
Lanham • Boulder • New York • Toronto • Plymouth, UK

First Rowman & Littlefield paperback edition 2014

Published by Rowman & Littlefield
4501 Forbes Blvd, Suite 200, Lanham, MD 20706
www.rowman.com

10 Thornbury Road, Plymouth PL6 7PP, United Kingdom

Library of Congress Cataloging-in-Publication Data Available

ISBN 13: 978-1-56699-277-0 (pbk: alk. paper)

♾™ The paper used in this publication meets the minimum requirements of American National Standard for Information Sciences—Permanence of Paper for Printed Library Materials, ANSI/NISO Z39.48-1992.

Printed in the United States of America

Cover and text design by Keith McCormick and Katty Montenegro Sakoto. Cover illustration by Tacoumba Aiken.

For Aaron and Lindsay,
partners in song

CONTENTS

PART III. Moving toward Culturally Conscious Worship

FIGURES

FOREWORD

I have often said that I live by worship, and yet it is killing me! With just a bit more exaggeration, one could also say that the church lives by worship, yet its worship is killing it! Worship, witness, and service are the three essentials of the life and mission of the church. Yet too often, particularly in mainline denominations such as my own, worship seems to have lost its flavor—or, almost as bad, has become the battleground for warring groups apparently convinced that the salvation of the church will be brought about by a more "contemporary" form of worship or by returning to supposedly "traditional" forms.

Such debates have led to the publication of an enormous number of books and manuals on worship. Most of these are how-to books. They seem to take for granted that we already know what worship should look like, and therefore they simply barge ahead with suggestions and testimonials about how to do it. Quite often, such books build on the experience of a "successful" church—one that gathers a large number of worshipers and has amassed a wealth of buildings and other resources. Apparently there is no question but that the standards of success dominant in our culture are the standards by which to measure ecclesiastical success. Thus, while such books offer a great number of suggestions—some perhaps quite valuable—they offer no theological guidelines for measuring our worship practices by the standard of the gospel.

On the other hand, a number of profound and sometimes inspiring books discuss the *why* of worship. They seek to provide theological criteria by which worship may be guided and judged.

Some review the history of worship in ancient Israel, in the early church, and in times past. They offer a wealth of information and much material for reflection. But all too often they leave us wondering, What do we do now? This is not just a practical shortcoming. It is also theological. By speaking of worship in general, such studies fail to realize that worship, like theology, is always the worship of a particular group of Christians, in a particular place, at a particular time—in other words, that worship, like theology, is always contextual. The worship of a particular congregation is part of the worship of the entire church catholic; but it is also the worship of this particular congregation in this particular setting.

Precisely by combining the why and the how-to, Michael Hawn and his colleagues at Perkins School of Theology allow us to think about worship in ways that are both theologically informed and shaped by the emerging circumstances of our society, both catholic and contextual. They lead us into this new way of thinking by focusing on the paradigm of Pentecost and offering significant insights into the character of worship that is truly Pentecostal— "Pentecostal" not in the denominational sense, but in the sense of being patterned after the church's experience at Pentecost.

In this regard, the first chapter of this book is in itself worth more than many larger tomes on worship. Hawn weaves the experience of Pentecost with sociological and anthropological studies showing how different cultures approach matters such as time, space, relations, and power. Thus, Christian worship is placed within a dual context: its inner, permanent nature as the work of the Spirit in the church, and the growing multicultural society in which our churches find themselves. We do not travel a one-way street from Acts 2 to our present situation. Nor does the street run one way in the other direction, beginning with our present situation and then trying to find justification in the biblical text. Rather, we move around a circle. The biblical text shapes our reading of our situation, and our situation shapes the reading of the text. The present and growing multicultural context is read in the light of Pentecost, and Pentecost is also read in the light of the multicultural context.

When we look at the story of Pentecost in this manner, we see is a story of extraordinary communication. We have always known that Pentecost is a miracle of communication. What we are beginning to discover, however, thanks to our current multicultural setting, is that the miracle entailed a particular sort of communication.

Indeed, if the goal had been only a matter of ensuring that all those present in Jerusalem could understand the preaching of the disciples, the Spirit had two options. One would have been to enable all those present to understand the language of the apostles. In a way, this would have required a lesser miracle, for those who had come to Jerusalem from Cappadocia, Phrygia, and other lands were presumably able to function in the Holy City. The text itself implies that they were able to communicate in some common language, for we are told that they spoke among themselves and commented on what was taking place. Yet, this was not the option that the Spirit chose. Rather than allowing the entire crowd to understand the language of the disciples, the Spirit made it possible for everyone to hear "each in their own tongue."

This obviously required a greater miracle, but it also led to fuller communication. In its root meaning, "communication" was understood to involve much more than the transfer of ideas from one mind to another. The Latin *communicare* actually means "to make common," that is, to share. (This same meaning also lies at the heart of the much used and abused *koinonia*, which means "to share, to have in common," or *koinos*.) To communicate is to share. And to a degree that too often we fail to acknowledge, to share is to relinquish control. Thus, true communication of the gospel means that it is no longer the exclusive property of the original messenger, but is now fully shared with the other. When the Spirit let the various people in Jerusalem hear the message in their own tongues, the Spirit also paved the way for a church that would no longer be controlled by the original disciples in Jerusalem or their cultural successors. The Spirit was saying that the language and culture of a Cappadocian, Phrygian, or Mesopotamian were just as capable as the language and culture of the disciples of bearing and expressing the message of the gospel. What happened at Pentecost is not only that more people believed and eventually thousands were added to the church. What happened at Pentecost was that at the very moment of its birth, the church was crossing cultural boundaries in such a way that it would be just as much at home on one side of the boundary as on the other. The church is multicultural by birth.

If all this is true, then Pentecostal worship must cross boundaries, so that those from one side of the boundary will be as much at home in the church as those from the other side. And this in turn implies that in Pentecost worship, the gospel will always be shared in such a way that power and control are also shared and even relinquished by its previous owners.

This has been a hard lesson for the church to learn—or an easy one to forget through the ages. Examples abound. Perhaps the most glaring one was the insistence of the Roman Catholic Church that all must use Latin, even long after it had become a dead language and the modern languages had come to the foreground, and even in distant lands where Latin had never been spoken. But this is not only a Roman Catholic problem. It is also a problem for many of our so-called mainline denominations, where we constantly speak of the need to welcome diverse people and respond to the challenge of new cultures in our midst—and where membership continues to decline, and we make little progress in attracting new constituencies. It is our problem, because we wish to "communicate" the Gospel with our new neighbors, but we are not really ready to share it with them in such a way that they have as much ownership and control over it as we do. We convince ourselves that we are a welcoming people, that we really want different people among us; but in fact we want them only if they are ready to become like us, to adapt to our culture and traditions, our ways of being the church, our forms of worship. We want them to feel welcome in *our* church, forgetting that the church is never ours but is always the Lord's. Thus, what Hawn calls the paradigm of "cultural assimilation" is always our temptation and frequently our downfall.

The other options, what Hawn calls "culturally open worship" and "cultural partnership," are riskier and costly. They imply that the church will no longer worship exclusively as we are used to worshiping and will no longer be controlled by the people, tradition, or culture that have controlled it in the past. They also involve the risk that the new church that will emerge will err and assimilate inappropriate elements from the various cultures in which it is incarnate. Yet if this risk suggests the possibility of error and even heresy, not to take the risk implies the certainty of apostasy, for a church that no longer communicates the gospel—that is no longer willing to share the gospel in such a way that listeners may truly claim it as their own—is no longer the church born at Pentecost.

Certainly, there are many difficulties as we seek to worship in a way that affirms the multiplicity of cultures in our midst—and even the multiplicity of cultures throughout the world, for when we worship we must remember that we are part of a church that even as we gather is also worshiping in a myriad of other cultures and contexts. There are difficulties of language, for unfortunately the miracle of Pentecost is not repeated in its fullness every Sunday, and we must find ways to relate and join in worship across language differences.

At this point, Hawn and his colleagues are particularly helpful in that they emphasize the nonverbal elements in worship. Too often, in our meaning-oriented culture, we confuse meaning with significance. If we cannot understand the meaning of something—understand it as we understand a sentence or an equation—we think it is not significant. In worship—particularly in mainline Protestant worship—we focus on words. We act as if what is important is what the words say, what we can write down on a notepad and repeat to another. That this understanding is insufficient should be obvious as we reflect on our daily lives. The experience of eating a well-flavored meal cannot be expressed in words so that another can relive the experience by merely hearing the words; and yet it is an important, significant experience. What is true in everyday life is even truer in worship, for in worship we are by definition in the presence of mystery—and the experience of such presence can never be fully expressed in logical sentences. And yet, we insist on language, on verbal communication, on words we can understand, as if what we cannot understand would not be significant.

By attending to the nonverbal elements of worship, this book takes us beyond the questions of language—questions that are at

once too simplistic and unresolvable. Language is certainly important
and has a central place in worship. But worship goes beyond language and even beyond understanding. It is in this *beyondness*,
which includes meaning but also sees the significance of what is
beyond meaning, that true multicultural worship can take place.
Worship is indeed about words, but it is also about movement,
sounds, gestures, music, dance, symbols, and space.

All these observations, however, would remain only theoretical
if not for the fact that Hawn and his colleagues offer us four case
studies of congregations that are exploring ways to share in worship
across culture, race, language, generation, and other boundaries.
The case studies show that this sharing is not easy. Among recent
immigrants, just as was the case among those who came decades or
even centuries ago, there is the tendency to turn to the church as a
means to preserve culture, which in itself militates against true
cross-cultural communication and worship. Because a single
gesture may have different meanings in different cultures, there will
be misunderstandings and tensions. Yet even as a congregation
appears to be succeeding in dealing with its own multicultural
setting, the kaleidoscopic cultural changes that are taking place in
our society require that it constantly find a new starting point—to
bring in a new group, deal with a new generation, reinvent itself
and its worship one more time. All of this, and more, becomes
apparent as we read the four case studies in this book.

Fully aware that what is before the church is a difficult task,
this book also offers concrete and strategic suggestions about how
to move toward a practice of worship that is more fully inclusive
of God's people. Without allowing us to forget the why, we are
offered a number of how-tos. These are very helpful, for they take
into account the life of actual congregations, with all the values
and difficulties inherent to that life. And yet they are how-tos that
are firmly grounded in the why of Pentecost. We are to do these
things, not because they will lead to a more *successful* church, but
because they are what the Pentecostal presence of the Spirit leads us
to do.

Difficulties remain. Hawn and his colleagues make it clear that
what they propose is not easy. They do not expect us to solve the

challenges of worship, to get the task done and then move on to something else. They are aware that this is a never-ending yet unavoidable task if the church is to be faithful to its nature and its calling. And yet it is important that we see the situation they describe not so much as a challenge as a promise and a chance to enjoy a foretaste of the promise. The church is a people looking forward to the day when God's purposes will be fulfilled. We live out of the promise of that day. It is a day when a multitude that no one will be able to count—out of every tribe, people, nation, and language—will sing hymns of victory to God and to the Lamb. We have not yet seen that day, but we can at least rejoice that through the multicultural situation of our 21st century, we are being allowed a glimpse of that day and even an opportunity—in the sort of worship proposed in this book—to gain a foretaste of it!

Justo L. González
Candler School of Theology

EDITOR'S PREFACE

HEALTHY CONGREGATIONS

Christianity is a "first-person plural" religion, where communal worship, service, fellowship, and learning are indispensable for grounding and forming individual faith. The strength of Christianity in North America depends on the presence of healthy, spiritually nourishing, well-functioning congregations. Congregations are the cradle of Christian faith, the communities in which children of all ages are supported, encouraged, and formed for lives of service. Congregations are the habitat in which the practices of the Christian life can flourish.

As living organisms, congregations are by definition in a constant state of change. Whether the changes are in membership, pastoral leadership, lay leadership, the needs of the community, or the broader culture, a crucial mark of healthy congregations is their ability to deal creatively and positively with change. The fast pace of change in contemporary culture, with its bias toward, not against change, only makes the challenge of negotiating change all the more pressing for congregations.

VITAL WORSHIP

At the center of many discussions about change in churches today is the topic of worship. This is not surprising, for worship is at the center of congregational life. To "go to church" means, for most members of congregations, "to go to worship." In his recent work

How Do We Worship? (Alban Institute, 1999), Mark Chaves begins his analysis with the simple assertion, "Worship is the most central and public activity engaged in by American religious congregations" (p. 1). Worship styles are one of the most significant reasons that people choose to join a given congregation. Correspondingly, they are central to the identity of most congregations.

Worship is also central on a much deeper level. Worship is the locus of what several Christian traditions identify as the nourishing center of congregation life: preaching, common prayer, and the celebration of ordinances or sacraments. Significantly, what many traditions elevate to the status of "the means of grace" or even the "marks of the church" are essentially liturgical actions. Worship is central, most significantly, for theological reasons. Worship both reflects and shapes a community's faith. It expresses a congregation's view of God and enacts a congregation's relationship with God and each other.

We can identify several specific factors that contribute to spiritually vital worship and thereby strengthen congregational life.

- Congregations, and the leaders that serve them, need a shared vision for worship that is grounded in more than personal aesthetic tastes. This vision must draw on the deep theological resources of scripture, the Christian tradition, and the unique history of the congregation.
- Congregational worship should be integrated with the whole life of the congregation. It can serve as the "source and summit" from which all the practices of the Christian life flow. Worship both reflects and shapes the life of the church in education, pastoral care, community service, fellowship, justice, hospitality, and every other aspect of church life.
- The best worship practices feature not only good worship "content," such as discerning sermons, honest prayers, creative artistic contributions, celebrative and meaningful rituals for baptism and the Lord's Supper. They also arise of out of good process, involving meaningful contributions from participants, thoughtful leadership, honest evaluation, and healthy communication among leaders.

VITAL WORSHIP, HEALTHY CONGREGATIONS SERIES

The Vital Worship, Healthy Congregations Series is designed to reflect
the kind of vibrant, creative energy and patient reflection that will
promote worship that is both relevant and profound. It is designed to
invite congregations to rediscover a common vision for worship, to
sense how worship is related to all aspects of congregational life,
and to imagine better ways of preparing excellent "content" and
"process" related to the worship life of their own congregations.

It is important to note that strengthening congregational life
through worship renewal is a delicate and challenging task precisely
because of the uniqueness of each congregation. This book series is
not designed to represent a single denomination, Christian tradition, or type of congregation. Nor is it designed to serve as arbiter
of theological disputes about worship. Books in the series will note
the significance of theological claims about worship, but they may,
in fact, represent quite different theological visions from each other,
or from our work at the Calvin Institute of Christian Worship.
Rather, the series is designed to call attention to *instructive examples
of congregational life* and to explore these examples in ways that
allow readers in very different communities to compare and contrast these examples with their own practice. The models described
in any given book may for some readers be instructive as examples
to follow. For others, a given example may remind them of something they are already doing well, or something they will choose not
to follow because of theological commitments or community
history.

By promoting encounters with instructive examples from
various parts of the body of Christ, we pray that these volumes will
help leaders make good judgments about worship in their congregations and that, by the power of God's Spirit, these congregations
will flourish.

John D. Witvliet
Calvin Institute of Christian Worship

PREFACE

Nora Tubbs Tisdale, professor of preaching, Presbyterian minister, and writer on worship, recalled in a sermon the comments of a New Jersey parishioner. She and this thoughtful, involved layman had just attended a church school forum on worship and multiculturalism. As they left, the layman reflected on all he had heard: "I chose this church because there were people like me here, music I liked, and a homogeneity that made me feel at home. Why now do I have to worry about how to make the church a welcoming place for all these other types? Don't they have their own churches?" Tubbs Tisdale responded to the layman's rhetorical question in her sermon: "The answer to his question, of course, is complex. As complex as Pentecost itself."[1]

In this book I attempt to respond to the Spirit of Pentecost as it moves in corporate worship. In my experience, the layman's observations hold true for many, perhaps most, who attend worship today. Attempts to reflect the Spirit of Pentecost in worship run the risk of tapping into a flood of responses ranging from insecurity with new forms to anger at those who would upset the established order and invade the worshiper's "comfort zone."

As a troubadour for global music and an instigator of cross-cultural worship for more than 15 years in a variety of denominational settings, including congregational, national, and international venues, I have, however, observed many faithful people who find that a taste of Pentecost in worship is refreshing and invigorating. I have seen an emerging pattern of response. After a service in which we have danced while singing an African song and passed the peace of

Christ silently to each other in a manner used by some Christians in southern India, teenagers have often come up to me to say, "I wish worship was like this all the time." Such a response might be expected from young people, one might say.

But what about the senior adults who display unusual grace as they dance to the same African song; or those who, needing walkers for mobility, move out into the center aisle and join the movement to the extent that they are able? I am astonished by the number of senior adults who also catch the Spirit of Pentecost during cross-cultural worship experiences.

The joyful and thoughtful responses of young and old in multicultural worship point to Joel 2:28: "I will pour out my spirit on all flesh; your sons and daughters shall prophesy, your old men [and women] shall dream dreams, and your young shall see visions." I have come to see how this passage confirms my work in cross-cultural worship with congregations. If people from a wide spectrum of ages respond to what I perceive to be the Spirit of Pentecost, then perhaps their affirmation is one indicator of a truly authentic movement of the Spirit.

All this said, cross-cultural worship is hard work. In this book I seek to help bridge the gap between the human tendency to prefer, on the one hand, ethnic and cultural homogeneity in worship and, on the other, a rainbow vision of the universal church proposed by theologian Justo González, "where all the colors paint a single landscape, where all tongues sing the same praise." González hopes for a time during God's Reign—*Gran Fiesta,* "when all peoples will join in joyful banquet, when all tongues of the universe will sing the same song."[2]

METHODS OF STUDY

In preparation for this book I worked with a team of consultants from the faculty of Perkins School of Theology, Southern Methodist University, in Dallas. Edwin David Aponte, a Puerto Rican American, is a professor of church and society. Evelyn Parker, an African American, is a Christian education professor. We, along with two Anglo master of divinity students, formed a diverse team in ethnicity, gender, and academic fields of study. We also represented a diversity of denominational perspectives, including ordained Baptist and Presbyterian ministers, a Christian Methodist Episcopal laywoman, and two future United Methodist ministers.

We engaged four United Methodist congregations in the Dallas area in our study. Each of these congregations was grappling with cross-cultural ministry either as a proactive mission or because the neighborhood was changing, and the newcomers were increasingly diverse. Two congregations were well established, one for almost 100 years and one for more than 35 years. Two congregations were newly organized at the time of this study, one in its second and one in its sixth year. The congregations also reflected varied ethnic constituencies. Grace United Methodist Church is a predominantly Euro–North American congregation that includes some black, Latino, and Asian members; it has a white male pastor. Agape Memorial United Methodist Church, a predominantly third- and fourth-generation Hispanic congregation with approximately 25 percent Anglo membership, was led by a Latino pastor. All Nations United Methodist Church is a mixed congregation with African Americans forming the largest group, followed by Anglos and some Hispanics. The pastor is an African American woman. Church of the Disciple is a largely Anglo congregation with a growing number of black members. At the time of this study the congregation was led by a white couple who served as co-pastors.

Each pastor chose a representative team of five, including staff and lay members, who met throughout the year 2000 to engage each other on the topic of multicultural worship. The congregational representatives and the Perkins research team worshiped and took meals together, toured one another's churches and neighborhoods, and studied common books on four weekends during the year. Drawing from Hartford Seminary's Congregational Studies Institute,[3] we placed our study of multicultural worship in the context of five "lenses" used in this program: theology, ecology (seeing the congregation in the context of its community), culture and identity, process (dynamics of congregational life), and resources. Each committee focused on preparing liturgies for World Communion Sunday and the Advent season, using the Perkins team as a sounding board for ideas and experiences. These were logical times to involve the congregations in multicultural worship. World Communion Sunday has a global focus, and Advent is the season of preparation for the Incarnation, during which God became manifest on earth for all peoples and all times.

Evaluating the experience, participants singled out the value of mutual support and the chance to discuss the issues raised in the study. An Anglo pastor appreciated the opportunity to talk to an African American female pastor about how his congregation could be more sensitive to the growing number of middle-class blacks in his neighborhood. A Latina nurse from Agape Church volunteered to work in the medical clinic at Grace Church, where her bilingual skills and medical training would be helpful. A predominantly Anglo congregation joined Agape in a work day to prepare a basketball and volleyball court for the children and young people in the largely first-generation Hispanic neighborhood.

These congregations expressed the pain and possibilities of any congregation seeking to plan worship with a diverse congregation. None of these were "United Nations" congregations, chosen because they had achieved a "rainbow" constituency. The Perkins team decided that it would be more realistic to choose congregations amid the struggle to capture the Spirit of Pentecost rather than to examine "mosaic" congregations already noted for their truly multicultural worship style.

The give-and-take between researchers and congregational representatives provided fruitful conversation and candid reflection and enriched the conclusions of this book.

A PREVIEW OF THE BOOK

Part I, "Is There Room for My Neighbor at the Table?," provides analytical tools for evaluating a congregation's cultural context. Part II comprises case studies of the four congregations that participated in the study. Each case study places a congregation's worship rituals in the context of its history, neighborhood demographics (congregational ecology), congregational constituency, and neighborhood programs. Members of the Perkins team wrote the case studies: seminarians Susan Knipe and Robin Stevens (Grace Church), C.

Michael Hawn (Agape Church), Edwin David Aponte (All Nations Church), and Evelyn Parker (Church of the Disciple).

Part III, section 1, "How Can We Keep from Singing? The Role of Musicians and Music in Enabling Multicultural Worship," examines one of the most crucial aspects of multicultural worship, musical leadership, and congregational singing. Part III, section 2, "Pentecost Renewed: 10 Strategies for Cultivating Common Prayer," offers specific guidance for congregations pursuing "culturally conscious worship," as defined by Kathy Black, an author whose research explores the range of cultural variations in United Methodist worship in the United States.[4] Finally, section 2 draws heavily on the experiences of the four congregations and what we learned from them.

A series of six appendixes offers specific process guidance. An extensive annotated bibliography suggests additional resources for various cultural contexts.

A NOTE ON ETHNIC TERMINOLOGY

Labeling ethnic groups is both difficult and unfortunate. Labels are usually inaccurate and misleading and, in some cases, demeaning. Acknowledging this fact, I face the conundrum of assigning labels to various ethnic groups in this book. The terms "African American" and "black" will be used interchangeably with the understanding that not all blacks in the United States are African Americans.

I will follow the practice common in literature of referring to people who have their ethnic roots in Spain (both full- and mixed-blood) but reside in the Americas, as Hispanics or Latinos. In the case of Latinos, the use of a single term—for example, Hispanics—does not reflect the diversity of cultures and nationalities present in the United States. The ambiguity of designation, on the other hand, reflects the uncertain position of Latinos in North American society. When appropriate, I will note specific countries and differences in gender.

Designating people of Euro–North American descent (it is too common to use "America" only in reference to the United States) is also problematic. In Texas and the Southwest, the term "Anglo" often distinguishes whites from other groups. Though *Anglo* refers technically to the English or issues related to the culture of England, I will use this regional term interchangeably with Euro-American to designate all white people in the United States. Once again, the Anglo label glosses over a diversity of cultures and nationalities.

Ethnic labels are not new. In Ephesians 2, Paul distinguishes between Jewish and Gentile Christians. Following Paul's lead that both groups become "one new humanity [in Christ] in place of the two (v. 15), this book explores the practical considerations of worshiping together in our diversity.

ACKNOWLEDGMENTS

I am grateful for receiving a Worship Renewal Grant from the Calvin Institute of Christian Worship, a program funded by the Lilly Endowment, and to the director of the Calvin Institute, John Witvliet, for his encouragement of this study and for his initial presentation of the project to the Alban Institute. Beth Ann Gaede, editor of this project for Alban, has been most generous with her time and skills, making the manuscript clearer in content and more readable in style. Copy editor Jean Caffey Lyles significantly improved the readability of the final manuscript and, as a fellow church musician with Texas roots, added important insights. Any inadequacies that remain rest squarely on the author's shoulders.

Perkins School of Theology supported me with a Scholarly Outreach Award, permitting me the time to pull together, reflect on, and prepare the manuscript for publication. Perkins also provided an ethnically diverse faculty and student body, as well as opportunities to lead and experience multicultural worship—a context that encourages fruitful and forthright discussions.

John Thornburg—hymn writer, worship consultant, pastor, and friend—read my major contributions (part I and part III, sections 1 and 2) and provided invaluable advice and gracious encouragement. I am grateful for the collegiality of Edwin Aponte and Evelyn Parker, with whom I can explore these complex issues in candor and depth. Susan Knipe and Robin Stevens were excellent partners in this study and made the practical arrangements with our four participating congregations.

Most of all, I am grateful to the four congregations that participated, allowing us to videotape, probe, and learn from their experiences—both painful and positive. These congregations are filled with faithful members who are willing to envision a more diverse way of "being church" and are led by committed ministers and church staff members who are willing to risk change inspired by the Spirit of Pentecost.

PART I

IS THERE ROOM FOR MY NEIGHBOR AT THE TABLE?

A few years ago I was in a meeting with the pastor of one of the most prominent African American churches in the Dallas area. He pulled me aside at one point and asked a provocative question. "Mike, we have an interesting situation that has developed over the last few years. When we built our church in its current location, the neighborhood was solidly African American. The neighborhood has been gradually changing since then, and now we're located in the middle of a largely Hispanic area. Our members drive in from all over the city. We've reached out to our new neighbors, and they're responding in many ways: they come to the clothes closet, use our food pantry, and use our child-care programs, but they don't attend worship. Is there anything we can do to encourage our Hispanic neighbors to participate in our worship?"

Hearing that pastor's account was an experience of déjà vu for me. Nearly 20 years earlier I had served as church musician for an Atlanta-area congregation located in what was then a neighborhood of "white flight." The Anglo congregation was attempting to maintain a vital ministry in an area where African Americans and Latinos were becoming our neighbors. The church provided a well-staffed and organized clothing closet and food pantry. Our preschool day-care program was racially integrated. Activities held in a beautiful gymnasium included a diverse group of young people from the area. Yet Sunday morning did not reflect the community's range of ethnicity.

At the dawn of the 21st century the diversity of the world is at our doorstep. While large urban areas come to mind first, even rural settings reflect this trend. I recall a recent discussion on National Public Radio about a radio station in rural Nebraska that had once been devoted to German polka music. Now the format is all-Spanish—¡Sí, todos! I visited a church in the mountains of western North Carolina where the director of children's choirs was attempting to meet the challenge of a sudden influx of Hmong children. My son told me of playing guitar for a Spanish mass in upstate New York each Sunday in the early 1990s for migrant workers from various parts of Central America. How easy it is to travel through the United States and find a wonderful "ethnic" restaurant—not just Chinese or Mexican, but also Thai, Salvadoran, Ethiopian, Indian, or Pakistani—run by a family of immigrants. These establishments cater to both Anglos and immigrants in the area—residents largely unnoticed by the majority population.[1] While the growing diversity of cuisine provides anecdotal evidence of demographic shifts, the "neighborhood" changed significantly during the last 30 years of the 20th century; it will become even more diverse in the 21st.

MELTING POT OR MOSAIC?

During the great waves of European immigration to the United States during the late 19th century and the first half of the 20th, "melting pot" was the dominant metaphor used to describe this phenomenon. Although the myth of the melting pot is alive and well, it is largely invalid and, for the most part, was never descriptive of the relationship between newer immigrants and those who preceded them. A melting pot in no way describes the earlier immigrants who arrived on our shores from the 15th through 18th centuries, and their encounters with Native Americans. Major urban areas in the United States still have neighborhoods consisting largely of the specific European immigrant groups that settled them in the 19th and 20th centuries. Cities like Chicago, Boston, and New York still reflect earlier migration patterns. A church musician in a Roman Catholic parish in New York told me that he had played funeral masses for nearly 40 firefighters and police officers following the terrorist attacks of September 11, 2001. Virtually all were second-, third-, or fourth-generation Irish Catholics whose parents or earlier forebears immigrated to the United States during times of political struggle and famine. This neighborhood was still intact. The concept of a melting pot never became a reality in much of the United States.

The church is often a center for ethnic activities and identity formation. A professor in Ireland told me of a trip to New York, where he attended the St. Patrick's Day mass at the cathedral named for the Irish saint. He commented that the Irish in New York are "more Irish" than those in Limerick, Ireland, where he taught. "I almost fainted when a soprano stepped up to the altar before the mass and sang, 'Oh Danny Boy.' This would never happen in Ireland." It would appear that a decision was made to reinforce cultural identity rather than to relate the music to the liturgy of the day.

In many congregations, members' fondness for specific songs reveals an underlying ethnic cohesiveness that has not melted into an indefinable, assimilated blandness. When I attended worship recently with a Christian Reformed congregation, five brothers sang from memory in Dutch a beloved hymn from the Netherlands (one of two Dutch-language hymns found in the *Psalter Hymnal*) on the Sunday after Thanksgiving. This song was a tradition in this church. Even younger members who did not speak Dutch understood some of the language and enjoyed this display of their ethnic faith heritage. At a conference in Winnipeg, Manitoba, with Mennonites, I was regaled at dinner with two favorite hymns sung in German, all stanzas, by memory. Immigrants to North America seem to have maintained a sense of ethnic origins even after several generations, especially in the church.

Some melting has taken place in the great pot of humanity that makes up the United States, but it is by no means complete. Rather than a homogenous soup in which all flavors have been assimilated into one indescribable taste, this soup is more like the Thai cuisine flavored by spices, vegetables, and a variety of seafood that make each bite an adventure. For many, assimilation of immigrants into a single cultural perspective is the goal.[2] The search for an overriding normative cultural ethos in the United States may be a vain quest. The varied roots of our population, however, provide a rich diversity that adds texture and variety to our lives. Rather than perpetuating the myth of the melting pot, I will offer another metaphor for our lives together—a cultural mosaic.[3]

The cultural assimilation suggested by the melting-pot metaphor does not describe the experiences of European immigrants arriving in the United States during the 19th and 20th centuries. The image may have even less validity for people of color in the 21st century. If Europeans found it difficult to conform, or to "melt" into the majority culture, how much more difficult is it for African Americans, Africans, Asians, and Latin Americans to be absorbed into a single deracinated culture? Is it desirable for Haitians, Taiwanese, Cubans, Nigerians, and Salvadorans to forego their worldviews and to assimilate into a unified ethos? Each culture reflects the diverse palette of the One who created all cultures.

A mosaic consists of thousands of tiny pieces, each with its own distinct hue and shape. Each has its own identity defined by size, color, shape, and texture. When these distinct fragments come together under the hand of a creative artist, a larger picture emerges. Complexity and diversity intensify this picture, especially when one sees the larger view. Does this "larger view" suggest that each piece has an identical role in the larger picture or reflects light in the same way? Probably not. Does it mean that each tiny fragment has an important part to play in the overall design of the mosaic? Yes!

Incarnational Worship

Worshiping together is an incarnational matter. How do we see God's presence among us? When Jesus came to live among us on earth, he came to a specific place, in a specific time, and to a specific convergence of cultures. By the end of the 20th century, the message of the gospel had been transplanted to virtually every corner of the world.[4] The gospel takes root in each culture in its own way. D. T. Niles, the Sri Lankan ecumenist, put it this way:

> The gospel is like a seed and you have to sow it. When you sow the
> seed of the Gospel in Palestine, a plant that can be called Palestin-
> ian Christianity grows. When you sow it in Rome, a plant of
> Roman Christianity grows. You sow the Gospel in Great Britain
> and you get British Christianity. The seed of the Gospel is later
> brought to America and a plant grows of American Christianity.
> Now when missionaries came to our lands they brought not only
> the seed of the Gospel, but their own plant of Christianity, flower
> pot included! So, what we have to do is to break the flower pot,
> take out the seed of the Gospel, sow it in our own cultural soil,
> and let our own version of Christianity grow.[5]

Niles's metaphor expressed a problem that he had encountered with
those missionaries who brought their own cultural perspective and
often could not separate it from the gospel they were spreading.
This metaphor has not outlived its usefulness. What is the nature of
the cultural soil that makes up the United States in the 21st century? Not all of it is like the rich black earth that I grew up with in
Iowa. Some of it is the sandy soil of the North Carolina coastline.
Some soil has the consistency of the red clay of Georgia. Some of it
reflects the rich volcanic ash of Hawaii. Some comes from the
tundra of Alaska. The United States has no uniform soil. Nor does
this nation have a uniform worldview among its citizens.

Culturally Uniform Worship

How then do we worship together? Several options are open to us.
One is to define worship from a particular cultural perspective—
cultural uniformity. This choice assumes that all those gathered are
on the same cultural page. They will all have common backgrounds
and ways of viewing the world. I do not suggest that faithful and
vital worship[6] cannot take place in congregations that are culturally
homogenous. I would make two observations, however. First,
cultural uniformity is much more difficult to achieve than it might
appear. Patterns of migration, global communication, and marriage
across ethnic and racial lines are so common that many, perhaps
most, congregations have members for whom English is a second
language. Congregations commonly include people who came from

a different section of the country, or were reared in another country or in a different socioeconomic context.

Second, generational differences have some of the same effects as varied ethnic perspectives within a congregation. Younger members have been shaped by a set of historical events different from those that formed older members. The change in formation is especially dramatic with the second generation—the children of immigrants —in whom the language and traditions of the parents give way, to some degree, to the dominant language and values of popular culture. Cultural uniformity may be harder to find than we think.

Cultural uniformity (or relative cultural uniformity) appears to lead to vital worship in some situations. From my experience such uniformity is usually found in a minority context where worship helps to maintain a cultural heritage. African American congregations, for example, may find that worship, at its best, reinforces the group's basic cultural values and identities. Because social realities threaten the fabric of a minority community, worship may reflect one cultural heritage and provide identity formation. The words of the African American pastor in Dallas suggest, however, that some black Americans may desire culturally diverse worship, in this case with Latinos. The case studies that follow in part II acknowledge that some blacks and Latinos seek culturally diverse places of worship.

Worship among expatriates may appear at first to be culturally uniform. I have been an expatriate who enjoyed worshiping abroad with other expatriates. Invariably a diverse group of expatriates gathers—people whose common denominator is their separation from home. But they probably would not choose to worship together in their country of origin. These apparently culturally uniform people usually end up being quite varied, their only common tie being that they all seek a Christian community away from home.

One danger of culturally uniform worship is that an ethnocentric perspective limits one's worldview. Culturally uniform worship may not prepare the body of Christ to encounter a diverse and complex society. There may be a place for worship as a refuge from the world, a setting where one feels comfortable with similar-minded folk, but such worship runs the risk of excluding those who are different. While achieving a high degree of comfort through cultural uniformity, congregations that lack ethnic diversity may be cutting themselves off from the resources of those who might enrich them. Cliques are not a substitute for Christian community.[7] As John Thornburg, pastor and worship consultant, noted in a conversation, "Cliques provide security, but not transformation." True worship should enable worshipers to become transformed from being separate cliques to being the body of Christ.

Worship through Cultural Assimilation

A second approach to cross-cultural worship is that of cultural assimilation. This practice assumes a dominant cultural perspective that will become the common currency for all participants, regardless of experience or background. Once again, some congregations with vital worship operate knowingly or unknowingly under this assumption. Some worshipers seek out this approach, because they prefer the cultural ethos of the dominant group. All who become faithful to Eastern Orthodox tradition, regardless of cultural heritage, will participate in a liturgy that has remained remarkably consistent since the schism between the Orthodox and Latin churches in 1054 C.E., with little regard for cultural change or location. Worshipers would probably be quite disappointed if that liturgy were changed. The dominant group in U.S. churches may vary. It may be a Gen X group holding a "praise and worship" contemporary service. Or it may be a predominantly African American fellowship having a "gospel" service. The dominant group may be made up of middle-class Latinos with roots primarily in Mexico. The dominant ethos may be that of Anglo mainline Protestantism.

Churches that knowingly or by default adopt a perspective of cultural assimilation may nonetheless be sensitive to the needs of the community. When congregations are located in urban or even inner-city areas, they often provide significant services to the community—for example, medical clinics, clothing, food, or counseling. When it comes to the gathered assembly on Sunday morning, however, people from the community may be welcome, but only if they assimilate into the worship patterns of the majority culture. Minority people often perceive an inconsistency between the words spoken—"All are welcome here"—and the nonverbal communication. Nonverbal signals include the numbers of minority persons in leadership, worship style, and artwork reflecting only the congregation's majority culture. While an unwelcome spirit may not prevail toward those beyond the majority culture, a sense of noblesse oblige may separate the strangers from the church when worship or decor or noninclusive leadership announces, "We are glad to do things for you, but you are not really one of us."[8]

Culturally Open Worship

A third position is that of cultural openness. A culturally open congregation will display a spirit of receptivity toward the community's cultural diversity, even though the congregation has a distinct cultural majority group. The difference between cultural assimilation and cultural openness is the degree to which people with differing values and backgrounds are included in decision-making processes of congregational life.

A posture of cultural openness will not only provide needed services or ministries for neighborhood residents but will also include people from the surrounding community in decision-making roles in the church. It will also try to honor the cultural heritage of these newcomers in the worship life of the congregation. In essence, the majority group allows its worldview to be altered by the minority constituency in decision-making processes and in worship. (The final section of this book will offer strategies for moving in this direction.)

Worship in Cultural Partnership

Finally, a congregation may reflect a cultural partnership. A cultural partnership takes place when no clear majority dominates and culturally diverse members reflect the surrounding neighborhood and work together in a shared Christian community. A cultural-partnership congregation develops something new in worship. Participants are "no longer strangers and aliens, but [all] are citizens with the saints and also members of the household of God, built upon the foundation of the apostles and prophets, with Jesus Christ himself as the cornerstone" (Eph. 2:19-20).

A congregation that reflects a cultural partnership has responded to the vision in Ephesians. Cultural tensions have been with the Christian church since its inception. This passage reflects a tension that existed between Christian Jews and Christian Gentiles. Jewish Christians may have felt that they were nearer to God than Gentile Christians were. Paul rejects this distinction. He states that Christ "has abolished the law with its commandments and ordinances, that he might create in himself one new humanity in place of the two, thus making peace, and might reconcile both groups to God in one body through the cross, thus putting to death the hostility through it" (Eph. 2:15-16). Christ, the imaginative artist, creates a mosaic (one new humanity) out of the disparate cultures of the world. Few congregations have fully embodied this model, but the vision of a cultural partnership offers rich possibilities for worship.

A spectrum of these four approaches toward culture and worship appears in figure 1. As an initial step in congregational analysis, a congregation may find it helpful to convene a representative group to discuss where on the spectrum it falls. The congregation's position on this spectrum does not necessarily indicate that its worship lacks vitality or is inadequate. It may suggest, however, that

Figure 1
Moving toward Culturally Conscious Worship

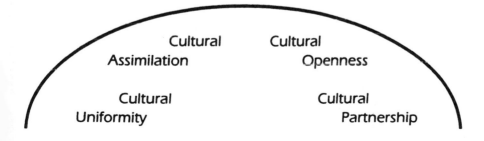

the congregation is not living out the biblical imperative to include
strangers and aliens in its worship and to incorporate them fully
into the body of Christ. A lack of inclusion of others may also
indicate a kind of liturgical provincialism, suggesting that a congregation is missing the potential to pray more fully and deeply. In this
book we seek to encourage worship that more fully embodies the
diversity of God's creation as reflected in the humanity around us.

I realize that I may be treading on uncertain, even dangerous,
ground at this point. Who am I to decide whose worship is "adequate" or "vital"? It is God's province, not mine, to make such
judgments. Let me risk some criteria for vital worship that I believe
have a biblical basis and seem to have been concerns of the church
since its birth at Pentecost. This list is not meant to be all-inclusive
or to reflect a deep theological rationale. That is a project for
scholars who write books devoted solely to this topic.⁹ Is the
Word—heard, recited, and preached—central? Is there an abundance of bread, wine, and water as signs of God's grace? Is the
leadership inclusive in gender, age, socioeconomic status, and
ethnic origin? Are strangers and aliens welcome? Do the people
pray in word and song for their needs and the needs of the world?
Does the congregation, gathered locally, have a vision for the world
and its potential? Does the congregation confront injustice and evil
on its doorstep and beyond? Is the congregation a witness for the
gospel (good news) of Jesus Christ? Does worship have one eye on
the present condition and the other on a future of wholeness and
oneness in Christ? Perhaps these questions may guide you as you
begin to analyze your congregation's vision, ministry, and role in
the community.

BIAS AND PREJUDICE

Before looking more specifically at the ways that worship and
culture intersect, let us clarify an important distinction between
bias and *prejudice*. Bias and prejudice are natural parts of the
human condition. In any cross-cultural encounter both will likely
come into play. Stepping totally outside our culture of origin is

impossible. We will always have a bias toward the cultural context that shaped us. Few people learn to function equally well in two cultures. In most cases those who do are members of co-cultures (sometimes called subcultures)[10] within a broader society. Children of missionaries are often bicultural. They may learn to be totally at home in the country in which their parents serve, speaking the language of this country from birth with no trace of an accent. In this case the children of missionaries are part of co-cultures as expatriates of the United States. They also become native English-speakers, living from infancy with their parents and among other missionary families. Many of my seminary students, members of minority groups within the United States, function equally well within the majority culture and in their culture of origin. These people are truly bicultural.

Those who live in cultures beyond their culture of origin tend to become self-conscious about their bias. Culture consists of a matrix of complex symbol systems that provide a means for people to participate in society. By preserving, transmitting, perpetuating, and developing knowledge and other ways of knowing, symbol systems "make meaning," enabling people to relate to one another.[11]

A healthy bias acknowledges other worldviews and presupposes other equally valid cultural ways of making meaning. Cultural bias becomes prejudice when it assumes an exclusive posture toward other cultural perspectives—when there is only one right way to view the world.

If a congregation moves from cultural uniformity toward cultural partnership, it is unlikely that individual members will give up their cultural biases. Members of a congregation will, however, develop self-consciousness about their bias and remain open to others' perspectives. Whereas prejudice leads to exclusion of other views, a healthy bias is a posture of inclusion. Cross-cultural consultant Eric H. F. Law talks about inclusion as a process of extending our boundaries to include others:

> Inclusion is a discipline of extending our boundary to take into consideration another's needs, interests, experience, and perspective,

which will lead to clearer understanding of ourselves and others,
fuller description of the issue at hand, and possibly a newly
negotiated boundary of the community to which we belong.[12]

Throughout this book, I assume that culturally diverse worship is
an act of inclusion in which one's own cultural biases have value
but must at times be modified for the sake of others' biases as all
extend their boundaries. Each fragment of the mosaic has its own
beauty but is also enriched by its relationship to the whole. Culturally conscious worship[13] leads congregations toward a community
that reflects the "one new humanity" presented in Ephesians 2. This
new humanity values the dignity and perspective of each person.
Worship that emanates from this diverse body of believers is greater
than the sum of its parts. The mosaic of a culturally diverse congregation in worship reflects the face of God from whom all cultures
come.

THE INTERACTION OF WORSHIP AND CULTURE

Before we propose strategies for enabling culturally conscious
worship in local congregations, it may be helpful to look at the
more general interplay between culture and worship. Nearly everyone agrees that worship and culture relate to each other, but defining this relationship is more difficult than it might appear at first
glance. Of the models available for describing this interchange, the
Nairobi Statement on Worship and Culture[14] (1996) offers perhaps
the clearest guidance for the broader ecumenical church. (A summary of the statement appears in appendix A.) The Nairobi Statement is helpful because it draws on a global perspective for its
conclusions.

Although prepared under the auspices of the Lutheran World
Federation, the Nairobi Statement is ecumenical in its approach. It
draws upon the research and insights of Anscar Chupungco, a
Filipino Benedictine priest who has taken a primary role in devel-
oping the relationship between the prescribed ritual of the Roman
Catholic mass and the ways the mass may reflect cultures around

the world. "Inculturation" is one of the terms used to designate the interaction between liturgy and culture since Vatican II (1963–1965), when major reforms took place in Roman Catholic worship. While its title and context seem far removed from local churches and their struggles with culture, it is a remarkably brief and practical document. The Nairobi Statement offers four major perspectives about the relationship between worship and culture: (1) Worship as Transcultural; (2) Worship as Contextual; (3) Worship as Counter-cultural; (4) Worship as Cross-cultural.

Worship as Transcultural

The transcultural significance of worship focuses on those qualities and theological assertions that should be present in Christian worship regardless of cultural context. (Quotations that follow are from the Nairobi Statement, found in appendix A.) The resurrected Christ, "through whom by the power of the Holy Spirit we know the grace of the Triune God, transcends and is indeed beyond all cultures."[15] Celebrating rites of Christian initiation (baptism) and Eucharist (communion) emanate from the church's understanding of the centrality of the resurrected Christ. The Bible in all of its translations throughout the world bears witness to the story of salvation; "biblical preaching of Christ's death and resurrection has been sent into all the world." Christian worship is a principal action of the church across cultures. Christian worship responds to the shape of the Christian Year. In particular the observance of Lent/Easter/Pentecost—and to a lesser degree, Advent/Christmas/Epiphany—transcends cultures.

Specific "practices" are also transcultural, including "readings from the Bible, ecumenical creeds, recitation of the Lord's Prayer, and Baptism in water in the name of the Triune God." The Nairobi Statement also identifies a particular pattern of worship, or *ordo*, which provides a shared structure across cultural lines. This fundamental shape is sometimes called a fourfold pattern of worship and can be found in many denominations. According to the Nairobi Statement the pattern is:[16]

Service of the Word
1. [T]he people gather,
2. the Word of God is proclaimed; the people intercede for the needs of the Church and the world.

Service of the Table
3. [T]he [E]ucharist [communion or Lord's Supper] meal is shared, and
4. the people are sent out into the world for mission.

The prayers of intercession for the church and the world are a hinge between the Service of the Word and the Service of the Table.[17] A discussion of the essential or transcultural elements of worship may prove fruitful for a local congregation embarking upon culturally conscious worship. Such an interchange may yield more common ground among diverse cultural groups than one would expect. Styles may vary. A congregation struggling with cultural diversity in worship, however, should identify those theological assumptions and practices that are central to the congregation's common experience. It may be best to treat the discussion provided by the Nairobi Statement as a general guide. Church leaders should encourage the people to voice their understandings of transcultural worship first and then use the statement to fill in the gaps. In my experience, discussions around this topic often prove to be vigorous and informative.

Worship as Contextual

All Christian worship is contextual. Just as Jesus was born in a specific cultural context at a unique point in time, so does each worshiping community exist in a specific cultural setting and time. God's grace does not come to us in an unembodied form direct from the mind of God. This is not to say that we cannot sense God's powerful presence at any given moment. We also experience God's grace through culturally conditioned practices such as gathering with other members of the body of Christ, reading the biblical witness of Christ's work among us, and sharing the sacraments.

Our response to God's grace in acts of Christian corporate worship, however, depends upon some degree of common cultural currency. The Sunday gathering of believers on the day of Christ's resurrection—the Lord's Day—seems to be a transcultural feature of Christian worship. We gather, however, in varied ways and need to be able to relate to each other as the *ekklesia*—the people of God called together in Christ's name and, according to the vernacular Greek, to intercede on behalf of the needs of each other and the world. When worship is both transcultural and contextual, a dynamic relationship exists between the universal church and the local congregation, a crucial dynamic for culturally conscious congregations.

A congregation with little sense of the universal church runs the risk of ethnocentric worship that values local practices to the exclusion of other ways of worshiping—in other words, prejudice. Local cultural practices allow congregations to worship in meaningful ways. If these practices become too myopic, a congregation risks taking on characteristics that are not consonant with the transcultural practices of the church universal. Without a dynamic connection between local and universal church, a congregation runs the risk of sectarian practices so culturally specific that few others can relate to them.

A helpful exercise with a congregation is to explore the dynamic relationship between local and transcultural practices. Where are the connections? In what ways does a congregation express its contextual identity in worship? Look at the broader fourfold pattern. Are there important gathering practices in your congregation? Some gather early with food. Some gather by singing. Some gather with lively conversation. Some gather in silence. Some gather with the sounds of an organ.

Look at the proclamation of the Word. How many lessons are read? Who reads them? Are they sung or spoken or both? Are they enacted (dramatized or danced)? From what location are the scriptures read? How do the people respond to the reading of scripture? Do they bring their own Bibles, or are Bibles provided in the pews? How long is the sermon? Where is the sermon delivered (from behind the pulpit or in front of the chancel at floor level)?

How does the congregation respond to the one who delivers the sermon (verbally, silently, physically)? What is the focus of the sermon (life stories or narrative events, exposition of scripture, practical application, or a mixture of these)? Each cultural context proclaims the Word in its own idioms and practices, offering many ways to participate in and to share the gospel.

When administering the sacraments, many cultural variations are possible. In a baptism, how much water is used? How is the water administered? How is the peace passed before the eucharistic prayer begins? What elements are served during communion? In what manner are they administered? Who may serve communion? How is the table prepared? What nonverbal symbols of the culture enrich the administration of the sacraments? What cloths cover the table? What kind of bread is served? What music (if any) accompanies the celebration of the sacraments? Is the music congregational, choral, or instrumental?

How do people depart from worship? Do the presiders precede the people or follow them? What blessings are used? Who delivers them? Is the closing music congregational, choral, or instrumental? Does the congregation remain seated during the postlude or depart during the postlude?

Worship as Countercultural

The Nairobi Statement asserts that worship is countercultural. We are reminded of the transforming nature of Christ's incarnation. Romans 12:2 is a centerpiece of the countercultural principle: "Do not be conformed to this world, but be transformed by the renewing of your minds, so that you may discern what is the will of God—what is good and acceptable and perfect." Christ came to redeem a world that had fallen away from God's vision for humanity. Each culture has its own manifestations of sin, be they envy, greed, oppression, lust, or a host of others. The incarnation was a countercultural corrective to the prevalence of evil in all cultures. All cultures as well as those who participate in them are in need of Christ's transformation. Christ's incarnation, death, and resurrection form the model for the process of cultural transformation. In

Christ's incarnation, we recognize that the Holy One is among us. In Christ's death we die to our sinful nature and rise as new creatures with the resurrected Christ. The experience in the early church of entering, being immersed, and rising from the baptismal waters is a dramatic symbol of this transformation.

While all cultures and peoples are a part of God's good creation, all cultures have practices that are hostile to God's desires for humanity. In an attempt to employ meaningful elements from various cultural settings in culturally conscious worship, one must discern what aspects of culture strengthen the gathered body of Christ and what elements may be contrary to God's created order. The Nairobi statement provides some guidance: "cultural patterns which idolize the self or the local group at the expense of a wider humanity, or give central place to the acquisition of wealth at the expense of the care of the earth and its poor." To these cautions I would add rituals that, by either their use or their omission, render some in the community voiceless or invisible by denying their worth as children of God. The enactment of some rituals and the architecture of some places of worship may foster segregation by limiting participation. Some worship practices may imply classism by reserving the roles of presiding or assisting in worship for those of a certain age, gender, socioeconomic position, or race. In some traditions, adherents may need to examine the balance between lay and clergy leadership. While these roles are not interchangeable, clergy presiders may fail to invite laity to take significant roles.

As in the other sections of the Nairobi Statement, it may be helpful for members to do a cross-cultural audit of worship. Do aspects of worship exclude some or fail to promote a transformation of those gathered into the body of Christ? Are some voices not heard? Are some spaces inaccessible? Do children and young people participate in worship in meaningful and ongoing ways? Do the various worship leaders reflect the constituency of the church and its neighborhood? The church has the opportunity to deliver a strong countercultural word to a world where globalization has meant the assimilation of all cultures into a single normative popular western culture. This society assimilates those cultures that have less access to economic power or channels of communication.

In contrast, a culturally conscious congregation finds a place for all at the table and values the perspective of each person.

Worship as Cross-cultural

The final section of the Nairobi Statement speaks to worship as cross-cultural. The theology underlying this section is that "Jesus came to be the Savior of all people. He welcomes the treasures of earthly cultures into the city of God." This section stresses the importance of "music, art, architecture, gestures and postures, and other elements of different cultures" and declares that elements of cultures should be respected when used in other places in the world. Although the cross-cultural dimension of worship is an important element in the culture/worship dynamic, the section on this topic in the Nairobi Statement lacks the specific guidance of the others. One purpose of this book is to offer more specific strategies for achieving a cross-cultural style of worship.

STYLE, PIETY, AND WORSHIP

Every cultural context, every congregation has its own piety or style, a way of expressing itself corporately that gives meaning to worship. Every congregation does and says things in a particular way. Linda Clark, Joanne Swenson, and Mark Stamm identify piety as "the corporate inner life of the church, made visible in its worship, fellowship, and mission. Piety is a function of both reflective and 'prereflective' assumptions and commitments about God's being and action, and about the proper shape of the Christian life."[18] A congregation's style is an outward manifestation of its piety. On visiting a congregation for the first time, one might be acutely aware of how the outward style indicators reflect a congregation's "corporate inner life."

- How are people greeted?
- Does the presider wear vestments?
- How do the choir and other worship leaders enter the worship space?

- What music is sung? Is it fast or slow, loud or soft?
- What instruments accompany the music?
- Do people move and sway or stand still when they sing?
- How are visitors (strangers) made welcome?
- What is the role of silence in worship?
- What is the shape of the worship space?
- What symbols are displayed?
- How is the communion table prepared?
- How do people receive communion?
- How is the scripture introduced?
- What does this congregation call the worship space—sanctuary, auditorium, nave/chancel?
- Is a printed order of worship used?

Many questions in this list focus on observations about the nonverbal ethos of worship. Yet the answers are important to worshipers. They form a matrix of impressions reflecting the style and the inner piety of a congregation. One might say that style in many ways tells us how a congregation prays together. By praying together, I am referring to prayer in the broadest sense—invocation, praise, adoration, confession, intercession, communion and baptismal prayers, and blessing. Worship consists of more than prayer—for example, the hearing of the Word—but prayer is one of the most important responses to the Word, whether read in scripture or preached in the pulpit.

Each congregation has its own way of praying together, of being the church gathered. Many of our hymns are prayers of invocation, petition, or praise. Some traditions chant the psalms as prayer. Some cultures connect prayer to specific physical postures or movements. Proponents of culturally conscious worship propose to incorporate diverse worshipers with many ways of praying into a unified worship experience. The vision of oneness in Christ that pervaded the early church still haunts us, especially as we look around and see the diversity of our neighbors.

How can we avoid a knee-jerk reaction when we encounter the worship of others? How can we avoid judging too quickly with "I like it" or "I don't"? Worship is not an exotic dish to which we can respond with an immediate "yum" or "yuck": more is at stake than our taste buds. Can a congregation develop a sense of self-awareness that acknowledges bias without prejudice? Let us look more specifically at style and the interlocking patterns of words and actions that make up how a congregation prays together. Examining four general areas may shed some light on meaning in cross-cultural situations. These are

- sense of time,
- nonverbal cues,
- role of written versus oral traditions,
- and relationship between the leadership and the congregation.

This is by no means a comprehensive list, but it should offer insight into the complexity of cross-cultural worship experiences.

Sense of Time

Congregations have different senses of time. Obviously worship services in various cultures or traditions may be relatively short, or considerably longer. An Anglo mainline Presbyterian service may last precisely 60 minutes; an African American National Baptist congregation may go on for two hours or more. This sense of time extends to how the congregation gathers before the service and lingers afterward. Some may attend Sunday school before the service and remain for dinner after the service, making it a four- or five-hour event. Others gather only for the worship hour. The relative length of a service is a significant cross-cultural component. People in a congregation with many Africans or African Americans may not feel that they have had a valid worship experience unless the service has lasted for at least two hours. An Anglo mainline congregation may value worship that gets "to the point" of the sermon quickly and cuts back on the "preliminaries." When people with different expectations of time participate in the same liturgy, the quality of their experiences may differ radically.

As important as the length of the service and the amount of time spent at church may be, people of diverse cultures also differ

in their overall sense of time. Anthropologist Edward T. Hall distinguishes between "monochronic" and "polychronic" senses of time.[19]
Some congregations have a monochronic view of time—that is, a
linear perspective in which one aspect of worship leads to another.
Euro-Americans often share this perspective, believing that time is
a commodity that can be saved or wasted or made up or lost. A
monochronic sensibility leads to a more individual awareness of
time—I might be late. Am I too early? Am I taking too much of
your time? Singing a traditional hymn in which the stanzas lead
from one to another in sequence may lead to a monochronic
musical experience.

Other congregations have a polychronic sense of time.[20] Polychronic time is more relational and less sequential than monochronic. For those on polychronic time, being with others is never a
waste of time. Time is more cyclical than linear. Those on cyclic
time tend to savor the moment and to set aside for a while those
issues that drive people in a linear fashion. Building community is
as important as gaining information and insight from the sermon.

Many communities that function on polychronic time make use
of cyclic musical structures—which are open-ended and built
around repetition, unlike traditional linear hymns. Their open-
ended quality allows the assembly to sing them until the whole
community is participating. Cyclic structures generally involve
physical response to music. Because cyclic songs are primarily aural
and do not require hymnals, singers tend to internalize the words
and music quickly and often respond physically to the repetition.
Music making then becomes not only aural but also a visible
expression of community when the people move together as they
sing. We will return to the possibilities and limitations of linear and
cyclic musical structures in part III, section 1, as well as how they
might enhance various parts of worship.

Nonverbal Cues

A second important area for those new to culturally conscious
worship is learning to recognize nonverbal cues. Euro-American
congregations are often more "tuned in" to what is said or written

and give little attention to nonverbal modes of communication. For many other cultures, the word, written or spoken, must be verified by what is done or displayed. A congregation may express verbally, for example, an open and welcoming spirit to strangers but neglect to confirm that welcome in nonverbal actions. A predominantly Euro-American congregation that wishes to include in its worship more African Americans or Latinos from the community loses credibility when nonverbal communication fails to complement verbal greetings. If those in the majority culture display only white representations of Christ, lack symbols meaningful to other cultural contexts, or allow insufficient time in a service for worshipers to greet one another, what is seen may contradict what is said.

Developing sensitivity for nonverbal forms of communication in other cultures may require that those from a dominant culture assume a minority role in another cultural context. An African American congregation that wants to welcome Latinos in the community into worship may find it helpful to send representatives in small groups (two or three at a time) to visit Latino congregations. To gain some perspective on nonverbal forms of communication, the visitors should observe for several weeks to develop some skill in negotiating the ritual practices of another cultural group. After a few weeks they will feel somewhat more at home. At first, many visitors will suffer "liturgy shock"—a disorientation in a new worship setting. This sense of confusion is the result of not understanding the rites (words) and rituals (actions) of an unfamiliar cultural group. Visitors may not know when to stand or sit, sing or be silent. Those from outside the congregation may not understand why certain rituals are performed and what they mean. If the liturgy incorporates other languages, visitors may be confused by the vocabulary used or the meaning of words.

Visitors in cross-cultural worship situations may also become disoriented by the general "soundscape" of the new worship environment—by which I mean all the ways that sound communicates the style and piety of the community. The presence (or absence) of children, the musical instruments used, the volume of congregational singing, the extent of back-and-forth between the minister and the people, the way the congregation gathers (for example, silently with an organ prelude, or with group singing), and the use of deliberate periods of silence—all these affect the soundscape. (Appendix B offers suggestions for observing worship in other cultural settings—a process designed to increase congregational sensitivity to how people worship in other cultures.)

Written versus Oral Traditions

Churches of some cultural traditions use a detailed printed order of worship, while others use none. I have observed that some African American congregations have a brief order of worship, perhaps a little more than a half-page, but embellish or take liberal detours from the printed order. This practice is typical of congregations with a polychronic sense of time—but not because the congregation has no set rituals or because the community is less literate. Detours from the printed order are usually a way of building community and strengthening identity. Some observers might believe that this expansion wastes time, or at least fails to use it efficiently. Congregations with a strong oral tradition are likely to sing more music than is included in the worship bulletin. When a moment of celebration or lament becomes apparent to the community, a song may emerge that suspends time and gives voice to common joy or concern. In congregations with a strong sense of oral tradition, it is not uncommon for sermons to include singing.

Anthropologist Jack Goody offers additional insights in his recent study *The Power of Written Tradition*. Learning through oral means is more intergenerational:

> Oral learning 'entails a greater amount of showing, of participation. Hence the world of childhood is less segregated from that of adults. Children sit or play around when discussions and performances are taking place, absorbing at least the general atmosphere of these activities and occasionally, if they listen attentively, some of their content as well. Much more learning depends upon the voice, upon face-to-face interaction. Whereas in literate cultures an individual can go off by himself with a book, in oral cultures a partner is needed as narrator or instructor.[21]

My experience in worship in varied settings around the world affirms Goody's experience. A predominantly oral worship setting tends to be more intergenerational and interactive than a setting dominated by paper and print. Worship that depends on literacy may exclude those at both ends of the age spectrum, those who have not yet learned to read and those whose eyesight is failing.

Lest my observations appear to be a judgment against prayer-book traditions, let me add that longtime Episcopalians have often internalized the complexity of *The Book of Common Prayer* through private devotional prayer and corporate worship. To the extent that Episcopalians have virtually memorized the rites and ritual actions of the prayer book, these have for such worshipers become oral texts. They have in effect freed themselves from the prayer book to participate as though they were living in an oral culture. Visitors who have not gained this proficiency may suffer liturgy shock when confronted by a prayer book, an order of worship, and a hymnal.

Once again, these observations do not indicate that vital and faithful worship takes place more effectively in one setting than in another. The relative balance of oral versus written tradition in worship may be a challenge for culturally conscious congregations as they learn to worship together. Avoiding this issue, however, may hamper full participation by people of diverse cultures.

Leadership and Power

Diverse ethnic groups bring with them culturally conditioned understandings of those in authority and leadership. An acquaintance with different perspectives may assist a congregation in dealing with perceptions about leadership and power. Anthropologist Geert Hofstede provides insight into this issue with his concept of "high-power-distance" and "low-power-distance" cultures.[22] People of high-power-distance cultures often perceive themselves as relatively powerless in the face of a powerful elite group that controls decisions and wealth. They perceive this elite to be at the top of a pyramid, the broad base of which contains the vast majority of the people who feel, by virtue of limited educational opportunities and economic potential, that they have little opportunity to make significant changes in decision-making structures.

Low-power-distance cultures, by contrast, usually have an
upper class and a larger middle class. More people in these cultures
have educational opportunity and economic potential and, as a
result, believe that they have access to power and decision making.
The concept of power distance is a significant dynamic in multicultural congregations. A middle-class Anglo congregation (a low-
power-distance culture) may have difficulty understanding why
recent Filipino immigrants (from a high-power-distance culture)
seem not to be interested in invitations from Anglo members for them
to join in decision-making processes. A Filipino view of authority
may make Filipinos less likely to question authority or even to
participate in the kinds of decisions that were made by leaders in
their culture of origin. Figure 2 provides a list of high- and low-
power-distance countries derived from Hofstede's research.

Figure 2

High-power-distance Countries	Low-power-distance Countries
Belgium	Australia
Brazil	Austria
Chile	Canada
Columbia	Denmark
France	Finland
Hong Kong	Germany
India	Great Britain
Mexico	Ireland
Peru	Israel
Philippines	Netherlands
Singapore	New Zealand
Thailand	Norway
Turkey	Sweden
Venezuela	Switzerland
	United States

Eric H. F. Law, an Asian American Episcopal priest from Hong
Kong, offers helpful conclusions based on these data.

1. The majority of recent immigrants to the United States come
    from high-power-distance countries, specifically from parts
    of Asia and Latin America.

2. Although the United States is a low-power-distance society in
    general, some people in America may assume the posture of a
    high-power-distance culture. This is especially true of those
    with less education and lower incomes. Many people of color
    in the United States may join the majority of recent immigrants
    in responding to multicultural situations as people from
    high-power-distance cultures would.
3. The perception of high power distance may persist for several
    generations after an immigrant arrives in the United States.[23]

People from high-power-distance contexts may have difficulty in
claiming an equal role in decision making even when this role is
offered and expected of them by others in the group. Those from
low-power-distance cultures often become frustrated with people
from high-power-distance situations. Even when people from low-
power-distance cultures verbally offer power to those from high-
power-distance cultures, people from those cultures may choose to
remain silent. Law suggests group processes by which those who
may feel voiceless can find a voice in culturally diverse groups. (One
of these processes, "mutual invitation," will be explored in the final
section of this book.) Developing an environment of cultural
equality is essential for worshiping in a way that reflects a cultural
mosaic. Those who value equality in relationships must be conscious of others who have accepted inequality as a circumstance
over which they had little control. Worship based on a cultural
partnership requires that each group become conscious of its
cultural biases and that all groups avoid the ethnocentric behavior
of attempting to assimilate others into a liturgical melting pot.

HIGH- AND LOW-CONTEXT CULTURES

A final area of analysis as we look at the landscape of cross-cultural
communication is the difference between high- and low-context
cultures. Anthropologist Edward T. Hall has also developed an
approach to cultural context and meaning that is essential for those
who pursue culturally conscious worship.[24] This point of view may
help those planning cross-cultural worship to understand some of

the complexities of communicating effectively to all who gather, regardless of cultural perspective.

Hall asserts that different cultures rely to greater or lesser degrees on cultural context for meaning. While all cultures have a cultural context, low-context people are less aware of their context, even to the point of assuming that they are either without a clear cultural perspective or that their cultural values are universal. Low-context cultures reflect a strong priority for individuality. While having many associations and encounters with others, the desire for individuality limits the number of people with whom one can have a deep relationship. Low-context cultures value efficiency in communication and therefore use an explicit code, usually spoken or written, to transmit most information. Using a written or spoken code—that is, language—as the primary mode of communication saves time, an important concern in many cultures. A low-context person makes changes easily and takes less time to establish a dialogue and receive information. Eric Law explains the dilemma well:

> Low-context systems may appear to be very inclusive at first because of their openness, without requiring any contexting time in order to relate to someone. The paradox is that they do exclude others, perhaps unintentionally, when they expect everyone to be low-context like them.[25]

E-mail may be the ultimate low-context medium of communication. I receive many e-mail messages, especially from colleagues or closer friends, that omit even the simplest of salutations associated with letters or in-person encounters. Even when I receive e-mail from a slight acquaintance or someone I don't know, the sender tends to keep the communication brief and to the point, avoiding "extraneous" information about family, weather, and personal circumstances.

High-context people value community relationships over individuality. Communication takes place as much through nonverbal gestures or movements as through oral or written expression. Touch and other nonverbal cues combine with briefer verbal messages to provide a highly contextual form of communicating.

Traditions of communication have been passed down for generations. Elders, the keepers of these traditions, attempt to ensure the
perpetuation of more elaborate nonverbal ways of relating. Because
of this role, elders often command a high degree of respect, even
veneration, in high-context cultures. Anyone who has experienced a
tea ceremony in Japan begins to understand the significance of a
highly elaborate nonverbal form of communication that has been
passed down for generations. Low-context people who are unfamiliar with high-context patterns of communication find it difficult to
understand nonverbal coded information that is not explicitly
explained. A high-context system lacks efficiency, from the perspective of those who are not accustomed to highly developed nonverbal forms of relating.

Two examples from high-context cultures may be helpful. I was
the guest of a Filipino extended family in a university community
south of Manila. The father of this family had traveled throughout
the world as a spokesman in his profession and had lived in several
countries as an employee of the United Nations. Virtually all of his
children and their spouses had earned doctorates or were working
toward doctoral degrees. The extended family community was so
important that all attempted to gather every weekend if possible.
Such gatherings seemed to me more like family reunions. Given the
rather cosmopolitan nature of this family, I was interested to see the
persistence of traditional ways of greeting. I observed, for example,
the traditional ritual of *mano-po* each morning as all children and
female spouses knelt in front of the father and touched the back of
his hand to their foreheads as a sign of respect. This respect was
further evident when the father assumed his role as a deacon in his
local Catholic parish. Those who greeted him on Sunday morning
before mass offered much more than a brief "hi" and a wave. Many
extended a hand, in the *mano-po* tradition, out of respect for his
role as a lay leader in the church and his age. This gesture was a very
high-context way of greeting.

I experienced even more elaborate rituals of greeting when I
lived for several months in western Nigeria among the Yoruba
people. As a low-context person, I expected specific routines to be
efficient and matter-of-fact. My most memorable culture shock

took place when going to the bank, a government office, or the post office. I hoped to be in and out quickly, but it was in these situations that my low-context expectations collided with the richness of high-context transactions. Exchanging money invariably became a 60- to 90-minute ritual. As my American dollars passed through a mysterious process involving several people, I observed that the Nigerians who entered the bank came with totally different expectations. While I sat rigidly fuming in a corner of the bank, the Nigerians were greeting each other, exchanging stories, swapping family information, discussing political events, and generally giving the gathering the air of a party. Indeed, they seemed grateful for the fortuitous encounters at the bank.

My Midwestern English reflects relatively few low-context greetings—for example, "Hi" or "How are you?" (often not waiting for a response) or "Good morning." The Yoruba language, however, has greetings that change every few hours through the day. Additional greetings are used for Sundays and special occasions. One must be highly aware of context to use the appropriate greeting at the correct time. When I see my African students on campus, they take offense if I do not spend extra time extending greetings and asking them how they are doing. I am much less likely to do this with my Euro-American students.

Returning to the e-mail example, note the high-context changes that have evolved with this generally low-context medium. Almost immediately, e-mail moved toward high-context adaptations with combinations of characters added to messages such as ;) or :) or :- that supplement the meaning of an otherwise low-context message. These "emoticons," or combinations of punctuation marks can indicate anything from a friendly greeting to a joke or sarcastic statement by the sender. Without these smiley-sideways faces, electronic mail may come across as bland or subject to misinterpretation. For example, upon reading a sarcastic statement, one may wonder if the sender is serious, unless a high-context clue does the work of vocal inflection or body language. Now digital photos and color are commonplace in ordinary e-mail messages, providing more high-context elaboration. Eric Law provides the following summary of low- and high-context communication styles.[26]

Figure 3
Characteristics of High- and Low-context
Communication Styles

High-context	**Low-context**
group-oriented	individual-oriented
rely heavily on physical context or shared context of the transmitter and receiver; very little is in the coded, explicit, transmitted part of the message	rely on explicit coding of information being communicated; less aware of contexts
spiral logic	linear logic
take time for "contexting" in the new situation	adjust to the new situation quickly
conflict may occur because of violations of individual expectations	conflict may occur because of violations of collective expectations
deal with conflict by concealment	deal with conflict by "revealment"
indirect, non-confrontational attitude	direct, confrontational attitude
"face-saving"	fact-finding
focus on relationship	focus on action and solution

Differences in high- and low-context cultural expectations often lead to conflict in worship. Two examples follow. One has to do with time in corporate gatherings. From the linear time perspective of a low-context person, some people appear to arrive perpetually late. The high-context person is as interested in the relationships that will be formed and renewed as he or she is in any "information" that may have been missed by arriving late. High-context parishioners are just as likely to remain for some time after the official conclusion of worship, and for the same reason, while low-context worshipers may leave soon after the benediction. To the high-context person, low-context people may seem insensitive to relationships, wanting to get down to the "business" of worship without taking time for proper greetings and showing deference to leaders. To the low-context person, high-context people may seem to be wasting time and failing to proceed efficiently in gatherings. Both have valid perspectives and can learn from each other.

Religious sociologist Nancy Ammerman notes that conflict is not necessarily negative if it leads to a better understanding between groups. Conflict may be a source of positive change.[27] Deep-seated misunderstandings arise and motives are questioned when people from different cultural backgrounds avoid open conflict and decline to identify the issues creating conflict, though underground or unspoken. For example, high- and low-context participants' differing expectations and sensitivities about a gathering time may lead to conflict. Although relationships are primary for high-context congregants, they also want to be challenged intellectually and to hear how God's Word applies to their experiences. Low-context people *do* enjoy and appreciate relationships. Though individualistic by nature, they come to church to be with other Christians and to participate in common prayer.

Another area that causes tension in relationships relates to the concept of "saving face" in figure 3 above. Because a high-context person tends to value relationships and to take an indirect, nonconfrontational approach, it is unlikely that he or she will disagree openly, especially with an elder or person in authority. This reticence is a sign of respect. The speaker would not want the authority or elder to lose face by being rebuked. Avoiding loss of face leads to what is often called the "conditional yes." Kathy Black notes:

> In some cultures, the relationship between two persons is so important that the person being asked would not openly refuse the request of another for fear of disappointing the other, hurting the other's feelings, or creating tension in the relationship. . . . Even if the person knows that he or she will be out of town on that particular Sunday, the relationship at the time of the request (when the persons are in face-to-face communication) takes

precedence over an unknown future date and time when the
parties will not physically be present with one another.[28]

Those skilled in high-context cultural communication may recognize nonverbal signals that indicate more clearly what a person
means by a given verbal response. Low-context folk can learn to
recognize high-context communication patterns and allow both
conversation partners to save face. What a low-context person may
gain by direct communication or confrontation may be lost in the
relationship with a person from a high-context culture.

High-context people may also learn that low-context people
who engage them in cross-cultural discussions will often "put all
their cards on the table" in what they say. Candor should not be
misinterpreted as rudeness. Clarity of verbal or written communication should not be confused with an uncaring attitude toward
relationships or the feelings of others.

All of the paradigms mentioned above—oral and written
tradition, high- and low-power-distance countries, high- and low-
context cultures—can be placed on a continuum of experience and
are present to some degree in most societies. Even highly literate
societies like the United States, for example, have a place for oral
experiences such as storytelling; music learned by ear from radio,
CDs, or computer-downloaded songs; and films that take the place
of, or supplement, books. Oral cultures also respect history, the
conservation of traditions, and the perpetuation of technical
information, even if it is transmitted by "wise men" and "wise
women" in the society and never appears in print. No single cultural perspective has a corner on knowledge or the best perspective.
We can all learn from each other.

IMPLICATIONS FOR YOUR CONGREGATION

In this chapter I have attempted to weave together some of the most
important strands in the cross-cultural liturgical landscape. Appendix C summarizes the concepts presented in this chapter in an
"Initial Worship Audit for Culturally Conscious Congregations."
Before attempting the strategies included in part III, section 2,

engage a representative group from your congregation in a process of becoming culturally conscious. The questions in appendix C will help you begin this journey. Steps to assist your congregation along the road toward a more culturally inclusive liturgy include:

1. Engage a representative and balanced group from your congregation and neighborhood (including age, gender, socioeconomic status, and ethnicity).
2. Use the audit.
3. Read and discuss the case studies.
4. Study the two sections in part III, developing a hierarchy of strategies from the final section that suits your situation.

You have probably concluded by now that cross-cultural communication and culturally conscious worship are hard work. You may also wonder, "Why should we try?" As Kathy Black points out, the birthday of the church at Pentecost began as a multicultural gathering. People were not segregated from one another by ethnicity or cultural perspective.[29] Extant records from the early centuries of the Christian church reveal repeated pleas for the Holy Spirit to make the church one body in Christ. At the turn of the 21st century there seems to be a renewed energy to claim the spirit of Christ's early followers.

Thomas Long, author of *Beyond the Worship Wars: Building Vital and Faithful Worship*,[30] has reported that most of the vital and faithful congregations he observed were ethnically diverse. The diversity ranged from a smattering of various ethnic groups to a virtual United Nations gathered for worship.[31] Many of the 10 characteristics of vital and faithful congregations he proposes are also important in shaping strategies for culturally conscious congregations.

We now look at four congregations that have, to varying degrees, become more culturally conscious about their worship. Two of these congregations are relatively new, having been started two and five years before this study. The two other congregations have long and established relationships with their neighborhoods—neighborhoods whose ethnic make-up has changed significantly. The younger congregations were established with a clear mission that included ethnic diversity. The older congregations have been drawn toward culturally conscious worship by their circumstances. Whether motivated by the intent to do mission or by changing demographics, their journeys may offer strategies, motivation, and companionship for the long journey for other congregations that seek to become more culturally conscious.

PART II

MULTICULTURAL CONGREGATIONS AND EXCELLENCE: FOUR CASE STUDIES

Some say that it does not work. Others say that it cannot be done. What a number of people in the pews, pulpits, denominational offices, and seminary classrooms in the United States are talking about is the possibility of creating a truly multicultural Christian congregation. Some say that nothing more than tokenism can be accomplished by "forcing" together people who do not want to worship as one. Others say that in any attempt to form a culturally diverse congregation, one cultural group will always dominate, overwhelming any smaller group. Some are cynical about the possibility of creating multicultural churches and argue that Christian congregations grow best when they are most homogenous and have a common worship style shared by all. Their thesis is that similarity produces growth—so why resist uniformity? Occasionally one also hears the complaint that the calls for multicultural congregations are nothing more than examples of "political correctness" and therefore a passing fad pushed by a faction within the church.

Perhaps advocates of homogenous church growth, skeptics, and opponents of multicultural congregations "protest too much"? Pervasive cynicism about multicultural congregations can mask an uncomfortable reality for Christians in the United States. As Charles Foster and Theodore Brelsford observe about historic "mainline" denominations:

> To this day, most of the congregations in these denominations remain among the most segregated of contemporary institutions.

> Although denominational leaders decry the lack of racial and
> ethnic cultural integration at the local level, they have given little
> attention, funds, or time to the implementation of a culturally
> diverse vision of community in the congregation.[1]

Within the context of cultural diversity, the quality of congregational ministry may erroneously be judged by standards borrowed
from the mainline Anglo culture—standards that may not take into
consideration the importance of diversity for Christianity. Indeed,
the contemporary search for "excellence" has itself become a cottage
industry that influences the larger culture.

Excellence in congregational ministry rarely is understood to
include the cultivation of and appreciation for cultural diversity.
However, part I illustrates that society in the United States is not
culturally monolithic, and that the church must search for more
ways to promote growth other than through cultural uniformity.

Certain denominations and associations, including historic
mainline, evangelical non-Pentecostal, Pentecostal and charismatic,
and fundamentalist groups often argue that the "most effective"
congregations are those whose members belong to the same ethnic
group (or are at least perceived to be part of the same group). But
these denominations and associations usually shy away from the
more difficult task of shaping multicultural congregations. When
excellence is measured solely by numerical growth, expansion of
programs, and construction of new facilities, a pervasive assumption prevails that multicultural congregations work against such
growth and standards of excellence.

Faulty concepts of excellence in ministry ironically build upon
faulty assumptions of the nature of the gospel and of Christian
ministry. Missing is an understanding that the countercultural call
of the gospel often means following a path that does not follow the
conventional wisdom or the most popular trends. The countercultural call of the gospel requires that we use a set of criteria for
excellence that is not valued by the business and corporate community, by higher education, or even within established ecclesiastical
traditions that stress the way things have usually been done. Those
discussing excellence in ministry, including culturally conscious

worship, should be wary of adopting definitions from the corporate business culture or theories of congregational redevelopment that lift up uniformity.

What would congregational excellence through diversity be like? Of primary importance is an understanding that the church is the body of Christ as revealed throughout the world. Furthermore, an understanding of excellence in congregational life and ministry that grows out of this biblical understanding of the global church will lead us to receive the gifts of people from all cultures and to work diligently to welcome those who are different from the majority group in socioeconomic status, cultural background, and political perspective.

In addition, the diverse gifts people of different cultures bring to the church include fresh perspectives on sharing faith and responding to the needs of the world, as well as new understandings of worshiping together—insights that may not be available to more culturally uniform groups. Finally, culturally conscious worship is a significant aspect of being the body of Christ at work in the world, one that will result in attaining congregational excellence through cultural diversity.

When we understand that Christ's church is global, it becomes clear to us that culturally conscious worship is a significant aspect of reaching congregational excellence through cultural diversity. Such worship is challenging, even in the abstract. A concrete way to understand excellence in ministry more clearly is through case studies of congregations engaged in ministry. Congregations that wrestle with diversity in day-to-day life and attempt to learn from experience are to be admired. Such are the four congregations in the following case studies. Each has a distinctive story to tell on its journey toward culturally conscious worship. None is perfect, nor has any reached the destination of liturgical diversity. These congregations include faithful Christians in a certain place and time trying to offer a witness in their respective communities. I am grateful for leaders' and members' willingness to talk about their struggles in this forum. It is my hope that your congregation may identify with one or more of these congregations and learn from their decisions about how to be the body of Christ faithfully in their setting. The description and analysis of each congregation should be viewed as a work in process and not as a finished project. We join each at a particular point on its journey toward cultural consciousness in ministry and worship.

CASE STUDY 1

OUT OF MANY, GOD MAKES US ONE: GRACE UNITED METHODIST CHURCH

Susan Knipe and Robin Stevens

Close to the heart of downtown Dallas stands a picturesque Gothic
Revival structure. Grace United Methodist Church is an elegant
testimony to a glorious past. Its highly visible tower and spire serve
as a beacon to a culturally diverse east Dallas neighborhood,
though they are dwarfed by the skyscrapers of Baylor Medical
Center, five blocks away. It is hard to walk past Grace without
pausing to admire the magnificent stained-glass windows that
depict the gospel story. The Grace congregation has endured many
struggles over the past 100 years. While the gospel scenes in the
windows have not changed in a century, the community surrounding the church has changed considerably. The stories of individuals
that compose the history of Grace are as varied as the colors of the
windows. These stories find unity in the worship of the Holy One.
Welded together, they create an art work of love and perseverance
that has carried this urban congregation through tough years.
Countless faithful people who believed in the significance of
Grace's ministries kept its traditions alive. Serving the community
amid world wars, a roller-coaster economy, and an ever-changing
neighborhood, the people of Grace have sought ways to honor God
and survive.

THE GRANDEUR OF GRACE

Located at the corner of Junius and Haskel, Grace United Methodist Church is a historic landmark just east of downtown Dallas. Its
tower and spire serve as a reference point for navigating the neighborhood. In front of the church is a small park bench surrounded
by a well-kept flower bed. Because the primary parking lot is
behind the building, the back entrance has become the main access
to the sanctuary. Worshipers may have feelings of awe and reverence as they enter Grace, taking in the splendor of the stained-glass
windows that dominate the sanctuary. The windows are a large part
of Grace's identity; and they preserve its story, rich in tradition. The
magnificent woodwork in the sanctuary contributes to the gran-
deur, and the chancel area inspires awe. Elevated above the congregation are majestic organ pipes and the pulpit in the center of the
chancel. Grace's pastor, the Rev. Dr. Charles Cox, commented, "The
magnificent pulpit changes the way one preaches."

Construction of the French Gothic Revival building dates to
1903. In 1925 the orientation of the worship space was changed
from east/west to north/south. According to John Gill, organist-
choirmaster at the time of the study, "The choir loft end of the
sanctuary was added at that time, and the seating capacity [was]
almost doubled. The current organ was also installed in 1925." Until
recently, the only other modification to the building was the addition of its educational wing, also in 1925.

Although it does not have the oldest church building in east
Dallas, Grace is the longest continuing congregation in the area.
Renovations to preserve the historical landmark began in 1986 with
restoration of the organ. Other improvements have included the
installation of an elevator; new electrical wiring, and air condition-
ing; addition of new office space and a new choir room; provision
of a nursery and more rest rooms; construction of facilities for the
Agape Medical Clinic and Open Door Preschool; restoration of the
parlor, classrooms, sanctuary, fellowship hall, and kitchen; and
enhancements to the church exterior.

A space formerly used as an office was made into a small prayer
chapel, an annex to the hospitality room. This cove has an altar and
a couple of dozen chairs; it is large enough for a very small wed-

ding. The chapel is a quiet, reflective spot paneled from floor to ceiling. The congregation's goal is to complete all restoration work in time for its centennial in 2003.

NEIGHBORHOOD DEMOGRAPHICS

During the early 1920s, Grace was considered an "all-white, silk-stocking" congregation whose members included "mayors, business leaders, and affluent Swiss Avenue residents."[1] The wealth of past members is still a source of pride; old photos of prominent parishioners of a bygone era hang on the church office wall. Many of the wealthiest families owned homes along prestigious Swiss Avenue, the first neighborhood in Dallas developed with specific zoning regulations for new homes. Those who gathered on Sunday morning included local and statewide political leaders.

As the demographics of the neighborhood shifted, so did the social status of the worshipers. Beginning in the late 1920s, apartment buildings were erected within walking distance of the church; the average income of neighborhood residents dropped. Initially occupied by Caucasians, these buildings over time became homes for people of color. As suburban life beckoned after World War II, the nearby area was rezoned for multifamily dwellings, allowing the large homes on Swiss Avenue to be subdivided into apartments and to decrease in prestige. Substandard apartment dwellings were also added after the war. By the mid-1970s many of these buildings were owned by slumlords. Segregation remained the norm for most congregations, and Sunday morning worship attendance dwindled as longtime members left the neighborhood and newer residents did not feel welcomed by the church and its ministries.

By the late 1970s Grace was facing the threat of having to close down. The broadening of the church's ministries to the neighborhood and the renovations that began in the mid-1980s were both responses to this situation.

COMMUNITY CONNECTIONS

Community involvement has been a priority throughout the history of Grace Church. Activities included rolling bandages during World War I, offering classes for cooking rationed food during World War II, and creating a food pantry and a clothes closet in the 1970s that gave birth to the ministry of the East Dallas Cooperative Parish (EDCP). In its efforts to meet the needs of the changing neighborhood, the EDCP has become "a national model of neighborhood service and congregational renewal."[2] Grace takes part in the cooperative parish with Christian congregations of several denominations. Each location is host to one or more ministries serving neighborhood needs. Through this cooperative effort, disadvantaged people in East Dallas are being served more effectively than through individual congregational programs. Service to the community is an important focus for the people of Grace and, as John Gill, the longtime minister of music said, "We see the importance of reinventing Grace every three or four years in this constantly changing urban area."

Figure 4
Demographic Overview:
Grace United Methodist Church

Population within a 1.5-mile radius: 313,856

Males: 49.7%
Females: 50.3%

Population 19 and under: 31.3%
Population between 20 and 54: 50.7%
Population 55 and older: 18.0%

White: 42.5%
Hispanic/Latino: 44.0%
African American: 10.8%
Other/Mixed: 2.5%

Owner-occupied housing units: 54.6%
Renter-occupied housing units: 45.4%

Source: Census 2000 <www.census.dfwinfo.com>

Grace houses the Open Door Preschool, which serves primarily children from non-English-speaking homes—Mexican, Mexican-American, Central American, Cambodian, and Vietnamese families—and are taught English as well as other skills they need for success in public schools. The school also offers English classes for the children's parents.

The East Dallas Legal Clinic was born out of the dream of Judge Merrill Hartman, a Dallas family court judge whose law firm offered free legal services for those without financial means; he also encouraged other firms to do pro bono work. As a result of his efforts, a legal clinic at Grace Church (the second such site established) was opened in 1983.

The East Dallas Legal Clinic at Grace has experienced continual growth; it handles civil cases, including matters of family law, immigration, taxes, wills, and bankruptcy. On two Thursdays each month volunteer lawyers, provided through Legal Services of North Texas, offer counseling and other services, including negotiation, preparation of forms, and representation in court.

Another of Grace's outreach programs comes in the form of health care. Three days each week, the Agape Medical Clinic treats low-income patients free of charge. Although the patients are primarily from East Dallas, some come from other parts of the city to receive minor medical care. Dr. Barbara Stark Baxter, a research allergist, a graduate of Columbia Medical School, and a member of Highland Park United Methodist Church, began this clinic in 1984 to provide health care to working, low-income people who were unable to secure health care elsewhere. The Rev. Dr. William Bryan, at that time pastor of Grace Church, noted that the then Dr. Stark was the first physician to desensitize pregnant women's allergies to penicillin so that their sexually transmitted diseases would not infect their infants. Several physicians and nurses now volunteer. One year 3,200 children were served. Part of Dr. Bryan's ministry there was to dispense anti-lice shampoo. The clinic is outfitted with equipment for minor care and a pharmacy that dispenses essential medicines to clients. Translators assist medical staff as they offer urgent care ranging from immunizations to check-ups, aided by volunteer church members.

Another of Grace's vital programs is its Asian ministry, reaching out to Cambodian and Vietnamese refugees who have settled in the neighborhood. The Rev. Pa Pan, the nation's first Cambodian United Methodist minister, was educated with funds provided by Grace and the cooperative parish. Pa operated a full-time Asian ministry out of Grace until the mid-1990s, helping immigrants find jobs and adjust to life in the United States.

For several years Grace hosted a Zen center in its educational wing. A room was adorned with candles and icons; the center offered weekly meditation sessions. According to Grace pastor Dr. Cox, "Zen meditation offers centeredness for a lot of people. Grace is what churches should be about, breaking down the walls between people." When the Zen center bought its own space, the classroom was freed up for a new activity. Art Spirit, a ministry to the artistic community of Dallas, led by a United Methodist minister, uses art as a focus for prayer. Art Spirit uses the classroom to display art in media ranging from a quilt to paintings and Orthodox icons. By hosting outside programs, Grace has adapted to being a "small church with a big building," Cox noted.

Grace Church is situated amid a growing Hispanic population, as evidenced by the many commercial signs in Spanish on shops and other businesses in the community. Other ethnic minorities live in the area, and a homeless shelter is nearby. Apartment buildings close to the church are home to many low-income and working-class people. The nearby Swiss Avenue district, once the habitat of Grace's elites, is now part of a Dallas urban-renewal movement. Many of the large old homes are being renovated by a varied group of upper-middle-class owners. The close proximity of East Dallas to the downtown business district makes Swiss Avenue a desirable location for professionals who choose not to live far out in suburbia. New construction, including urban lofts, is also in the picture. Townhouses selling for $190,000 and up replaced some of the low-rent apartments. Low-income residents have been forced to find new homes as older structures are razed or remodeled, and the new or refurbished housing commands high rents out of their reach.

Health-care agencies have a strong presence in the community. Five blocks from Grace is Baylor University Medical Center, one of the top medical teaching centers in the country. Its skyscrapers dominate the skyline as well as the neighborhood. An apartment complex is available for the families of patients who need long-term medical care. A kidney-treatment center is located across from the church. During the week, traffic is heavy on surrounding streets, with mass-transit bus service available.

Across the street from the church is the fenced-in urban academic complex of Criswell College. This school has been a respected institute of Bible-Belt conservatism for decades.

DEMOGRAPHIC MAKEUP

At the time of this study, Grace averaged 110 worshipers on Sunday mornings, with a membership roll of about 275. While many congregations in the area are about the same size, Grace contrasts sharply with large suburban churches boasting thousands of members. Current statistics represent a significant decrease in the size of the congregation from earlier years. Grace is predominantly Caucasian, a contrast to the immediate neighborhood. Euro-Americans make up approximately 80 percent of Grace Church's membership; the remaining 20 percent consists of African Americans and Asians. Several biracial families are a part of Grace. The average age of members falls between 45 and 50; those figures reflect a congregation whose average age is gradually declining. Until the recent addition of a children's sermon, few children and youth attended worship.

The congregation includes openly gay and lesbian members, some of whom are residents of the nearby revitalized housing area. According to Dr. Cox, one-third of the active members are gay men or lesbians, and these members account for a third of the church's financial support. Their participation has had a dramatic effect on both the building restoration and the general revitalization of Grace. The majority of the choir consists of gay and lesbian singers who prefer to avoid single-issue churches. This inclusiveness is the touchstone of diversity for this congregation, and it is closely tied to the successful hospitality extended by many members. Hospitality extended to gay and lesbian members at Grace is extended in turn by them to other groups in the community.

Income levels vary greatly among church attenders. Homeless folk may wander in on any given Sunday; in contrast, some members commute from the affluent neighborhoods and suburbs of Dallas. Some commuters have long-standing ties with Grace; other worshipers drive to Grace because they want to support the ministries of an urban church that embodies ethnic, social, and economic diversity. Some low-income and working-class people who live in nearby apartment complexes also make Grace their church home. All are welcome, regardless of income level.

WORSHIP AT GRACE CHURCH

Grace follows a traditional fourfold pattern of worship (see part I). Greetings and announcements are followed by a responsive call to worship. Hymns are from *The United Methodist Hymnal* (1989). After the opening hymn, the congregation participates responsively in a prayer. "Greeting One Another in Christian Love" (passing the peace) follows, and people turn to each other with handshakes or hugs and brief conversation. The choir sings an anthem. Then comes a prayer offered by the pastor or lay leader, voicing the joys and concerns of the congregation, and concluding with the Lord's Prayer said by all. During the offering, the choir sings another anthem; then comes the Doxology, sung by all ("Praise God from whom all blessings flow"). After the reading of the morning scripture, the pastor delivers a sermon. Holy Communion follows. The service ends with a closing hymn, benediction, sung response, and organ postlude.

Worship Planning Process

The pastor and the choir director typically plan the weekly worship services. The worship committee focuses on major observances like Advent, Christmas, and Easter. On occasion this group also is responsible for worship outside the Sunday schedule. Dr. Cox said he believes that the design and dignity of the sanctuary set the tone for worship. He voiced great "respect for [the] traditional" atmosphere of the sanctuary. The current order of worship reflects the pastor's traditional leanings and his desire to maintain what he called the "integrity and centeredness" of worship.

Achieving a balanced ethnic perspective in worship planning, as well as in leading the congregation generally, can be difficult. A Latina member commented, "[The] leadership is very white." Even though some members are black, "it is rare for a black person to achieve any management position within the church," said one white female member. Some suggested that in the past, minorities named to committees were tokens. They were usually not well educated about their role, and they rarely attended meetings. Others differed with this perspective, noting that African American members, though fewer in numbers than other minority groups, have had regular roles on committees. Asians, especially Cambodians, have been the largest minority group. Although they have been invited to participate on committees, a language barrier has limited their participation, even when translation has been available. Now there is an effort underway to achieve a more multicultural balance.

The minister of music recognizes that it is difficult to incorporate first-generation Cambodians into the congregation because of culture and language differences. While efforts to integrate adults should be continued, he said, he has "always felt that our best chance would be with the children. Our children's Sunday school program has recently been entirely revamped to meet the special needs of the Cambodian children. Getting them to sing in a children's choir is the next step. We have great hopes for these kids."

Distinctive Features of Worship

For Grace members, the most important aspects of worship are fellowship, passing the peace, and Holy Communion. The fellowship after the service includes a coffee time with light refreshments in a hall adjacent to the sanctuary. Coffee hour in effect extends the service beyond the hour allotted and provides valuable time for introductions and conversations among the various groups.

Passing the peace is a joyful ritual that takes three or four minutes. Worshipers exchange hugs and brief conversations; many move out of the pews to greet others. Though this joyful time expresses the inclusive nature of the congregation for most, the pastor reported that some folk have let him know that for them, "It's a little bit too much forced friendliness." Curiously, choir members do not generally leave the loft to greet other worshipers. While the practical reason is probably that the choristers need to be in their places for the anthem, the practice may contribute a non-verbal note of disunity. The traditional architecture, placing the choir far from and much higher than the congregation, contributes to this sense of separation. One layperson noted, "I wish the choir were closer." The minister of music confirmed that it is impractical for the choir to leave the loft during the passing of the peace because of the time it takes, but he encourages the singers to move through the congregation greeting people after the service.

Grace Church celebrates Holy Communion weekly; congregants see this sacrament as a vital part of worship. Recent pastors have encouraged weekly Eucharist. Though the rite is shortened on most Sundays to include essentially the words of institution, the full text is spoken on the first Sunday of each month and on other celebratory occasions; at those services the musical responses are sung.

THEOLOGICAL FRAMEWORK

The motto of Grace, "Out of many, God makes us one," reveals the theological presupposition central in the life of the congregation. The weekly celebration of Eucharist enacts the unity the congregation desires. Receiving the bread and the cup sets this gathering apart as a Christian group. The Lord's Table is a leveling place for all Christians, a perspective that Grace Church celebrates with pride. Gays commune alongside straights; homeless people kneel beside upwardly mobile first-time home buyers; children come forward with retirees; Asians share the meal alongside African Americans. All kinds of faces are visible, challenging the congregation to value the diversity in the family of God.

A United Methodist understanding of the gospel stresses that God's salvation is offered to all. A song, sung at the end of each worship service, written by choir member Carol St. George to Beethoven's tune *Ode to Joy*, reflects this inclusive spirit:

Praise to thee, O Joyous spirit,
  God of beauty, God of love.
Send us forth in love and service
  with the grace that makes us one.
Sanctify our daily living;
  grant us strength of heart and soul.
In God's likeness we, united,
  share the peace that makes us whole.

A theologically trained lay member said the parting song "describes who we are and defines our theology."

The open communion table relates to the hospitality offered after the service. "The motivating force for Grace is hospitality, theological vision, and survival," said a seminary intern. The hospitality of open communion extends to serving refreshments after the Sunday service. At Grace, hospitality is a means to congregational revitalization. The weekly extension of welcome is a wellspring of hope for the future of Grace Church.

Stewardship of the building and a major renovation of the sanctuary are the most tangible results of the theology at work here. Plans are now being realized to remodel the large room adjacent to the sanctuary used for the "Grace Gathering" coffee fellowship after worship. In a time when many churches have added large-screen projectors, theater-style spotlights, and stages to highlight "praise and worship" bands, Grace restored the beautiful old stained-glass windows, stripped off whitewash to expose the original woodwork, and polished the chandeliers. Attending to the building, raising funds for its renovation, and restoring it to its former glory make a theological statement that Grace Church is here to stay in this community. Though the neighborhood may change, the congregation intends to continue its journey, offering social services and spiritual direction, and living as a welcoming congregation. By renovating and repairing the windows, organ, and sanctuary, and by restoring the fellowship room to its historic style, the congregation is reclaiming the traditional values that have sustained it for nearly 100 years.

Like many older American congregations, Grace finds a sense of preserving Christian tradition central to its theological task. Grace leaders and members have vowed to remain faithful through ethnic, socioeconomic, and demographic shifts in the community. Through its community ministries Grace is a beacon of hope for many who have nowhere else to turn. It is a place of service for those who prefer a vital congregation struggling in a diverse urban setting to the comfort of a homogeneous suburban neighborhood. Since the conception of Grace, God's active presence has been a driving force behind the momentum of its programming. God is active in the lives of young children through the ministry of the preschool. God is present in the healing hands of doctors and nurses who work in the clinic. God abides in the search for justice offered through legal services.

CHALLENGES AHEAD

The congregation's desire for diversity is reflected in its motto, "Out of many, God makes us one." Grace continually tries to reach out and serve the diverse community that surrounds the church. The community that Grace Church serves through its outreach ministries is much different from the group of worshipers who attend on Sunday. "Some still see Grace as a segregated congregation but admit that the majority of the congregation would be shocked to be identified as segregated," noted a longtime member of the worship commission. "Segregation at Grace is not always a racial issue, but it is sometimes an economic one," she continued. Most of the congregation would say, 'We are glad they are here. . . . What happens when *they* outnumber *us*?'" Another member of the team summed up the dilemma not only for Grace, but also for other congregations in similar circumstances:

> Each year, thousands of people from other lands come through our doors because of [our] outreach efforts. Most don't attend services at Grace, but we make sure to have a presence among them so that they know they are always welcome. I believe that no matter how good our intentions are to be inclusive, many are simply uncomfortable with people [who] are, in many cases, so different from us. It's not a matter of racism or bigotry, but rather a natural human response—one that can be had just as easily by those on one side or the other. The question is "What to do about it?"

The experiences of Grace Church raise fundamental questions that challenge all congregations. Grace has admirably attempted to maintain a balance between revitalizing its rich heritage and responding to the needs of a diverse community. Many congregations have folded under similar circumstances. Despite heroic efforts and careful theological discernment, some members are still haunted by questions about the congregation's future identity in light of its cultural heritage.

A congregation requires much time to absorb the effects of community change. Though some Grace people are nervous about the reasons for changes in neighborhood demographics and their possible effect on the congregation's future, theological reflection provides an anchor for members' concerns. The struggle, according to one member, is how to make Grace more appealing to the unchurched of the neighborhood. For some seekers, the traditional style of the architecture, combined with the liturgy and the warmth of the people, may indeed lend a sense of "sanctuary," a place of rest for world-weary wanderers. For others, the restoration of the stained-glass windows may not be a use of resources that connects with their cultural background. The rich sounds of the restored organ may not resonate with their musical heritage.

As the surrounding neighborhood is experiencing a surge in revitalization, Grace seeks to preserve its tradition while embracing a diverse neighborhood. The pastor sees Grace as a "happy, joyful place" where people can come to "feel good about themselves and life, . . . with the worship helping them to get through the week." The church is trying to reinvent itself as the neighborhood changes. Hymns are becoming more diverse. "Music does a better job than the spoken word in delivering the message," Dr. Cox observed. For World Communion Sunday, people wore their native dress, Afghan bread was served at communion, and the liturgy from the World Communion literature was used. At the end of the service, worshipers formed a circle around the sanctuary, all holding hands—a diverse group of people coming together as one in Christ.

The refurbished stained-glass windows are back in their places with the light of Christ shining through them. Grace also seeks a restoration of a different sort, that of realizing its vision and identity as a new community reflecting the diverse face of the Creator.

Joining hands with neighbors on Sunday mornings as well as on weekdays requires not only open hearts, open doors, and open minds. It also requires outstretched hands, ones that will go out into the neighborhood to bring new people in, not just opening the church doors to welcome those who come. The challenge of Matthew 25 is existential rather than theoretical for Grace Church: How do we clothe the naked around us? How do we feed the hungry in our midst? How do we care for the sick on our doorstep? The very name of this congregation—Grace—reflects the desire of these people to share God's love. It is by God's grace that this church has struggled through the tough times and continues to stand, uniting hearts in celebration of the congregation's 100 years. Members share God's grace with those who come to Grace, while seeking to understand God's plan for them as a diverse church.

LA FAMILIA
AGAPE MEMORIAL UNITED METHODIST CHURCH

C. Michael Hawn

If you enter Agape Memorial United Methodist Church on a Sunday morning from the parking lot, you may find yourself coming through the back door leading directly into the *cocina* (kitchen). As you walk through the *cocina* into the fellowship hall, you will hear a buzz of conversation in Spanish or English or "Spanglish" as people share greetings and *abrazos* (embraces). Some women may be preparing food in the *cocina* for a *comida* (dinner) after the second service. A table is spread with juice, coffee, and an assortment of *pan dulce* (sweet Mexican rolls) and doughnuts. The fellowship hall is set up with tables and chairs. Across the room is a wall of pictures of Sunday School classes, awards, congregational photos, and other memorabilia. Entering through the kitchen reminds one of coming into the home of a beloved *tía* (aunt) and feeling the welcome of the extended *familia*.

Agape (pronounced "ah-GAH-peh") Church is located on a tree-shaded street just a few blocks from a busy connecting road. Parking is also available on the street in front of the church. Many folk park there, and some walk to church from nearby homes. At the door an usher greets you, gives you an order of worship, and directs you into the sanctuary. Just off the narthex is a small room where some gather before church. If you arrive just as the English-language second service is beginning, you may have to weave your way into the service through the choir, minister, and worship leader, as they wait to enter in procession during the first hymn. A child serving as acolyte walks slowly and carefully with a candle lighter down the aisle toward the chancel area. The organist plays a prelude. A sense of reverence prevails as worship begins.

HISTORY OF THE AGAPE CONGREGATION

Agape Memorial United Methodist Church began as the Floyd Street Mission under the Dallas Board of City Missions in 1930. The congregation became the Latin American Mission as a part of the Rio Grande Annual Conference of the Methodist Church in 1948. The Rio Grande Conference is a Spanish-language, nongeographical judicatory that includes Texas and New Mexico, overlapping six predominantly Anglo annual conferences. At the Floyd Street Mission, worship was conducted in Spanish because most members spoke only Spanish. More important, the congregation's identity was shaped as a Mexican (rather than Mexican-American) church, a mission for Mexicans temporarily north of the border rather than a congregation fully integrated into the culture of the United States.

The mission became a constituted congregation in 1948 as the Latin American Methodist Church. It then merged in 1965 with Mary King Methodist Church, an Anglo congregation. Mary King Church had a vision of becoming a larger congregation in the community. Its facility at that time, however, was small. At the time of the merger, the Hispanic members of the amalgamated congregation were fully assimilated and virtually all bilingual.

In 1990 a second union took place. The merged Mary King Church united with Capitol Memorial United Methodist Church, a member congregation of the denomination's North Texas Annual Conference (as was Mary King). Capitol Memorial, an aging, mostly Anglo congregation that could no longer maintain its facility, found that many of its members were moving to the suburbs as the neighborhood became increasingly Hispanic. The uniting congregations became Agape Memorial United Methodist Church. Capitol Memorial had a better facility and became the home of the newly formed congregation. Though Agape was situated in a Hispanic neighborhood and the majority of the members were Latinos, the English-language service was the dominant worship hour. As a Latina member said, "We lost some members in the merger, but won with the increased resources of the combined congregations." Agape Church today is the product of the uniting of a Hispanic mission and two Anglo congregations.[1]

The Rev. Minerva Carcaño, former director of the Mexican American Program at Perkins School of Theology and a member of Agape, discussed the process leading to the merger.

> I once asked some of the Agape leaders, Hispanic and Anglo, how they had been able to merge into one congregation. They told me that it had been over the work table in the kitchen. They had faced resistance to the merger, and many of them wondered whether the merger would work. But, as they had dinners and other church projects and worked together in the kitchen, sharing their stories, struggles, dreams, and hopes as people of faith, they discovered that they weren't so different from each other after all. At the kitchen table they grew to know, respect, and eventually love each other.[2]

Agape Church has enjoyed a long-standing relationship with Perkins School of Theology, Southern Methodist University. In addition to Minerva Carcaño, one of the congregation's prominent members is Dr. Roy Barton, a 1957 Perkins graduate who returned in 1974 to be founding director of the theology school's Mexican American program. He held that post for 21 years. This relationship is a point of pride for the congregation. Perkins is a leading theological school for the training of Hispanic ministers both in its master's-level degrees and in the "course of studies" program. The latter, a Spanish-language certification program, offers courses for future ministers who either have not attended college or who are older than 35 when they begin their theological studies. Perkins offers a lectureship each year in Hispanic theological education in honor of Dr. Barton, an event in which many Agape members participate.

Since the merger of the two congregations, Agape has continued to hold membership in the Spanish-language Rio Grande Conference, but not in the predominantly Anglo North Texas

Conference. According to Dr. Paul Barton, pastor of the congregation briefly, the decision was a point of contention in the newly merged Latino and Anglo congregation. At Agape, Latinos make up 70 to 75 percent of a total membership of about 240. The congregation holds two worship services each Sunday, a Spanish-language service that ministers mostly to older bilingual members who prefer to worship in Spanish, and a later English-language service that includes families with children and youth. These services are virtually identical in format. Another indication of the dual Anglo and Hispanic identity is reflected in the pew racks. The mostly English-language *The United Methodist Hymnal* (1989) sits alongside the denomination's Spanish-language hymnal, *Mil Voces para Celebrar: Himnario Metodista* (1996). (Its title echoes Charles Wesley's hymn "O for a thousand tongues to sing.") On most Sundays the same hymns will be sung at both services in the respective languages.

Members recognize that pastors of Agape must be fully bilingual to be effective in ministry to the congregation and neighborhood. For this reason it can be difficult to appoint a minister when a pastoral vacancy occurs. During this study, the congregation was led by an experienced, semi-retired interim minister, the Rev. Moisés Yáñez. An interim pastor, though not unheard of, is unusual in the Methodist appointive system.

Agape has a "cordial relationship" with the community, Dr. Barton noted. This relationship is evident in the vital ministries that the church conducts in the neighborhood. Barton observed that "the church building itself is a part of the church's witness," by which he means that Agape's location in the community bears its own witness.

NEIGHBORHOOD DEMOGRAPHICS

Agape Church is located in a neighborhood in east Dallas near *el centro* (downtown). The church is surrounded by brick and wood-frame homes, many well over 50 years old, and is near a number of apartment complexes. Part of Agape's challenge is to relate to the residents of several well-maintained two-story apartment buildings within walking distance of the church.

Businesses within a few blocks of the church often have signs in both English and Spanish. For example, there are several *lavanderías* (self-service laundries), a *carnicería* (butcher shop), *panaderías* (bakeries), a *supermercado* (supermarket), a popular, inexpensive, authentic Mexican restaurant (Cuquita's), and a smaller food shop (Amigo's Food Market). Other businesses that cater to Spanish-speakers include Compadres Taquera (a billiards establishment), income-tax firms, and small shops specializing in wiring money to Mexico and El Salvador. These establishments are thriving primarily on the business of first-generation Latino immigrants who support family members back home. A few blocks away, but still in the neighborhood, are larger strip malls, a common sight in Dallas. They include two large national Latino supermarket chains (Fiesta and Carnival) and a host of mainstream franchises such as Blockbuster Video and McDonald's. While a diverse ethnic clientele frequents these businesses, most are geared to the needs of Latinos.

The area around Agape Church is rich in religious diversity as well. Three Baptist churches are within blocks of the church, each reaching a distinctive ethnic population. Iglesia Bautista El Mesías (the Messiah Baptist Church) is directly behind Agape, reaching Latinos from the neighborhood. Ebenezer Baptist Church is a few blocks away. It includes African American members as well and offers classes in English. The largely Anglo Ross Avenue Baptist Church is the oldest Baptist congregation; its roots in this area predate the influx of Latinos over the years.

Other religious communities nearby include a Roman Catholic congregation; the Asamblea Apostólica de la Fe en Cristo Jesús (the Apostolic Congregation of Faith in Jesus Christ); a Latino Seventh-day Adventist Church; and an Eritrean Orthodox Church, a congregation of Ethiopian immigrants. The Comunidad de Esperanza (Community of Hope) houses a child-care center.

COMMUNITY CONNECTIONS

At the top of worship bulletins at Agape is a church motto—"Un Iglesia para Nuestra Comunidad" (A Church for Our Community).

Agape Church has a tradition of reaching out to the community. The Rack, located in a house adjacent to the church building, offers low-cost second-hand clothing to neighborhood residents. The church also sponsors the Not Home Alone after-school program for children in the neighborhood. The Casa Feliz Centro para Ancianos (Happy House Senior Adult Center) meets weekly in the church fellowship hall, providing a gathering place for neighborhood folk to eat, read books and magazines not available or affordable to them, and socialize. The recently added concrete court next to the church is used by the community for basketball or volleyball and as a place for church and community fiestas.

One of the challenges of Agape is to relate to the Anglos and African Americans in the community, though they may be on the decline. A Latina member observed, "Agape has Anglo members but no real focus on reaching out to Anglos or African Americans or other English-speaking [people] in the community." Developing multicultural identity through culturally conscious worship may be one way to help Agape reach out to the community in fresh ways. Figure 5 provides an overview of the demographic picture of Agape's neighborhood.

DESCRIPTION AND IDENTITY

A broader perspective on the characteristics of Hispanic congregations offers clues for understanding the identity of Agape Church. To be a Hispanic Protestant in the United States is to be a "double minority" person. First, a Hispanic Protestant is in a minority by virtue of ethnicity and perhaps language. Second, Hispanic Protestants are part of a religious minority, since most Hispanics throughout the United States and the Spanish-speaking world are Roman Catholic.[3]

Being a double minority may contribute to a sense of marginalization. Justo González, a Cuban-American church history professor and leading Hispanic scholar, refers to the marginal state of Hispanics as "liv[ing]... at the hyphen"—that is, the hyphen in the middle of Mexican-American or Cuban-American.[4]

Many Hispanics are also racially mixed—*mestizo/mestiza* (Spanish and indigenous parentage); or *mulato/mulata* (Spanish

Figure 5
Demographic Overview: Agape Memorial United Methodist Church

Population within a 1.5-mile radius: 369,577

Males: 49.3%
Females: 50.7%

Population 19 and under: 30.5%
Population between 20 and 54: 51.1%
Population 55 and older: 18.4%

White: 47.2%
Hispanic/Latino: 41.3%
African American: 8.0%
Other/Mixed: 3.5%

Owner-occupied housing units: 54.2%
Renter-occupied housing units: 45.8%

Source: Census 2000 <www.census.dfwinfo.com>

and African parentage) rather than *criollos* ("pure" Spanish descendants). In-betweenness runs through every aspect of Hispanic experience in the United States.

La Familia

Agape shares many characteristics with other mainline Hispanic Protestant congregations in the United States, especially those that are Presbyterian or Methodist. Rubén Armendárez, a Texan Presbyterian and former professor and administrator at McCormick Theological Seminary, Chicago, identifies some of these characteristics. The first is *La Familia* (the family). "The Hispanic Protestant congregation can be accurately described as a family group. The membership of the congregation is usually composed of from one to three identifiable large families who are related to one another through marriage."[5] Agape Church reflects this pattern. In describing the most important aspects of the church, a longtime Latina member said, "Agape is my home, my family." A very active Latina church member with a young family repeated this theme. "Agape is a special community and family that is willing to reach out and spread love to the neighborhood." At the core of the founding members was Sam Moreno, still an active member, and his mother, now deceased. Sam married one of five sisters from Mexico. Each of the remaining four sisters married; their families, including husbands, have been active in the congregation. Most are still living and attend regularly, along with some of their children and grandchildren. Though Sam Moreno and his kin make up the largest extended family in the congregation, other two- and three-generation families are members of Agape.

Armendárez noted, "Other smaller family units also join those large families through marriages or through what is known as *padrinos* or *madrinas* (godfathers or godmothers) or *compadres* or *comadres* (coparents)."[6] This pattern is also evident at Agape. It is not surprising that the Agape team in the study group for this project chose to name its chapter "La Familia." The extended family is both a reality and a metaphor for relationships among the members.

An interesting aspect of Hispanic Protestant tradition is the term used to address each other in church—*hermanos* or *hermanas* (brothers or sisters). This usage not only relates to a sense of all members as *familia* but also serves as a distinctive term used by Hispanic Protestants but not by Hispanic Roman Catholics.[7] As one Latina noted, "Catholics tend to live out their faith experience more individually and personally, while Hispanic Protestants understand and live their faith experience more communally." *La familia* shapes the identity of a Hispanic Protestant congregation in almost every way.

Lenguaje (Language)

Hispanic congregations are often bilingual, speaking both English and Spanish. "This bilingual condition and experience is a natural expression and a reality with which they live daily," Armendárez noted.[8] Agape has two worship services, an earlier one in Spanish and a later one in English. Though many, perhaps most, of the members are bilingual, only rarely is English used in the Spanish-speaking service or Spanish in the English-speaking service. Although "Spanglish" is common in conversations outside of worship, it is rare in worship.

González observed, "Older people and more recent immigrants tend to prefer Spanish, while many in the younger generations prefer English. . . . The resulting [dynamic] in congregations is quite interesting, and sometimes sad."[9] Agape fits this pattern to some degree. Teenagers often understand Spanish but resist speaking it. Therefore, Agape's Spanish-speaking service is attended primarily by a smaller number of senior adults, while the English-speaking service is attended by a wider range of generations. A Latina notes, "Bringing [the Spanish and English services] together and having one whole community of faith can be difficult at times. We have united services occasionally. These are OK, but the communication is not as good as it could be." Agape maintains a bilingual approach to ministry and an insistence on bilingual pastors to serve the influx of new immigrants into the neighborhood, on the one hand, and, on the other, to maintain contact with younger people who may not be totally bilingual.

Protestante (Protestant)

Armendárez's study of Hispanic Protestant congregations suggests that they articulate their Protestant perspective in specific ways. According to a list provided by Armendárez, Agape Church appears to be representative of Hispanic Protestantism:

- The Bible is central and normative for our faith.
- The Bible leads us to understand that we are justified and saved by faith.
- The Bible commands us to observe only two sacraments: Baptism and the Lord's Supper.

- The Bible teaches a personal relationship with God.
- The Bible teaches that Jesus Christ is our savior and the only intermediary between us and God.
- Prayer is a means of personal relationship with God.
- All people are sinful, and confession is to God alone and pardon comes from God.
- All people have an equal relationship with God.[10]

While these assertions describe many Protestants, most reflect the Latino experience of being a Protestant minority in a predominantly Roman Catholic cultural context—for example, justification by faith, only two sacraments, Jesus Christ as the only mediator. The final assertion, "All people have an equal relationship with God," may reflect an observation cited above: Latinos are a double minority in the United States and may therefore have been subjected to oppression and discrimination.

Justo González notes the prominence of the Bible in worship and emphasizes that Latinos read the Bible differently from Anglos because of their experience. Given the diversity of Spanish-speaking countries and cultures in the Western hemisphere, González is quick to assert that there is no one monolithic Hispanic perspective. Yet overarching themes come to the forefront when Latinos read scripture. These themes include marginality, poverty, mestizaje and mulatez (mixed-race people), exiles and aliens, and solidarity.[11]

The centrality of the Bible in worship is an important part of Hispanic Protestantism. Throughout worship, especially as a response to the reading of the scriptures and during sermons, the refrain *"La palabra de Dios"* (The word of God) is prominent. Like many Hispanic Protestant congregations, Agape hears all four lectionary passages each Sunday, including the psalm, often read responsively.

Being a "Methodist witness in the community" is also an important part of Agape's identity, according to one member. In a largely Hispanic neighborhood where most Latinos are Roman Catholic, Agape takes its Methodist connection very seriously. Mainline Hispanic *Protestantes* have a distinct and vital identity and are often more vocal about their specific denominational connection than are their Anglo counterparts.

Minoría entre Minoría (Minority within a Minority)

Armendárez notes some of the consequences of the minority-
within-a-minority perspective in the Hispanic Protestant church.
Besides being part of a cultural minority in the United States and a
religious minority among Latino Roman Catholics, the double-
minority reality affects the Latino Protestant perspective in other
ways. Hispanic Protestants are aware of their small numbers and
small resources.

> The sense and feeling of smallness in this sense, therefore, is
> confirmed by the fact that a large number of Hispanic Protestant
> congregations are small numerically and depend on financial
> support, either through local, regional, or national Anglo denomi-
> national bodies.[12]

Carcaño points out:

> Hispanic Protestants are minorities within their denominations as
> well, and face blatant racism and the majority church's difficulty
> in creating space for the gifts of other cultures. While there are
> those within denominations who valiantly struggle to create an
> inclusive church, there is yet much work to be done. These
> realities affect the psyche of Hispanic Protestant churches and
> their ability to be creative in worship and self-affirming of their
> own culture and what it can bring to worship.[13]

While Agape Church is proud of its neighborhood outreach programs and its ability to survive through several congregational
mergers, a feeling persists among some members that limited
numbers and financial resources prohibit them from doing all they
would like in the community. In relation to the growing influence
of first-generation immigrants in the neighborhood, however,
Agape seems to be a comparatively wealthy church. One Latina
noted, "Many in the neighborhood see us differently, and think that
they could not afford to go to such a 'rich' church."

Until recently many clergy and laity in the Rio Grande Conference have felt that they were second-class citizens, often under the
leadership of an Anglo bishop who might not understand their

situation. In 2000 a Latino bishop was appointed to lead the conference. Bishop Joel Martínez is a graduate of Perkins School of Theology and served many years as a pastor in the Rio Grande Conference. This appointment has been a source of great pride to Agape Church, which sent several representatives to his installation service.

Rio Grande Conference ministers rarely receive salaries as high as those of ministers in largely Angloju annual conferences. Armendárez noted, "As participants, the Hispanic Protestant congregations feel that they are underrepresented because of numbers and resources, which leads, as some have expressed it, to a sense of inadequacy—not with themselves, but 'because they have more and we have less.'"[14] While Agape Church may share some of these feelings, it has produced several strong Hispanic leaders in the denomination, both clergy and lay, and it is proud of the church's role and heritage in the community and beyond.

A discontinuity prevails at Agape between congregational ministries to the community and the presence of its members in the community. Armendárez makes an astute observation:

> [A] survey in one of the participating congregations indicated, overwhelmingly, that its own members recognize their lack of involvement in the issues affecting the community. . . . [M]ost members of these congregations do not . . . live in the community. A large majority . . . live outside and thus become commuters to church activities. In a sense, they are Hispanic aliens in their own communities and aliens to the neighborhoods to which they commute for church activities.[15]

Agape has over the years provided important services *to* the surrounding community—which now consists of large numbers of first-generation Latinos, predominantly from Mexico and El Salvador. As in the churches in Amendárez's survey, most Agape members are third- and fourth-generation Latinos who no longer live close to the church. Living outside the community creates a cultural and geographical gap as the church attempts to reach out to recent immigrants who live in apartment complexes near the church. A Latino lay leader at Agape noted the decreasing hands-on involvement of church members in ministries to the community. Increasingly, the church pays others to lead these ministries. The lay leader lamented the lack of "official involvement of the congregation."

Armendárez's survey of Hispanic Protestant congregations offers a general way to understand the identity, ministries, and worship of Agape Church. While Agape varies somewhat from the churches that participated in his survey, it appears to be similar in most respects to other Hispanic Protestant congregations. A closer look at Agape's worship offers a clearer understanding that Agape, though a predominately Hispanic church in a Hispanic neighborhood, faces many cross-cultural challenges.

A PATTERN OF WORSHIP

The Spanish- and English-language services follow a similar pattern with some variations. A typical Sunday's order of worship is as follows:

English service	**Spanish service**
Prelude	Preludio
Processional Hymn *(English service only)*	
Call to Worship *(may be a responsive psalm)*	Llamamiento a la Adoración
Hymn or Songs of Praise	Himno (o Cantos) de Alabanza
Invocation	Invocación
Apostles or Nicene Creed	El Credo Apostólico o Niceno
Hymn of Praise	Himno de Alabanza
Time of Fellowship and Announcements	Bienvenidos y Anuncios
Pastoral Prayer	Oración Pastoral (o Oración en el Altar)
Response *(sung)*	Responso *(sung)*
A Time for Children *(English service only)*	
Old Testament Lesson	Lectura del Antiguo Testamento
Anthem *(choir)*	Himno
New Testament Lesson	Lectura del Nuevo Testamento
Gospel Lesson *(all standing)*	Lectura del Evangelio *(all standing)*
Sung Response	Doxología
Sermon	Sermón

Offertory	Ofertorio
Special Music	Música Especial
Invitation	Dedicación de las Ofrendas
Hymn	Himno
Benediction	Bendición
Recessional Hymn	
(English service only)	
Postlude	Postludio

Communion is celebrated on the first Sunday of each month. On these Sundays, earlier parts of the service are modified, and the order following the sermon varies:

Sermon
Requests for Concerns and Prayers
Invitation to Prayer
Confession and Pardon
Offering
Special Music
Dedication of Offerings
Anthem
Thanksgiving and Communion
The Lord's Prayer
Breaking the Bread—Giving the Cup
Dismissal with Blessing
Recessional Hymn
Postlude

Distinctive Worship Practices

The presence of a choir affects the order of worship in the English-language service, which includes processional and recessional hymns and the addition of an anthem. A children's sermon is also included in the English service. From time to time a quartet sings special music in the Spanish service. During the time of this study, the interim pastor worked with a Perkins Seminary student from Mexico to introduce the singing of *coritos* (shorter Spanish-language choruses) in the Spanish service as a way to attract the Hispanic immigrant community to the Spanish-language service.

An important feature of both services is the use of a lay leader (*Lider de Adoración*). Women and men share in this responsibility.

This position is an important one in the Hispanic Protestant church. A Latina member noted, however, that some Hispanic pastors in other churches become acculturated to Anglo ways and do not use a *Lider de Adoración*. Some liturgical activities may not be listed in the order of worship. These include the lighting of the candles during the prelude, an occasional greeting (passing of the peace) among the congregation, and an invitation to kneel at the altar during the pastoral prayer. The service order may vary in detail from week to week but generally follows this pattern.

The worship committee has attempted to play an active role in worship planning, especially during special seasons. A representative of the Agape worship committee preferred hymns that correspond to the scripture. She also cited several newer hymns as her favorites including, "Here I Am, Lord," "Lord of the Dance," and "Sois la Semilla" ("You are the seed"). These hymns are found in both hymnals. Some committee members said they would like a greater degree of coordination between the committee and the pastor in worship planning. The part-time, interim status of the pastor may have reduced the time devoted to worship planning.

Joint bilingual services are held on Thanksgiving, Good Friday, and Christmas. The Christmas service features a choral cantata and does not include a sermon. During this study, an additional bilingual service was planned for World Communion Sunday in October. The choir sang a eucharistic hymn from Uruguay, "Hoy Celebramos con Gozo" ("Let us celebrate today with joy") that reflected a fiesta spirit. Participants from both services sang *coritos*, normally used only in the Spanish service. The Latina seminary student found these changes refreshing. She hoped that the congregation would build on these successes by incorporating more songs, customs, and art with Hispanic cultural significance into future communion services and by having more joint bilingual services. Interim Pastor Yáñez said he felt that the joint bilingual communion allowed the congregation to experience a needed "unified worship service." Efforts were made to use Spanish and English in such a way that direct, repetitious translations were not necessary, producing a more flowing experience.

Bilingual worship services, however, require significant planning and often meet opposition. One Latina member noted, "There is a lot of resistance to bilingual services at Agape by Latinos because 'everyone understands English anyway.' This attitude makes it harder to reach out to the Spanish-speaking members of the community."

Both the seminary student and Pastor Yáñez said they believed that the response from the congregation to the joint bilingual communion service was positive. Though this evaluation is anecdotal, it may indicate possibilities for the future direction of worship at Agape, a way to help the congregation relate better to the community.

Music in Agape's Worship

During the time of the study, Agape's music director, an Anglo university music professor, moved out of state to take a new position. He worked well with the musical resources available and felt welcome and appreciated by the choir and congregation. Among the instructions he had received from the interim pastor was to teach the congregation new hymns, especially at the English-language service. He also formed a quartet to sing favorite hymns during the Spanish-language service. Accompanying him at the piano and organ were two capable volunteer musicians, rotating responsibility for service playing. Soloists from the congregation often sang during the offertory.

After the director's departure Agape did not have a regular music director for almost a year. Some individuals filled in from time to time, and a retired music director was secured to help the choir prepare a cantata for the traditional Christmas service. The choir, which ranges from eight to 15 members, practices weekly. Even if the singers were unable to sing an anthem, they took their responsibility as worship leaders seriously, entering in procession each Sunday and taking their places in the choir loft.

The seminary student played the guitar and made several attempts to introduce *coritos* in the Spanish-language service. Her leadership was enthusiastic, and she led with a clear, strong voice. Singing *coritos* was not the usual practice of the mostly older group that gathered for this service. These third- and fourth-generation

Latino Methodists were almost totally dependent on the English-language hymns in translation that they had grown up on. Many such Euro–North American hymns, translated into Spanish, appeared in the *Himnario Metodista* (1973). At the time of the study, few of the newer hymns found in *Mil Voces* were sung in worship. Older favorites that had also appeared in the earlier *Himnario Metodista* were standard fare in the Spanish-language service. An older Latina member of the worship committee lamented, "Some of the beautiful old hymns are not in *Mil Voces.*"

The use of various musical instruments relates to cultural identity. While an organ is common in Anglo churches, its use in Latino contexts may indicate a high-status congregation. Moisés Yáñez noted, "The organ is a powerful instrument. It is a symbol of the church's priorities. When Hispanics merged with the Anglos, they followed the Anglo pattern of worship." Like many Latino Protestant congregations, Agape lives in the tension between ministering to third- and fourth-generation Latinos (whose forebears came to the United States at a time when assimilation into the dominant culture was a high priority), and reaching first-generation Latino immigrants who are not assimilated. For long-established members, part of the cultural assimilation consisted of adopting many Anglo Protestant worship practices. These included the style and selection of hymns, the use of the organ, and other rituals of mainline Anglo Protestantism before the Second Vatican Council. Part of the identity of Hispanic Protestants was shaped by clinging to practices distinguishing them from Roman Catholics, such as singing hymns and placing importance on the Word (*La palabra de Dios*) in sermon and scripture readings. The underlying dynamics of the Hispanic Protestant "double minority" make the singing of favorite Anglo hymns in translation an even more important identity issue among third- and fourth-generation Hispanics. These were the hymns that Anglo Protestant missionaries first used to introduce Hispanics to the Christian faith.

It is natural for minority congregations to preserve the cultural priorities and values of older members. Justo González identifies the challenge well:

Often the congregation is the only place where the older generation of Latinos and Latinas have a voice—they are generally
disempowered in politics, and very seldom can they influence the
schools . . . their children attend or the curricula they follow.
Therefore, many older Hispanics are tempted to turn the church
into a cultural preserve, whose main function is to transmit the
mother culture to the younger generations. When that happens,
the younger folk—especially teenagers—resent being forced to
worship in Spanish and to follow the traditional culture, with the
result that as they grow up they often leave the church, at least for
a while. Thus, the generational conflicts that are so common in
the dominant culture—and which are not as marked in Hispanic
cultures themselves—become quite diverse in many Latino
congregations.[16]

The Agape congregation faces a dilemma, especially in dealing with
complex and varied generational musical preferences. Many recent
immigrants would be comfortable only in a Spanish service. However, the Spanish service offered at Agape is shaped by the musical
preferences of third-generation members who understandably
favor the hymns found in an earlier hymnal and, to some degree,
resist newer forms of music such as *coritos* that appeal to newcomers. The English-speaking service rarely uses any Spanish and,
though incorporating some more recent music, would not usually
reach recent immigrants from Latin America either.

Configuration of Worship Space

Agape has ample worship space. The chancel area is raised several
steps above the congregation. Some worshipers are bothered by the
great distance between the altar and pulpit in the chancel and the
people below. The fixed pews hamper the creation of more intimate
seating arrangements that would allow worshipers to see one
another. The piano and organ are behind the pulpit on the left side
of the chancel (from the congregation's perspective), and the choir
loft is behind the lectern on the right side of the chancel. The
communion rail, where people kneel to receive the elements,

separates the lectern from the choir; the large altar table, where communion is prepared, stands in the center against the back wall of the chancel except on communion Sundays, when it is moved forward. The wide gulf separating the organ and piano from the choir on the opposite side of the chancel is not ideal musically; the organist has difficulty seeing the choir director from the console, especially when the altar table stands between them. The seminary student noted that, in contrast to Mexicans who like to sit closer to the front of the church, a high percentage of the Agape congregation sits toward the back, creating a scattered feeling at times.

Ample wall space in the chancel area allows room for colorful banners. A series of distinctive banners reflects the changing seasons of the Christian year. Just to the left of the banners, on the chancel wall behind the pulpit, hangs a candle in a red glass holder. One member commented that the "Catholic eternal light" had always been there.

I attended a summer communion service that met in the fellowship hall because of an air-conditioning failure in the sanctuary. Folding chairs were placed in a semicircle around the hall. The altar had been brought in and placed level with and near the congregation. People sat much closer together and closer to the front in the smaller space. A woman lay leader (not common in Latino Protestant communities) assisted the pastor at the communion table. People passed the peace before communion with an ease and energy that I had not observed in the sanctuary. Commenting on their usual practice, one member said, "The greeting is not so important now at Agape." Thinking back on my earlier experiences in Methodist churches in Texas and Mexico, I observed that Agape did not practice an extensive greeting or passing of the peace. In many churches "the peace" is a festive seven- to ten-minute ritual. In the intimacy of the fellowship hall, Agape members shared a warm, vibrant, and extended greeting before communion. While it is difficult to judge the meaning of the warmer interchanges from this single experience, it is safe to say that the alternate space had an effect on worship that Sunday morning.

Agape's Worship Identity

Although Agape's worship style is influenced by the merger of a
Latino mission with two Anglo congregations, significant aspects of
the services reflect the underlying piety of the Latino majority. In
my conversation with several lay members, they cited what they felt
to be the three most important aspects of worship at Agape. The
first was coming forward to kneel for prayer during the extended
pastoral prayer. Both services share this pattern. Though this ritual
is not usually printed in the bulletin, those who wish to participate
are invited to come forward or know that this opportunity is
available to them. This practice is common in many Latino Methodist churches I have attended. Some congregations emphasize a
healing dimension for those who are ill. Many come accompanied
by close family members for support. Others use this time to make
the congregation aware of celebrations such as birthdays and
anniversaries.

A second significant feature of Agape's worship is the focus on
la palabra de Dios (the Word of God). These members contrasted
their emphasis on the Word to brief homilies offered in many
Roman Catholic churches. The importance of *la palabra de Dios* is
evident in the practice of having all lectionary lessons read. Though
this is not a practice unique to Agape Church among Latino or
Anglo mainline congregations, reading all the lectionary passages
may indicate an underlying personal relationship with scripture
along the lines cited earlier by Justo González in his *Santa Biblia*.
The Latino Protestant has a high understanding of the authority of
scripture as a guide for daily living and a source of hope.

The third issue raised in the conversation with Agape's members was the importance of ritual and the sacramental "power"
(role) of the pastor. "The importance of ritual" is perhaps another
way of saying that Hispanics value being together in worship and
engaging in those practices that form a marginalized and voiceless
minority into a community. The role of the pastor, one member
noted, is "like a priest" who voices before God the congregation's
joys, concerns, and sorrows, and applies biblical truths to their lives.
The pastor presides over the rituals of worship and helps to ensure

that they reflect the concerns of the people. Although pastors generally provide this function for their congregations, many Latino Protestant congregations emphasize the priestly dimensions of pastoral leadership.

A fourth significant feature of Agape's worship is the ample time allotted for sharing joys and concerns. Anyone is welcome to offer words of thanksgiving or requests for prayer. At times the sharing leads to brief testimonies. The pastoral prayer often follows, allowing the minister to voice the joys and concerns of the people in words of praise and petition to God.

CHALLENGES AHEAD

As I reflect on my experiences with Agape Church, I am struck by the congregation's warm hospitality. Though under interim pastoral leadership during the study and suffering from the loss of a music director for part of that time, the congregation continued to examine its relationship with the community and to meet the challenges with resolve and hope. One indication of Agape's firm commitment to being "A Church for Our Community" is the outside court for basketball and volleyball, which Agape built during the interim period on a church-owned lot adjacent to its building. During this time the congregation also continued its other ministries. Though not always knowing the answers, Agape wrestled, with the guidance of interim pastor Moisés Yáñez, with ways to reach apartment dwellers who were among the many first-generation immigrants to the area. Despite the lack of a permanent music director, the choir prepared music for the traditional Christmas worship service. Although valuing established rituals and traditionally separate English and Spanish services, the congregation demonstrated openness to trying new songs in a joint bilingual World Communion service.

The cross-cultural challenges facing Agape are different from those of other congregations in this study. Like sister Latino Protestant congregations, Agape must bridge the generation gap between bilingual older members and English-speaking young people. Agape must also relate to Anglo members who speak only English.

In addition, the congregation needs to relate to recent immigrants who speak only Spanish or, because they are just learning English, prefer to worship in Spanish. Most of these people are Roman Catholic, and increasingly others are Pentecostal. While its ministries to the community are vital, Agape's ability to worship with the community appears to be limited at this time. Although the cultures differ, Agape faces the same challenges that confront many established congregations when the neighborhood around them changes.

The Rev. Maria Luisa Santillán Baert, an ordained United Methodist minister and a member of the Rio Grande Conference, offers some general guidance to churches like Agape. She encourages the church to build on its heritage of attracting new people through "inspiring hymns, . . . dynamic preaching, . . . moving prayers, . . . powerful witnessing, and meaningful worship."[17] She encourages Protestant Hispanic congregations to rethink their resistance to all Roman Catholic practices and to incorporate those that may be meaningful to Hispanic Protestants as well. These practices, discarded by many Hispanic Protestants as non-Christian, include "Ash Wednesday services, candles, acolytes, *quinceañeras* [a party celebrating a girl's 15th birthday], and posadas [a Christmas procession particularly popular in northern Mexico and the southwestern United States portraying the Holy Family as its seeks shelter]."[18]

Santillán Baert also encourages the practice of having different kinds of worship, including "praise and prayer" services that focus on singing, recitation of favorite Bible verses, and testimonies. She explains, "Testimony services are those in which participants stand up one at a time and publicly testify in word and in song about their Christian experience and their faith journey."[19] Following the thinking of the Rev. Roberto Gómez, also a clergy member of the Rio Grande Conference, Santillán Baert encourages Hispanic Protestants to give a higher priority to Holy Communion, a practice that suffered among Hispanic Protestants because of its association with Roman Catholicism. "The de-emphasis of Holy Communion is a high price to pay to become Protestant," she commented.[20] Furthermore, Santillán Baert encourages the use of tortillas for communion bread as a cultural symbol that connects Eucharist with Hispanic culture.[21]

Santillán Baert also urges Hispanic Protestants to sing some of the rich hymns written originally in Spanish by recent Latin American hymn writers. She cites a list of Methodist writers who have become known ecumenically around the world in Spanish-speaking countries. They include Vicente Mendoza, Federico Pagura, Mortimer Arias, Raquel Mora Martínez, Raquel Gutiérrez-Achón, Pablo Sosa, and Manuel Flores. Many of the suggestions offered by Santillán Baert have been included in *Mil Voces Para Celebrar* and will be incorporated in a forthcoming bilingual *Hispanic Book of Worship,* edited by Bishop Joel Martínez and his wife, Raquel Mora Martínez (Abingdon, 2003).

Agape has a heritage of strong and visible leadership. It has demonstrated its resilience through a merger and its desire to witness and minister to the community. A young Latina church leader said, "We do not draw a line as to who can or cannot come to Agape." The challenge for Agape is to find a way for the neighborhood to feel this welcome spirit in its worship as well as its ministries.

CALLED INTO BEING:
ALL NATIONS UNITED METHODIST CHURCH

Edwin David Aponte

> For my house shall be called a house of prayer for all nations.
> (Isa. 46:7 NEB)

This scripture provides the inspiration for All Nations United Methodist Church. The congregation represents a small but increasing group of churches throughout the United States whose membership is ethnically diverse.

Plano, Texas, is an exurban city north of Dallas. Once a small town, Plano is now home to many corporations that wanted to move outside Dallas proper. The city eventually became the home of a snack-food giant, as well as varied information-technology and consumer-products companies. Sociologist Nancy L. Eiesland states: "Small towns, once perceived by long-time residents to be distant physically and culturally from the city, are frequently becoming 'exurbs,' that is, residential and service centers surrounding edge cities."[1] Plano's population grew from 72,331 in 1980 to 222,030 in 2000.[2]

Plano is a place of contrast, with wealthy corporate executives and working-class people living in the same town. Much of Plano is an affluent corporate community, despite downturns in information-technology industries. Some residents both live and work in

town; others commute to Dallas; but as in other exurban communities, many people commute to the other cities and towns outside
Dallas without ever going into the center city. Plano is divided
geographically by U.S. Route 75, also known as the Central Express-
way, a division that has economic overtones. The east side of Plano,
where All Nations Church is located, is the city's more culturally
diverse side. The racial/ethnic distribution of the city and the
neighborhood can be seen in data from the 2000 U.S. Census in
Figures 6 and 7.

The demographic information demonstrates some of the
differences between the east side and west side of Plano. Figure 7
provides an overview of the population within a 1.5-mile radius of
All Nations United Methodist Church.

Racial categories used by the Census Bureau for various ethnic
groups, especially Latinos, are still disputed by sociologists and other
observers. Even with possible discrepancies in racial attributions, it
is evident that All Nations Church is situated in one of Plano's more
racially diverse areas. Moreover, the congregation itself shows
remarkable racial and ethnic diversity, as seen in Figure 8.

According to the Congregations Project, a study funded by the
Lilly Endowment that focuses on multiracial churches throughout
the United States, a congregation is multiracial when "no one racial
group is 80 percent or more of the congregation."[3]

Figure 6
Demographic Overview: City of Plano, Texas

Total population: 222,030

White: 78.3%
Hispanic or Latino (of any race): 10.1%
Black/African American: 5.4%
Asian: 10.2%
Other/Mixed: 1.6%

Owner-occupied housing units: 68.8%
Renter-occupied housing units: 31.2%

Source: Census 2000 <http://www.census.dfwinfo.com>.

Figure 7

Demographic Overview: Neighborhood of All Nations Church

Population within a 1.5 mile radius: 19,317

Males: 51.9%
Females: 47.9%

Population 19 and under: 30.4%
Population between 20 and 54: 53.5%
Population 55 and older: 16%

White: 44.1%
Hispanic/Latino: 27%
African American: 8.8%
Asian 1.3%
Other/Mixed: 18.8%

Owner-occupied housing units: 62.4%
Renter-occupied housing units: 37.6%

Source: Census 2000 <www.census.dfwinfo.com>.

Figure 8

Demographic Overview: All Nations United Methodist Church

Membership: 140

White: 42%
Hispanic or Latino (of any race): 5%
Black/African American: 51%
Asian: 1%
Other/Mixed: 1%

Source: research conducted by Edwin David Aponte

CONGREGATIONAL LIFE

Like many communities in North Texas, Plano has many Christian churches. A snapshot of a Sunday morning reveals much about the congregational life of All Nations United Methodist Church, formed in 1999. On a typical Sunday morning in this diverse section of Plano, congregational music led by a choral ensemble precedes the worship service. The entire building is abuzz with activity as people move from Sunday school classes to worship. As the piano plays and the choir sings, people gather in the sanctuary. Though this church's music is influenced by African American hymnody, the choir is strikingly multicultural. Anglos, African Americans, and Latinos sing together. As one looks around the sanctuary before the start of worship, one can see in the people gathering in the pews a diversity in gender, race, and ethnicity, in dress (some quite casual and others more formal), and in age. The diversity at All Nations is particularly notable in comparison with the Anglo Baptist congregation that shared the building with All Nations at the time of this study.

As the congregational gathering music concludes, the robed, African American pastor, the Rev. Dr. Clara Reed, mounts the steps to the platform along with congregational leaders assisting in worship. Dr. Reed gives a warm greeting to all worshipers. She informs the assembly that All Nations is "Christian by faith . . ." and without a pause the congregation enthusiastically responds, " . . . diverse by design!" The liturgical dialogue is dramatic and unexpected to the first-time visitor. This congregational call-and-response at the start of worship is so smooth and powerful that one wonders if it is somehow scripted, and perhaps in one sense it is. In some way this phrase at the start of worship is a clue to the nature of the calling, life, and ministry of this multicultural congregation.

Conversations with members reveal, however, the depth of passion that this motto holds for them. A feature on the congregation in the religion section of the *Dallas Morning News* included these responses by members:

"We're exposing our children to the fact that in God's eyes we're all the same," said Mia Mbroh, an African American whose husband is African.

"When my grandchildren come to visit, this is where I want them to see me," said Bettie Adams, who is part of the church's white minority.

"We can meet different kinds of people and share with different people to show the love," said Ruby DeLeon, whose family is from the Dominican Republic.[4]

CONGREGATIONAL HISTORY AND VISION

It is clear that All Nations Church is committed to its mission of being a multicultural congregation. The congregation's identity is caught up in the vision "Christian by faith, diverse by design." Members have a strong sense of ownership of the vision articulated by the pastor. The name All Nations, though derived from the pastor's dream for the church, has become a shared vision for the entire congregation. "Christian by faith, diverse by design" is not only a Sunday morning call-and-response; it is a de facto credo of the congregation. Members repeat it often, both in and out of worship. It reflects the congregation's sense of self and how members hope to minister.

In 1998 the North Texas Conference of the United Methodist Church committed itself to plant 100 new churches by the year 2020. At the same time, Dr. Reed had a definite plan for establishing and leading a multicultural congregation. In discussions between leaders of the annual conference and the pastor, the conference's church-planting commitment and Dr. Reed's vision of a multicultural congregation led to a fruitful dialogue. The upshot was that All Nations became the first major project of the conference commitment to plant multicultural churches. Because it adopted the goal of becoming a multicultural congregation, All Nations has developed as a regional church rather than a strictly neighborhood church—a "niche" congregation attracting and serving those who are prepared to commit themselves to the countercultural goal of a multicultural congregation.[5]

Some members of the congregation spoke of an unformed sense of search or calling for this type of congregational life and mission—a longing that remained unarticulated until they came to All Nations. To others, coming to All Nations was a homecoming, although "home" was a place they had never seen before. As if by chance, a number of members had lived and worked outside the United States in the past. Some congregants have speculated that those who have tasted of a multicultural reality may continue to thirst for it.

Communal ownership of ministry seems to have been part of All Nations from its inception. The congregation started with 12 people meeting for a Bible study in homes. This small beginning was followed by a period when the congregation worshiped and held Sunday school classes in a rented movie theater with the smell of popcorn announcing that the service was about to end. All Nations is already in the third phase of its life and has grown into a congregation of 130 worshiping in a purchased facility of 34,000 square feet. As it grew in size and ministries, All Nations Church seemed to realize that its formation and growth did not happen in isolation from the larger church. A strong link remains between the North Texas Annual Conference and All Nations. Dr. Reed has followed a plan for developing a multicultural congregation within a United Methodist structure. All Nations' relationship to the denomination may be seen in the basic structure of worship, the organization of committees, and the mission it has to the community at large.

The congregation has members who have experienced a multicultural congregation elsewhere and want to continue participating in a diverse congregation. Many said that they joined the congregation because its diversity mirrored their own diverse family units.

Congregational life has also been characterized by a sense of family relationship from the outset. The origins of this characteristic seem to be found in the days of the initial Bible study group, but especially in the period when All Nations met for worship and Sunday school in a rented movie house. For some, this early period is recalled as a "golden era." The weekly setup and breakdown served as a community-building exercise. Preparing a secular space for Sunday School, caring for infants in a nursery, and worshiping together united people in a common task. Ensuring cultural diversity on all committees constantly reminded the congregation that each encounter at the church was another opportunity to learn from other cultural perspectives. A visitor to All Nations will experience community by participating in the passing of the peace, a ritual that lasts for at least 10 minutes during Sunday morning worship. At this church community it takes very little prompting to persuade the church archivist or a staff member to share photographs of social occasions or committee meetings. Though the congregation's history is brief, members do not want to forget the founding days. All Nations is a community where hugs and laughter are always present in and outside worship.

A DEVELOPING CONGREGATION

Through this basic credo, "Christian by faith, diverse by design," All Nations Church has found ways to create a shared identity that mobilizes members for service and outreach. The commitment of this small congregation has been focused and strengthened by its common goal of being a diverse Christian body. Without that shared commitment it would be difficult to create a worshiping community like All Nations. "I think the people who come to All Nations want to see the kingdom present," Dr. Reed said, referring to the congregation's diversity. "They aren't waiting for heaven."[6]

Financially, All Nations is still in its infancy. Half of its income comes from gifts of sponsoring churches and programs of the denomination's North Texas Conference. Recently All Nations purchased its 34,000-square-foot building for worship and education from a Baptist church—a remarkable achievement for a congregation of this age and size, and at this stage of its life. Members said the purchase reflected All Nations' hope and trust that God will make the congregation grow. And while church members say that a great deal of prayer went into the search and acquisition of the building, the purchase of the facility was accompanied by

bold envisioning, aggressive strategic planning, and shrewd negotiating, drawing upon members' skills and talents. After the initial
period when All Nations met for worship in homes and then in a
movie theater, the congregation now has a church building that it
can call home.

A Praying Community

In a profound sense that goes beyond pious slogans and "church
talk," All Nations is a community of prayer. Repeatedly both pastor
and members spoke of a deep and genuine dependence upon God,
as well as a belief in God's continual involvement in their lives. This
belief is evident each Sunday in worship when the prayers offered
by the pastor and the people reflect their dependence on God, who
they believe is with them in all of life's struggles and will show them
the way. During Sunday morning worship the pastoral prayer is
preceded by a time when members share not only their concerns,
but also their "praise reports" of how prayer has been answered.
Popular black gospel songs such as "I love the Lord," or "Give me a
clean heart" follow the pastoral prayer.

Other oft-repeated expressions of their beliefs are the statements "We've made it" and "We're going to make it," sometimes
uttered in tandem, statements that assert that God has been with
them so far and that God will continue to be with them in the
future. Prayer meetings are held regularly. Prayer is part of every
leadership decision of the congregation and, indeed, of every
meeting within the church. Worship is not limited to Sunday
morning, as meetings begin and end with a song and a circle of
prayer. Prayer permeates weekly Bible studies in homes, congregational community service, and the sharing of individual stories
(testimony) in worship. A widespread sense seems to prevail that
these and other activities of the congregation could not take place
effectively without prayer.

The congregation is christologically focused—that is, parishioners have a knowledge and experience of God in Christ that informs their common vocation. All Nations' diversity is part of its
ministry of reconciliation and influences the way decisions are

made. Furthermore, nurturing diversity is a communal spiritual discipline for many members. Another spiritual discipline is singing. Singing together in many styles and, increasingly, in several languages is an act of liturgical reconciliation. While the pastor offers strong leadership, the congregation's activities do not revolve around her. The laity have claimed a vision of communal discipleship which they try to work out by taking on roles and actions traditionally limited to the pastor.

One phrase heard at All Nations is "We don't have any conflicts." While many congregations say this, it may be true at All Nations. Upon close examination it does not appear that All Nations is naïve or in denial, or that this congregation avoids conflict. Rather, members seem determined to work things out together in an intentionally prayerful way. As difficult issues and tough questions arise among this diverse group of people, members testify about open and honest forums for sharing opinions and making decisions. Members of the congregation recalled that past struggles concerned issues, not personalities. Having a shared vision, vocation, and commitment helps All Nations Church seek out processes that to date have resolved any possibly debilitating conflict.

Encouraging the Laity's Voice

All Nations has made some strategic decisions in its young life. The decision to purchase a church building sooner rather than later gave the church time to draw upon the wealth of gifts and skills in the congregation, to devise strategies, and to negotiate a reasonable price for the building. All Nations shares the newly purchased building with a Baptist church that will soon move into its own new facility. The All Nations congregation is looking for ways to maintain its present church building until membership grows. This hope has led to the decision to seek a tenant after the Baptists move out. Though driven in part by pragmatic concerns, this decision has become part of a larger discernment process for the entire congregation. Members are searching for a tenant that would benefit from the shared use of the building, one that might not otherwise have access to space.

Many parishioners are highly educated and skilled in a variety of ways. Members freely share their vocational or professional expertise with the church. This willingness allows All Nations to handle many routine tasks and unexpected speed bumps with dispatch. Members offer their skills, for instance, in finance, strategic planning, and contractual negotiations. They also handle such roles as operating the sound system, participating in the music program, and giving lay leadership to committees in a way that enables the congregation to work as a unit. Christian education is managed by people capable and equipped to do so. The distinctive feature of All Nations is its conscious attempt to ensure representative ethnic diversity in all of these roles.

Congregational leaders are involved in leading worship, taking responsibility for long-range planning, teaching Sunday school, leading the choir, and working with outreach ministries. While it is true that most congregational leaders do some of these things, All Nations Church does not seem to follow the usual pattern of most racially and ethnically homogenous mainline congregations. In every aspect of its administrative and organizational life, All Nations has a diversity of people involved. The fact that All Nations also has sufficient diversity in its congregation to be able to implement diversity of leadership is also unusual. The leadership reflects the congregation's differences in culture, background, and class. In the area of administration, the role of the pastor appeared to us to be quite important, particularly in the manner and model of leadership. The way Clara Reed preaches and teaches is both well structured and gentle, and these characteristics carry over into administrative leadership and a shared sense of direction for the future. The lay leadership uses the pastor's manner and leadership style as a model. Dr. Reed's ability and training, and the foresight in her planning, accompanied by her willingness to pitch in with the mundane details of congregational life, were observed repeatedly by researchers for this study. Her willingness to participate as needed infects others in the congregation, especially the lay leaders.

The lay leaders appear focused and sure of their identity as members of All Nations church, working together toward a clearer understanding of their relationship to their community and to the larger denomination. The church's administrative structure reflects a conscious commitment to ministry that seems to be owned by the laity. All Nations Church has lay coordinators with specific responsibilities in worship, membership, ministry, discipleship, and administration.

While effective communication is vital to any congregation, All Nations seems to have made visible and intentional strides in improving communication. One example is the year's calendar of events. This calendar lists various meetings, worship services, and prayer times for the whole year. The church calendar is negotiated by the entire group so that anyone in the congregation can have input, lending a sense of group ownership of the project. This is an effective tool in the process of education, giving everyone a sense of what is happening in congregational life, keeping members' focus as a young congregation, and maintaining a tie to worship and ministry. The calendar is not viewed simply as a list of dates and events, but also as a declaration—of their shared calling and corporate identity—as well as a declaration of the ministries they are engaged as a result of that call and identity. To see the All Nations Church calendar solely as a communal date book misses the members' own understanding of how it functions in their life together. Members are informed about what is happening in their congregation, and they know how to obtain any further information needed.

Both the parishioners and the pastor cite the importance of teaching for their life and ministry together. In their "being church" together, genuine excitement is evident about growing in knowledge of the faith in a collaborative way. Teaching and learning take place in a way that all are perceived as both learners and teachers. Teaching about the Bible, Christian liturgy, and the seasons of the church is also woven into worship in an unobtrusive way, contributing to the developing congregational identity. Since part of the congregation's diversity is its inclusion of members new to the Christian faith, the fact that All Nations embraces the role of a "teaching church" is important for the construction and maintenance of a group identity. Membership classes are held every other month for four Sundays, reviewing the basic tenets of Christianity, United Methodism, and All Nations Church.

All Nations does ministry at a local homeless shelter. Other programs include the Esther women's Bible study, the Amigos after-school program, a prison ministry, Meals on Wheels, evangelism efforts, a weekly lectionary Bible study, a choir, the Disciple Bible study I and II (an intensive survey of Old and New Testaments), youth ministry, and revival services. As a congregation, All Nations United Methodist Church is relatively young, having recently celebrated its third anniversary. The congregation is clearly excited about its past, present, and future in ministry. Both pastor and people constantly speak of "our" ministry—that is, in a positively possessive sense. "Ministry" is not seen as something far and distant. For this group, ministry seems to be work in which all are person-ally and collectively invested. All Nations has four lay speakers who occasionally preach and reflect the diversity of the congregation.

WORSHIP

Although pastoral leadership is strong, a worship committee is active in the planning and carrying out of worship. The congre-gation's worship is vibrant and inclusive, as well as thematic. The pastor emphasizes that All Nations should be a singing church. Singing both in and outside communal worship is an important means for realizing the congregation's basic vision and call. Not only is singing a congregational spiritual discipline; it is a vehicle of teaching and community building. Learning new songs from a variety of traditions fosters unity among the members of this diverse congregation. The singing is also thematically connected to the lectionary passages for the day, providing an educational com-ponent to the service. What is preached from the Word is enhanced by song. The choir, though it also sings anthems, relishes its role as the singing teacher of the congregation. The worship committee is involved in planning a diverse worship time that is upbeat and lively, while also making time for quietness and reflection.

All Nations' worship consists of various styles—such as "tradi-tional" worship, "gospel," and "contemporary." There are no wor-ship wars here. The intentionally diverse community at All Nations recognizes that "traditional" and "contemporary" have different meaning for different people. Traditional music may be African American spirituals for some members, while for others classic Western hymns may reflect the tradition. Gospel music and praise choruses may represent contemporary styles for some, while a recently written hymn could be seen as contemporary for others.

In its commitment to be broadly multicultural, the congregation especially hopes to increase its Hispanic membership. Members have used some bilingual creeds and songs. While copies of *The United Methodist Hymnal* (1989) are available and used in worship, the hymn texts are also projected on a screen. The mixture of media used for singing—hymnals and screens—reflects the preferences of people from diverse liturgical and ethnic traditions.

Praise and thanksgiving are central characteristics of worship at All Nations. The selected music reinforces this emphasis, as do the pastor's calls for "praise reports." Dr. Reed is skilled at tying various components of the service together with brief comments. These comments not only give the liturgy a sense of flow, but also offer momentary opportunities for the pastor to educate the congregation about worship, an important task for a new congregation whose members come from many traditions. The liturgy has a set structure, yet there are moments when the pastor may offer opportunities for the congregation to participate, as special concerns or reasons for thanksgiving arise. Flexibility within a set structure is an important part of this congregation's worship.

Sunday morning worship begins with at least 12 to 15 minutes of congregational singing. In the worship leadership for most Sundays, All Nations tries to have four laypeople involved—two men and two women, two African Americans and two Anglos. Every Sunday an invitation to join the church is offered.

All Nations' desire to increase the number of Latino participants is understandable, especially in light of the church's location—in a neighborhood with a growing Latino population. The congregation recognizes that it now must face the challenge of language if it is truly to be a multicultural congregation. All Nations has committed itself to make the effort and to make it work. As one member of the congregation said, "It makes sense to be in relationship with people around you," a sentiment shared by others in the congregation. In addition to bilingual creeds and songs, the opening welcome and closing invitation are sometimes given in Spanish, and traditional Hispanic holidays are observed. Hispanic ministry appears to be a growth area for the congregation—one that seems to have wide congregational support. One tool used in this regard is the Hispanic Creed, written by Justo L. González, noted theologian and retired professor of church history at Columbia Seminary, Decatur, Georgia.

Un Credo Hispano

We believe in God, the Father Almighty
Creator of the heavens and the earth;
Creator of all peoples and all cultures;
Creator of all tongues and races.

We believe in Jesus Christ, his Son, our Lord,
God made flesh in a person for all humanity,
God made flesh in an age for all the ages,
God made flesh in one culture for all cultures,
God made flesh in love and grace for all creation.

We believe in the Holy Spirit
through whom God incarnate in Jesus Christ
makes his presence known in our peoples and our cultures;
through whom, God Creator of all that exists,
gives us power to become new creatures.

We believe in the Church
universal because it is a sign of God's Reign,
whose faithfulness is shown in its many hues
where all the colors paint a single landscape,
where all tongues sing the same praise.

We believe in the Reign of God—the day of the Great Fiesta
when all creation's colors will form a harmonious rainbow,
when all peoples will join in joyful banquet,
when all tongues of the universe will sing the same song.

And because we believe, we commit ourselves:
to believe for those who do not believe,
to love for those who do not love,
to dream for those who do not dream,
until the day when hope becomes a reality.[7]

Copyright © 1996, The United Methodist Publishing House.
Used by permission.

CALLED INTO BEING

All Nations United Methodist Church seems to embody the characteristics of culturally conscious worship. As a congregation, All
Nations has a clear sense of vocation that is tied directly to an
understanding of the gospel. "Christian by faith, diverse by design"
is the glue of this congregation and a chief characteristic of the
culture of this community. A concept of community—"we" rather
than "I"—is a tangible reality for this congregation, particularly as
expressed in the negotiated diverse worship and the engagement in
community ministry outside the church. At the core of the calling
of All Nations Church are a vocation, a commitment, and the
shared values of a ministry of reconciliation. A ministry of racial
reconciliation is particularly crucial in a society that continues to be
plagued by "the problem of the color line."[8]

Furthermore, All Nations is made up of people who share not only
a calling in ministry. In the working out of their ministry together in
their social context, they have also developed true and deep friendships.
In fact, it may be that one key to the success of their ministry efforts is
their genuine commitment to one another in Christian friendship.
This commitment necessitated courageous risk taking, exceptional
effort, and trust, which in turn produced greater trust and reliance
by the members upon each other in their common mission. Abiding commitment, trust, and mutual reliance have enabled them to
share their treasures within their common ministry.

All Nations United Methodist Church is keenly aware of many
of the challenges it faces as a congregation. Although it has the

formal support of denominational authorities and structures, members realize that some within the denomination are ambivalent, suspicious, or even hostile to All Nations' presence and continued existence. All Nations truly celebrates multicultural congregational life, particularly in its regular worship of God. At the same time, with very few models to follow, the congregation is blazing the trail for true multicultural worship in the United States. A certain amount of exploration and discovery takes place as members discover anew each week what multicultural worship means for them. As All Nations Church seeks to be true to its calling as a multicultural congregation, it is exploring what it means for an English-dominant, albeit multicultural, congregation to reach out to the growing numbers of bilingual and bicultural Hispanics. In the immediate geographic area of the church's ministry, many of the Hispanics are Spanish dominant. As All Nations explores this challenge, the congregation is addressing it initially through worship.

CASE STUDY 4

MISSION: POSSIBLE:
UNITED METHODIST CHURCH OF THE DISCIPLE

Evelyn L. Parker

Quiet. Serene. Tranquil. These adjectives describe my reaction to the United Methodist Church of the Disciple the first time I drove into its parking lot. A gentle breeze was the only sound that broke the silence. The stillness of the early Sunday morning was not pierced with the usual weekday sounds from the nearby corner shopping center with its grocery store, gas station, and video store. The years of sawing and hammering from the construction of new homes across the street from the church were replaced by the serenity of Sunday silence. The spacious church parking lot had several spaces labeled "Visitor Parking" adjacent to the front entrance. The parking lot and the church occupied only a third of the three acres of flat land that stretched back to the edge of another new residential subdivision.

As I walked toward the church, I heard a rippling of water from the fountain in front of the church. The gentle bubbling sound added to the restful ambience. I sensed with gratitude that I had come to a place of comfort.

The visitors' parking spaces and the fountain suggested that the congregation valued hospitality and hoped to welcome strangers in its midst. The spacious narthex was replete with information. One billboard was particularly eye catching, directing participants to their Sunday school classrooms. My eye was drawn to the various handouts, badges, flyers, and other resources on a table in the narthex in front of the church's main door. Male and female greeters approached and extended a welcome as I entered the sanctuary.

In the sanctuary the energy level was rising in anticipation of worship. The worship space held three sections of interlocking, blue-cushioned chairs with wire baskets underneath to hold Bibles and hymnals. The two large video screens hanging from the ceiling on either side of the pulpit displayed a listing of church activities. I suspected that I was about to experience a contemporary worship service. Candles of varied sizes were arranged on the communion table. Scarves of a palette of earth tones were draped around the candle bases and seemed to float down to the floor.

A grand piano stood close to the wall just left of the chancel area. Its position suggested that it was seldom used; an electronic keyboard was more prominent, level with the communion table and to the left of the chancel, suggesting that it was used often. It finally dawned on me that there was no pulpit but a fluid space resembling a stage, not the traditional divided chancel with a pulpit on one side and a lectern on the other. Light was focused on the stage/chancel. In the back of the sanctuary was a video projection room where several people were busily preparing for worship. I assumed that the recorded music that filled the air was controlled from the same room as the video images.

The walls of the sanctuary were plain, highlighting the importance of the communion table at the center of the chancel. The solidity of the light-brown walls was interrupted only near the ceiling by the black grid lines of the air-conditioning vents. The walls, the pews, and the stage/chancel all complemented the serene ambience.

As I glanced toward the stained-glass window high above the chancel, my tranquil mood became one of celebration. The space contained colors and shapes forming a somewhat abstract rendition of the Lord's Supper. All who were eating and drinking seemed to join in a celebratory banquet. Jesus had a darker skin tone, and others at the table were of multiple hues, suggesting people of varied colors representing all the world's races and nationalities.

The stained-glass window of the Eucharist declared that the worship space was sacred, inviting worshipers to participate with the people of the world in the holy supper. It also profoundly and tacitly conveyed the message that all people were welcome in the sanctuary.

For a year a small group of five or six people from each of the four congregations participating in our study met to examine the cultural implications of liturgy. During the first session, each group was asked to choose a title for a hypothetical book to introduce its church's journey of faith. Why would the small group from Church of the Disciple choose the title "Mission: Possible"? What events in this church's story would indicate that the church had engaged in a "Mission: Possible"? What was the relationship of "Mission: Possible" to the focus of this project, congregations concerned about developing cultural diversity in worship? A history of the Church of the Disciple addresses some of these questions.

A BRIEF HISTORY

In June 1993 the North Texas Annual Conference of the United Methodist Church appointed a clergy couple to a mission yet to be born in DeSoto, Texas, a suburb south of Dallas. Before the appointment of the Revs. Matt and Cammy Gaston, the conference had purchased eight acres of land on Cockrell Hill Road in DeSoto. The pastors' task would be to gather a new community of faith that would serve the communities of DeSoto and the surrounding area. Because of projections of new housing construction in the southern suburbs of Dallas, the United Methodist conference wanted to anticipate this growth by starting a new congregation. From the beginning conference leaders had a sense that this should be a culturally inclusive congregation.

Matt and Cammy Gaston canvassed DeSoto and the surrounding area with brochures in preparation for the first Sunday service, inviting residents to the new mission. In addition to those seeking a church home, people from area United Methodist congregations volunteered to "seed" the new church. Heidi and James Horton, at that time members of the Duncanville United Methodist Church, were among those who volunteered to help start the mission. The congregation began by meeting in a cluster of house churches, including the home of the pastors as well as homes of various members of the congregation. The Hortons' home became the site of the congregation's eight o'clock prayer service held for 20 minutes every Sunday morning, as well as for fellowship. An average of 20 to 30 people met each Sunday morning. On some occasions the attendance reached 50.

In August 1994 the congregation was chartered as the United Methodist Church of the Disciple, with a further descriptive statement, "A Community of Faith." The intent was to express clearly to everyone the relational nature of the congregation. (In many new United Methodist congregations, especially those that use more contemporary worship styles, the word "community" is used to express the nature of the congregation. The rationale is that "church" may not communicate well to the unchurched.) Like the 12 apostles of Jesus, the founding members too were his followers, people on the way, sometimes filled with fear, doubt, and confusion. The congregation wanted to affirm its identity as a community of disciples who were learners, followers, and teachers, banded together in their faith journey.

In the early stages, participants in the mission would also visit other churches for two or three worship services each month. In October 1993, the church newsletter published a prayer and worship gathering schedule that included caravan trips to First United Methodist Church, Sachse, Texas, a predominantly Anglo congregation in a neighboring suburban township, and St. Luke Community United Methodist Church, an African American church in south Dallas. The educational ministry of the new mission featured several series of classes, which usually met in the home of the Gastons. In October the pastors played host to members as the couple taught a series titled "The Nature of the Church." Families from area United Methodist congregations who agreed to "seed" the mission attended the Bible study in the co-pastors' home. They met weekly from July 1993 until the church building was erected in January 2000.

One of the pastors organized and led a 10-day recruiting effort called "Phone-a-thon Prospecting." Adult and teenage volunteers called residences in DeSoto, Cedar Hill, and Duncanville, asking two questions: "Are you currently active in a church" and (if not) "Would you like to receive some information on a new United Methodist church beginning in our area?" The call for volunteers, both adults and teenagers, was published in the October 4, 1993, church newsletter. The pastor emphasized to potential volunteers that Christ calls Christians to reach out to "those who do not know God through the care and love of a church home." The goal was to determine quickly who within a five-mile radius might be interested in the new community of faith. The workers expected 27 new families of the 6,000 reached to join them in their first worship service. A goal of 5 percent to 8 percent of the families called was based on the estimated number of people without a faith community and the large number of established churches in the five-mile radius.

The initial membership of the congregation consisted of 27 families. In addition to James and Heidi Horton and their six-year-old daughter, Genny, these families included several with elementary-school and teenage children. Work, prayer, and fellowship characterize the building blocks of this congregation. Their pastors encouraged them to work at bringing others into the new congregation, to pray for the growth of the community, and to play together after hard work. Examples of the congregation's play included a party for both teenagers and adults on the church property after a local football game, and a family camp-out at Cedar Hill State Park. A laundry list of task forces published in an October 1993 newsletter, was headed, "Lord I want to be a Christian . . . in my work, in my wor-rk," adapting the text of an African American spiritual. These groups included shepherd leaders responsible for the nurture and care of small groups of congregants, prayer chains, children's and youth ministry, worship, music, welcome, building, grounds, moving equipment and supplies, task forces, and administration work.

Providing educational and pastoral ministries for members of the community of faith was enhanced by sermons focusing on congregants' self-understanding as disciples of Jesus Christ called to servanthood. A strong commitment to mission and outreach emerged early in the life of the congregation. The Halloween 1993

"Trick or Treat Can Goods" drive for the Dallas County food pantry is an example of how this mobile congregation sought to serve the community.

The first five months of work, prayer, and play in the DeSoto area and the reality of a "house church" similar to that described in the New Testament culminated on December 5, 1993, when the young congregation held its first Sunday school and worship service in the main ballroom of the DeSoto Holiday Inn. Financial support for this temporary worship site came from several United Methodist churches in the region. The motel ballroom was transformed into the sanctuary of the Church of the Disciple, complete with liturgical trappings. Flowers were given by sister churches, and the congregation's first banner was displayed. It was described in the worship bulletin: "The Holy [S]pirit (dove) gives faith to each disciple and continues to sanctify (flames) or develop us as we learn to live a life of love and obedience to the Good Shepherd–Redeemer (staff and cross) Jesus Christ." The Holiday Inn ballroom was the congregation's temporary sanctuary for two months.

In February 1994 the congregation began to worship in the Seventh-Day Adventist Church of Duncanville and DeSoto. It was a new facility on Cockrell Hill Road just north of the congregation's property, where its future church building would stand. The mission worshiped in the Seventh-Day Adventist Church for six years. During this time members of Church of the Disciple expressed hopes and dreams of having their own building in which to worship and provide ministries. The pastors and the congregation focused on making their dreams realities. Congregants of all ages participated in the planning. Paper and crayons were distributed to both children and adults. They were asked to draw their vision of the new church. Their drawings expressed their theology of joy and servanthood. In its plans for the future building, the congregation worked to capture its identity as a community of disciples journeying together as learners, followers, and teachers. A theology of inclusion of all God's people began to influence the architectural design.

The theology of inclusion was most fully expressed in the evolving design for a stained-glass window to be created for the future sanctuary. Tom Gibson, a member of the congregation, designed the window, using as his model a picture of the Last

Supper that hung in the pastors' home. Gibson's design captured
the vision of the original congregation's desire for an inclusive
church, where all people were welcome to become disciples of Jesus
Christ. Jesus, with dark skin tone and Arabic features, became the
central figure welcoming all people to his table. The disciple figures
would depict people of all cultures and races from around the globe
lifting their hands in joy.

From 1997 to 2000 a core group of members, basically members
of the 27 original families, were involved in the construction of the
new building. The congregation moved into its new church home
in January 2000. This major accomplishment included construction
of the stained-glass window, with the help of members of the
Ramona United Methodist Church in California, the home church
of one of the pastors. In fact, members of Ramona took Tom
Gibson's design for the window and cut pieces of colored glass for
the Texas congregation to assemble. The pastor's mother and a few
members of the California congregation brought the pieces of
stained glass to Texas. Over a weekend the sister churches worked to
assemble and hang the window by matching numbers on the pieces
of glass with numbers on a pattern. This undertaking proved to be
most rewarding for Church of the Disciple's children, youth, and
adults.

During the period from 1993 to 2000, the congregation developed varieties of ministries designed to serve people both in the
congregation and outside it. The United Methodist Women took
flight with programs that included guest lecturers on global missions. Church of the Disciple youth sponsored international mission trips, helped with garage sales to raise mission money, joined
in "Walk for the Cure" to help provide money for cancer research,
participated in a weeklong stay at Arkansas Heifer Project Ranch,
and volunteered with the DeSoto Community Outreach Center.

In May 1995 the congregation instituted its first churchwide
garage sale to raise money for mission work. Members were encouraged to go through their closets, drawers, garages, and attics
and bring whatever they hadn't used for years. Congregants were
urged to bring their "stuff" because they knew they wouldn't need it
and "God will get the glory." During the garage sale the Disciple
United Methodist Men provided hot dogs, nachos, and soft drinks.

The United Methodist Women prepared baked items. The sale organizers arranged for a bloodmobile to be on site to encourage members and visitors to donate blood. Over the years profits from the churchwide garage sale have increased. In May 1999 the congregation raised over $5,000 for mission work. Other events include mission trips to international locations and an "Amigos Day," an annual day for repairing homes of low-income Dallas County families. Youth and adults also participate in the interfaith housing coalition, which assists families in securing decent housing, as well as food supplies, and provides tutoring services, arts and music programs, and group outings for children.

Children take part in the Workshop Rotation Sunday school, which includes a children's Bible Bowl, and game-show Bible learning experiences for third- through sixth-graders. Educational and recreational ministries for youth include vacation Bible school; church camp; "Chrysalis Flights," a program of faith formation for youth; and the practice of hosting other youth groups for drama and musical events.

Adult educational ministries began with the inception of the congregation, usually featuring short- and long-term study groups. Disciple Bible Study, a course whose participants commit to a 39-week survey of the Bible, has been a staple of adult educational ministry in the congregation. In May 2000 the congregation partnered with two African American United Methodist churches, St. Paul and St. Luke Community, both in Dallas, to conduct a "satellite" Disciple Bible Study, a popular denomination-wide program. Church of the Disciple was a convenient site for members of those congregations living in the southwest Dallas County area. Because of space shortages in the other congregations, Church of the Disciple provided classrooms; St. Paul and St. Luke provided leadership. Partnering with African American congregations is one of the ways that Church of the Disciple has increased its visibility among black people moving into the community.

Church of the Disciple has also developed new adult Sunday school classes, such as the Disciples Journey Class for newcomers to the community of faith 20 years of age or older. The Seekers Sunday School Class is for both couples and singles ranging in age from 25 to 40.

The music ministry of Church of the Disciple is the most culturally and racially diverse ministry in the young congregation. Regina Lee, keyboardist for Church of the Disciple, came to the congregation in April 1999. She said it was difficult for her as a black woman to come to a predominantly Anglo church and "integrate" her style of music into the worship service. Lee sometimes worked with Alicia Owens, an Anglo, and the two referred to themselves as "Ebony and Ivory" when they sang duets. The music team works at providing a variety of musical experiences for the congregation, including Christian quartets and a band, as well as hymn sing-alongs.

The congregation's identity experienced tensions as the reality set in that the church was situated in a rapidly changing area with over 50 percent affluent African Americans. In August 2000 one pastor wrote about the constituency of the neighborhood in a letter to the congregation: "The congregation is unsure how it feels about that [demographic] and the path its pastors are taking toward multiculturalism." This letter suggested that establishing a culturally conscious congregation is a process rather than a goal that can easily be achieved. While the congregation was envisioned from the beginning as an inclusive congregation, that vision needed to be revisited continually as new members joined. There are no quick solutions for churches that hope to be multicultural. Developing culturally conscious congregations is often a case of two steps forward and one step back.

NESTLED IN SOUTHWEST DALLAS COUNTY

The exterior of Church of the Disciple's building is made of a Texas Hill Country variety of Austin stone. The church is one block south of the intersection of South Cockrell Hill Road and Beltline Road. Located at that intersection is a recently completed shopping center with an Albertson's Grocery Store, Express Gas Station, Blockbuster Video Store, and several small businesses.

The church is nestled amid an area of tremendous growth and development in southwest Dallas County. New homes under construction flank the church in every direction. Many houses are priced from $100,000 to $140,000, with some up to $300,000. For the Dallas area, these are the prices of middle- and upper-middle-class homes. Some of the older homes in the neighborhood are located north of the church on Pleasant Run Road. These homes are usually built on many acres of land, allowing them to maintain some separation from the newer homes. These homes sell for $1 million and up. The older homes are often those of longtime wealthy residents, many of whom built country homes in a location that was considered far from the city of Dallas at the time of their construction. The newly built homes and those under construction, east and west of Church of the Disciple, are owned predominantly by African American residents who are new to the community, having moved as the suburbs of Dallas expanded south. Newer freeways make it possible for them to commute to work in downtown Dallas.

Several newly built churches—seven within a 1.5 mile radius—also surround the Church of the Disciple. These ecumenical neighbors include three Baptist churches, a Nazarene church, a Lutheran church, a nondenominational church, and the DeSoto Seventh-Day Adventist Church, which leased its space to Church of the Disciple while it was without a church building.

Besides the new churches and the homes under constructions, Church of the Disciple is surrounded by several schools. These include Chestnut Hill Day School and Child Care Center, Cockrell Hill Elementary School, and DeSoto West Junior High School.

Over the past seven years the congregation of Church of the Disciple has grown from its original membership of 27 families. During May and June 2000 the Sunday school attendance averaged 112 people, and worship averaged 220. Worship attendance has grown by 19 percent since 1999.

The congregation is mostly European-American with a few African American families and even fewer Hispanic families. A few racially mixed couples attend, mostly Hispanic and Anglo. The families of Church of the Disciple are largely middle-class and upper-middle-class. For the most part, these families reflect an even distribution of child, teen, and adult generations. The absence of college-age members is consistent with statistics in most Protestant mainline denominations. Of the adult membership, middle-age adults between 35 and 50 make up the largest group.

The demographics of Church of the Disciple contrast with the neighborhood demographics. As indicated earlier, neighbors living adjacent to the church are well over 50 percent affluent African Americans. The fact that Church of the Disciple provides space for Disciple Bible Study for members of St. Paul and St. Luke Community United Methodist churches suggests that the new homeowners in the neighborhood have long-standing commitments to communities of faith located far from southwest Dallas County. St. Paul and St. Luke are regional congregations in Dallas, as far as 20 miles from DeSoto. Their members travel faithfully on Sunday to church in Dallas but do not care to drive so far during the week, when traffic is much heavier, for other activities such as Bible study. Perhaps Church of the Disciple's African American neighbors participate in the trend of many churchgoers across the cultural and ethnic spectrum, driving long distances from their homes to their churches. Some evidence of this trend exists among a few of the members of Church of the Disciple. Several members who were

Figure 9

Demographic Overview: United Methodist Church of the Disciple

Population within a 1.5 mile radius: 5,669

Males: 48.6%
Females: 51.4%

Population 19 and under: 32.9%
Population between 20 and 54: 53.5%
Population 55 and older: 13.4%

White: 45.6%
Hispanic/Latino: 8.0%
African American: 43.4%
Other/Mixed: 3.0%

Owner-occupied housing units: 93.2%
Renter-occupied housing units: 6.8%

Source: Census 2000 <www.census.dfwinfo.com>.

residents of the DeSoto area have moved to other suburbs but still journey back to Church of the Disciple for Sunday worship and other church activities.

During the early 1990s the housing industry in southwest Dallas County started to boom because a government science laboratory was slated to be located in Waxahachie, just over 15 miles from DeSoto. DeSoto, Cedar Hill, Duncanville, Ovilla, and Red Oak were expected to be the bedroom communities for employees of the laboratory. When the laboratory project was terminated and the expected new residents did not materialize, many houses in the area became available at bargain prices.

WORSHIP AT CHURCH OF THE DISCIPLE

I began this chapter by describing the peaceful and serene atmosphere I experienced from the time I walked across the parking lot and into the sanctuary. I also related my first experience of the stained-glass window in the sanctuary, its colors and jubilant images. I wondered if the juxtaposition of images of tranquility with images of celebration was intentional and integral to worship at Church of the Disciple. After experiencing worship there on several occasions, I have concluded that the ambience was created intentionally. I believe the peaceful atmosphere from the parking lot to the fountain to the narthex prepare all who come for joyous worship. The peaceful ambience of the church prepares one for a worship celebration. Though for some this combination might be jarring, a spirit of celebration suits this young congregation attempting to attract African American and Anglo members of the community.

The celebrative quality permeates all of worship. The liturgy is organized around three larger sections: "We Gather in Praise and Prayer," "God Calls to Us," and "We Respond to God." The first section begins with celebration music led by a music group called Notes of Praise or by some other segment of the worship team. The tradition of singing praise songs began with the first formal worship service at the DeSoto Holiday Inn. Celebration music is usually followed by the welcome, call to worship, affirmation of faith, children's time, call to prayer, pastoral prayer, and the Lord's Prayer. Occasionally, baptisms and special recognitions are interspersed between praise songs and prayers.

Besides the worship team and Notes of Praise, guest musicians are often invited to worship, where they sing not only celebration music but also songs in other styles interspersed throughout the worship service. Music is important to the worship life of the church. The congregation uses a variety of music styles, from classic hymns and African American gospel songs and spirituals to "Contemporary Christian Music" (CCM), a distinctive current genre. Regina Lee, the keyboard player, adds a touch of African American gospel music throughout the service. Congregational singing continues to take an important role in the life of worship. Early musical leadership focused more on the praise team and less on congregational singing. Even though some are concerned that the church is "not yet a singing congregation," music has a central role in making the worship service one of celebration. More recently (2002), a church-music student from Perkins School of Theology has assumed leadership of the church's music program. He is the most skilled musician in the church's brief history and knows how to work with the praise team, develop a more traditional choir, and encourage congregational singing. He is also proficient in a variety of musical styles from classical to current musical expressions.

However, music has also been a point of contention. Some members became discontented with various styles of music and decided to leave the community of faith. They sought a "high church" worship style— with large choirs and more formal music. These people left the church after realizing that the majority of the community values a variety of music styles that suit their informal approach to worship.

"God Calls to Us" is a time in worship that includes giving offerings, reading scripture, and hearing the sermon. In many liturgical traditions offerings are seen as an opportunity to respond to God. Though placed earlier in the service than in some churches (a common practice in the South, where Southern Baptists have a strong influence on United Methodists and churches with a more congregational polity), offerings at Church of the Disciple are a part of God's call to discipleship and the needs of the community and the world.

Sermons are usually followed by "reflection music," except on communion Sundays. It is eliminated then to conserve time; music suitable for celebration of the Lord's Supper takes its place. On the Sundays that I visited Church of the Disciple, the preacher never stood behind a lectern. Sometimes he or she stood on the sanctuary floor rather than the chancel stage. When preaching in the chancel area, Matt or Cammy Gaston would stand in front of the communion table, the focus of the chancel. Some members have commented that the communion table enhances worship because of its "solidness and centrality" and because it is "massive, friendly, a gathering place."

The chancel has been the site of drama on several occasions, though not often enough for some members. In a church newsletter (July 2000) Alicia Owens celebrated the gifts of Diane Balay and Company, who performed a Good Friday drama. Balay has been a member of the community of faith for six years and wears a number of hats in addition to drama director.

"We Respond to God" is a time that usually includes an invitation to Christian discipleship, an invitation to mission and ministry, and a musical and spoken benediction. The invitation to Christian discipleship is a priority in worship. During the final song, people are invited forward to make a profession of faith, to make a commitment to a specific ministry of the church, or to become a member of the congregation. Likewise, mission and ministry are extremely important. Matt or Cammy Gaston invites worshipers to participate in the many mission events and forms of ministry that Church of the Disciple offers.

Church of the Disciple has two pastors who share in the responsibilities of the worship celebration. Both sit in the front pew along with the musicians and other worship leaders. One of the Gastons usually serves as the primary liturgist, while the other preaches. However, the worship service clearly depends on many people to lead and to welcome guests. For example, young people may read the scripture, rising from their place in the pew, or families may lead a litany together. While the pastoral leadership is strong, one has a vivid sense that laity and clergy share worship leadership equally.

The fountain in front of the church also plays a role in worship. It is used for baptisms and, on occasion, for rituals in which Christians recall their baptism. For example, one worship service ended at the fountain, where the people gathered around and heard the words "Remember your baptism" as they felt water splashed on them by the pastor standing in the fountain. The fountain functions, I discovered, not only as a graceful addition to the church's landscaping but primarily as a baptismal font.

The stained-glass window also has a significant place in worship. Several members commented with pride about the window in the sanctuary, observing that it enriches worship with its "timeless messages" and its images of "connection, working together, and love." Diane Balay commented that the stained-glass window enhances worship because "it was made by our own hands. It embodies a theology that is important to us—God welcoming all people to his table of fellowship." I believe Balay's comments express central theological themes important for this congregation, especially in light of members' concern to become more ethnically and culturally diverse.

Given the high percentage of African Americans in the immediate community, the congregation has worked hard to relate to African Americans through Bible study and common work projects such as an interfaith housing coalition. Staff members have so far included one African American. Rigorous efforts to hire additional African American staff have not yet succeeded, but attracting more black employees remains an important priority for the congregation. The range of musical styles in worship includes African American gospel songs and spirituals, along with other types of hymns and songs. Sermon themes also reflect, on a regular basis, the importance of cultural diversity. The project team from Church of the Disciple participating in our study chose the chapter title "Mission: Possible" to describe team members' vision of a multicultural congregation and the work that is gradually helping this hope to become a reality.

WHY "MISSION: POSSIBLE"?

Church of the Disciple has considered carefully the age-old question "What's in a name?" Early in its history the congregation gained much practice in responding to this question as members explained why the congregation decided on the name United Methodist Church of the Disciple. Co-pastor Matt Gaston captured the sentiments of the congregation in the October 1993 newsletter. He connected these 20th-century disciples of Jesus Christ, located in southwest Dallas County, with Jesus' disciples of the New Testament, who numbered far more than the band of 12, and many of whose names are unknown to us. More important, the name of the church describes who the members are and what they do. An early church bulletin began the welcome statement by saying, "We are a community of faith which seeks to live the life of a disciple of Jesus Christ—in other words, a life of joy and servanthood." Members of Church of the Disciple are followers of Jesus Christ with human flaws, yet faithful in service and joyful on the journey. "Servanthood" and the joy of a shared community are key theological themes in the life of the congregation and serve as two pillars that theologically support this church.

Servanthood and mission are words that describe the first theological pillar. From its inception the congregation sought to reach out in service to the poor and the downtrodden in southwest Dallas County and in other parts of the world. As they worshiped in house churches, the DeSoto Holiday Inn, and the Seventh-Day Adventist Church, the congregation sought to carry out its commitment to serve the people of the area through a vision to create a diverse community. This commitment to service was tested severely between 1997 and 2000, the times of planning and construction of the church building. Even in the midst of burnout, a core group of the community of faith was able to persevere. As the church was being built, members of the congregation came after work to clean up after construction workers or to provide carpentry for specific projects. Over the seven years of its existence, the congregation has built homes for the poor with Habitat for Humanity, purchased livestock for poor families in Central America through the Heifer

Project, provided aid for the people of Honduras, organized and
participated in medical mission trips, and financially supported an
orphanage in Puerto Escondido, Mexico. Many of these acts of
service continue today. For example, the annual garage sale raises
funds for the orphanage in Puerto Escondido. An offering of $500
was sent to the orphanage each month. Mission connects all generations of the church. Children, youth, and adults all participate in
serving the local and global community, either collectively or in
their age-level groupings.

The life of joy that this congregation seeks is most concrete in
worship. This time of adoration and praise to God is described as a
celebration. The inclusion of a variety of musical styles, the use of
drama, attention to the aesthetics of the sanctuary, and the practice
of setting the mood for worship through projecting words or
images on the screen, using computer software—all indicate a
commitment to joyous celebration in worship. The stained-glass
window, designed by a member of the congregation from a Hispanic plaque that had hung in their pastor's home—a window
made by their own hands, filled with festive and joyous expressions,
and celebrating the fellowship of all peoples of God—is symbolic of
the joyous life that abounds for this congregation.

A life of joy is also evident in the congregation's commitment to
mission. Those who participate in mission projects, as well as those
who have responsibility for the committee on mission, do their
work in a spirit of joy.

Why then did the members of the study team title their chapter
"Mission: Possible," and how does that title connect with developing cultural diversity in worship? I believe that "Mission: Possible"
is a hope-filled statement from members who served as the core
group during the first six years of Church of the Disciple. Members
of this group saw their hopes realized as their numbers grew, as
mission projects increased, as the church was being built. The
stained-glass window "built by our own hands," as Diane Balay
noted, is tangible evidence that missions are possible. Balay, the
Gastons, and several other members believe that Church of the
Disciple can become culturally diverse and that worship is the
venue for expressing hospitality to the stranger. The stained-glass

window is the starting point for showing hospitality to the stranger right in the doorway.

The Gastons were appointed to another congregation in 2000. The new minister has continued to reach out to African Americans in the community with some success. Several new African American families have been visiting, and some have joined.

PART III

MOVING TOWARD
CULTURALLY CONSCIOUS WORSHIP

HOW CAN WE KEEP FROM SINGING?
THE ROLE OF MUSICIANS AND MUSIC IN
ENABLING MULTICULTURAL WORSHIP

From the beginning of the Christian church, music and musicians have been a source of controversy. Leaders were concerned about musical styles—"we don't want music influenced by pagan practices." The early church fathers were uneasy about the secular influences of musical instruments—"don't let pagan instruments into the church." Early church liturgists were worried about dance in worship—"it's pagan." Male presiders were apprehensive about who was permitted to sing—"only men and boys need apply for the choir (women remind us of pagan rituals)."

Yet, music, especially song, has also evoked and sustained our prayer in Christian worship from the beginning. It touches us to the bone and shapes how we talk to God and how we perceive that God talks to us. When one worships with a congregation, one discovers that every congregation's worship service has its own "feel," or ambience. This "feel" is made up of many aspects: How do people greet one another? What is the shape and nature of the sacred space? What kind of presence do the presiders exude? What sacred symbols and community signs are visible? All of these are important, but one key aspect of the "feel" of worship is the nature of the musical sounds that integrate with all that is seen, said, and done.

My purpose in this section is to bring to light issues that arise in regard to making music in culturally conscious worship:

- Who leads music in culturally conscious worship?
- What qualities do culturally conscious musicians need to lead worship?
- Why is the experience of congregational singing so important in culturally conscious worship?
- What kind of music should be sung?
- How should this music be chosen?
- What additional resources are needed to sing cross-culturally?
- What is the role of the choir or, for that matter, who *is* the choir in culturally diverse music making?

The answers to these questions seem fairly obvious in a familiar cultural and musical context. They are less obvious when we sing music from different traditions—each with its own heritage of sounds, styles of leadership, and ways of integrating music and liturgy.

INTEGRATING MUSIC AND WORSHIP

Music is a kind of aural, or audible, lubricant that mingles with everything else that is going on. It sounds in space, but the sounds do not take up space. I call this quality *valence*—that is, the capacity to unite, interact, or react with other aspects of the environment. "Valence" is a term primarily associated with chemistry. According to the *American Heritage Electronic Dictionary*, it refers to "the combining capacity of an atom or a radical determined by the number of electrons that it will lose, add, or share when it reacts with other atoms." While a listener may experience music in isolation from other aspects of the environment—for example, while listening alone with headphones to a fine recording of an orchestra—the experience is not the same as hearing the orchestra in an acoustically vibrant and beautiful concert hall. The live experience of watching the conductor evoke the sounds from the musicians, hearing the violin section play in perfect unison, or seeing all the string players draw their bows in exact precision—these cannot be duplicated. Recordings have their place, but live music making is a singular experience that cannot be duplicated fully by other means.

Live music making in worship has the character of valence as the experience of sound permeates rites (the words said) and rituals (the actions performed), creating a liturgical chemistry that is greater than the sum of its parts.

I recall an African service that incorporated singing throughout the communion rite. The people sang as a colorful cloth was placed over the table and a procession of dancers accompanied the communion elements forward. The choir hummed beneath the opening of the Great Thanksgiving, leading the congregation directly into the singing of the *Sanctus* (Holy, holy, holy). Following the words of institution, the choir began humming again under the prayer invoking the presence of the Holy Spirit, leading directly into the singing of the Lord's Prayer by the congregation. The singing continued as people moved in procession to the table to receive the bread and wine. Music permeated the communion liturgy, much as incense permeates the worship space of an Orthodox Church after the icons have been reverenced.

ENLIVENERS OF WORSHIP

The role of the musician needs special consideration in culturally diverse congregations. In the four congregations studied, a common thread was the quality of musical leadership and the ability of each musician to capture the congregation's vision of inclusiveness in sound each Sunday. Church musicians have always had particular titles—cantor, Kapellmeister, organist-choirmaster, director of music, precentor, song leader, minister of music, or worship leader. But this office is so important to the experience of culturally conscious worship that a new title, free of traditional Western connotations, may be needed. I propose a broader range of responsibilities and possibilities, and suggest that the primary musical presider in culturally conscious worship be called the "enlivener."[1] Michael Warren, a Roman Catholic educator, uses this term to describe a person who embodies the traditions of a faith community and attempts to explore the community's fullness by sharing its faith heritage in poetry, songs, rituals, and artifacts. Warren distinguishes between the enlivener and the "bureaucrat." The bureaucrat reduces the richness of a tradition to programs, ideas, and logical categories

of thought. Lifeless structures may transmit the facts or key events
of a particular tradition, but often do not relate a liturgical heritage
to the life of today's worshipers, "distort[ing] the tradition rather
than disclosing it."[2] Enliveners do not manage programs; they
engage people.

What is the difference between an enlivener and a Western,
classically trained church musician? In many cases, there may be
little difference. Many church musicians have assumed the role of
enlivener either intentionally or through intuitive insight. Others,
however, view their ministry of music primarily from the perspective of specialized musical ensembles that sing for the congregation
rather than as a ministry that involves the entire congregation in
more than pro forma music making. Musical ensembles (instrumental and vocal) play important roles in worship, but they are not
a substitute for the congregation as a "choir of the whole."

TASKS OF THE ENLIVENER

The first task of the enlivener is to bridge the gap between the
established choir (choral ensemble) and the choir of the whole—
those in the pew—so that all may join together in praise to God.
The first role of the choral ensemble is to help the congregation
find its voice. An ensemble may also sing choral music to God that
the congregation cannot sing because of its difficulty.

Establishing a strong congregational choir may enlarge the
vocational understanding of the choral ensemble. First, in numerous cultures around the world, the choral ensemble and the congregational choir are less separated in function than they are in many
churches in the United States. While choral ensembles in Africa, for
example, may sing individual selections separate from the congregation as a part of choral offerings to God, the people often claim
the choral ensemble's anthems for themselves when the anthem is
repeated during the weeks that follow. Furthermore, it is not unusual for the choral ensemble's music to take a musical shape or
structure that allows the people to participate in some way, even
during the first presentation by the choir. They may be able to sing
the refrain with the choral ensemble or move to the rhythm of the
music. (I will say more about the importance of musical structure

later.) One can experience this approach in many African American churches as well. Since the culturally conscious congregation will be singing world song in worship, the ensemble singers should incorporate into their vocational perspective the role of teachers of the congregation's song as well as singers of anthems to God on behalf of the congregation. The first task of the enlivener, then, is to establish the congregation as the primary choir of worship.

Teaching the Congregational Choir

Second, the enlivener assumes this position on the merits not only of musical ability but also of an ability to relate to the congregation as a teacher. As a part of their vocation, enliveners will use their singing voices to teach the congregation to sing its song, rather than to sing solos on behalf of the congregation. The voice should be clear, confident, and true to pitch, but does not need to have a "trained" quality. Trained singers may be very good enliveners, but their voice and manner need to be invitational in tone. The enlivener's voice says, "Please sing with me," rather than "Listen to me." An operatic singer who has been trained to sustain a full sound over an orchestra may not understand the role of the enlivener. A clear and inviting folklike vocal quality is often best.

The enlivener's relationship with the congregation depends on trust. The congregants must trust the enlivener to lead them into unfamiliar musical waters with the hope that the songs they learn will teach them to pray in new ways and enable them to feel a greater oneness as the body of Christ. To this end, teaching new songs should be done efficiently, accurately, and engagingly. Knowing how to break down a song into component parts—text first, tune only, one phrase at a time, using responsorial or echoing techniques—is essential. Appendix D describes a process for teaching a new song to a congregation. The teaching process for a new song assumes that the people learn most successfully voice-to-voice rather than instrument-to-voice. Piano and organ are poor substitutes for an engaging voice in teaching new songs. If you want people to sing, teach them to sing by using your voice. Instruments may be helpful in giving a starting pitch or providing harmonic support once the people learn a song, but nonvocal accompaniments should not overpower the singers or become a crutch upon which the singers are dependent for making music.

Enliveners not only teach the music and words of the song but also offer insight into the song's meaning and original context. Many songs sung in worship come from Christians of a different place and time. It may be helpful to think of the song as a prayer that other Christians have shared with us. Possible questions for the enlivener include: Under what circumstances was this sung prayer first uttered? Who sang it? How was it used in worship? How might a prayer from another cultural context enrich or broaden our way of praying? The enlivener may ask these questions both for sung prayers from centuries past and for current songs that come to us from another part of the globe.

Let us take two examples. In the United States, congregations often sing Martin Rinkart's great hymn "Now thank we all our God" during a Thanksgiving service. While this is certainly a possible use of Rinkart's text and its joyful, sturdy tune, a time of national thanksgiving had nothing to do with the hymn's origins in 1663. Here is the first stanza, as translated by Catherine Winkworth in 1858:

> Now thank we all our God
> With heart and hands and voices,
> Who wondrous things has done,
> In whom this world rejoices;
> Who, from our mothers' arms
> Has bless'd us on our way
> With countless gifts of love,
> And still is ours today.

At first glance, it is not apparent that this hymn was written during the Thirty Years' War, in a time of utter devastation, starvation, famine, and disease. "In all things give thanks" (Eph. 5:20) seems to be an underlying theme of this hymn.

The second stanza:

> O may this bounteous God
> Through all our life be near us,
> With ever joyful hearts

And blessed peace to cheer us;
And keep us in his grace,
And guide us when perplexed,
And free us from all ills
In this world and the next.

This stanza is more petitionary in tone: *keep* us, *guide* us, *free* us.
But to the casual singer, it does not begin to communicate the
situation in which Rinkart as a minister performed last rites for
scores of people nearly every day, numbering in the thousands,
including his own family.

The final stanza is doxological:

All praise and thanks to God
The Father now be given,
The Son, and him who reigns
With them in highest heaven,
The one eternal God,
Whom heav'n and earth adore;
For thus it was, is now,
And shall be evermore.

From the horror of the Thirty Years' War comes a beautiful doxology of gratitude to God. The final stanza praises the triune God—
the substance of a Christian doxology and God's abiding and
eternal love—"For thus it was, is now, and shall be evermore."

When we sing this hymn, we join with Christians who have
struggled through some of life's greatest horrors, survived in the
shadow of death, and found hope in the face of hopelessness. The
strength of the vigorous Reformation melody, sung by a congregation, brings with the singing the promise of hope and God's abiding presence. When worshipers engage this hymn fully, they join the
saints in singing of an eternal God who is ever present.

The South African freedom song "Siyahamba" originates in oral
musical tradition.[3] The common translation is "We are marching in
the light of God." This song has been sung by many congregations
and choirs around the world in recent years. People enjoy singing it
and, on occasion, find themselves moving to its engaging rhythms.
Who sang it first and under what conditions? This song wells up

from the wretched abyss of an oppressed people. Under apartheid, it was illegal for black South Africans to gather in public except under the strictest of conditions. Armed police stood by to enforce this system of subjugation by beating, maiming, and even killing those assembled. Throughout history, singing has been one of the most important ways of uniting an oppressed group. Roger Hudson, a Methodist minister in South Africa, reminded me that singing is also a way for oppressed people to keep from being dehumanized. Only living people can sing. The need to find hope in the face of oppression is the social context for "Siyahamba."

Like African American spirituals, many African songs contain an implicit code within the composition that communicates to the initiated while avoiding offense to those in power. The text of "Siyahamba" appears as a simple statement of joy. While this is the most obvious message, there is much more to this text. "We are marching" is a statement of unity. The text does not say "I am marching." Few individuals could stand up to the wrath of apartheid alone.

"Marching" is a verb of action. It is not a verb for silent victims, but one of defiance and hope. It encourages an active response rather than a passive acquiescence to the fear that must have been on the minds of apartheid-era singers. "The light of God" provides a direction for those marching together. Throughout southern Africa, the "light of God" is code language for a future hope. Black and white South Africans who joined in antiapartheid gatherings singing "Siyahamba" were not just basking in the sun, but singing in defiance of pervasive oppression and in the hope of a future free from fear and full of promise.

These two examples illustrate how the enlivener might put a face on a song, share some of the song's context in appropriate ways, and then invite the congregation to join these Christians past and present in their sung prayer. Petitions for God's mercy by Christians in any place or time are the petitions of all Christians. Musical praises offered by Christians in any age, from any culture, enhance our praises today. Just as the enlivener merges the choral ensemble with the congregation into a unified choral voice, the enlivener brings the voices of saints past and present into harmony with local congregations.

Relating the People's Song to Worship

A third task of the enlivener is to relate the people's song to the broader experience of worship. It is not sufficient just to sing a good song in worship. A good song, well taught and appropriately integrated into worship, in itself unites those gathered as the body of Christ. Returning to the concept of valence, music—sung, played, or danced—has a capacity to weave itself into the fabric of an experience and to transform individuals into a vital singing, praying community.

How shall we pray this song? It may be a prayer of invocation or praise, adoration or petition, intercession or thanksgiving, blessing or sending forth. In all of these situations and more, what can be said may also be sung. Words spoken to the community may have power, but words sung by all the people shape the community's identity. To paraphrase 1 Corinthians 14:15, people will sing with spirit if they understand what they are to sing and why they are singing it. Integrating the congregation's song into worship is part of the work of the enlivener.

Embodying the Congregation's Song

Enliveners need also to embody the songs they teach. Many songs from the world church reflect cultures in which dance is a natural form of expression. While enliveners will teach a wide variety of literature, those who teach songs from dancing cultures should invite the singers of the congregational choir not only to lift their voices but also to dance their sung prayers more fully.

For Euro–North American congregations, dancing while singing may present obstacles. Many Westerners may have difficulty imagining cultures where singing and moving are integral experiences. For congregations striving to be more culturally conscious, moving and singing encourage hospitality and solidarity with those of other cultures who more naturally engage in this practice. Practicing a fully embodied song offers culturally conscious congregations fresh possibilities.

African cultures often assume that music is a combination of playing drums, singing, and dancing. The musical experience lacks authenticity when one of these is not present. In some Asian contexts, especially in Southeast Asia, dancing is also a natural cultural expression. South and Central American cultures as well as Caribbean practices are similar.

Although the cultures mentioned above are not the only ones that assume movement to be part of music, many of the places where Christianity is growing most rapidly are dancing cultures—especially in what many call the "southern" world. Some estimate that the southern world includes two-thirds of Christians today (65 to 70 percent) compared to the northern (Euro–North American) world where Christians make up 30 to 35 percent of the total Christian population. These percentages reflect a rapid change in global Christian demographics from 1950, when approximately 70 percent of Christians lived in the northern world. Given the cultural mosaic that pervades much of the United States, culturally conscious congregations will encounter Christians from dancing cultures in the two-thirds world.

For many descendants of Euro–North American cultures, resistance to movement while singing and praying may be strong at first. Some may feel self-conscious or inadequate because they lack experience. It is natural for congregations to feel vulnerable when exploring culturally conscious worship. It is helpful for enliveners to acknowledge the experience of vulnerability as a way to reach out and identify with others, especially minority groups, who may also feel isolated and vulnerable. The enlivener creates a safe space where experimentation is allowed and we can laugh at ourselves.

Euro–North Americans also worry about offending those from other cultures when they attempt to embody sung prayer through movement. Allowing ourselves to be vulnerable is the key to relating to others once again. If we allow those among us who have more experience to become our teachers, then we have leveled the liturgical playing field and are moving toward becoming a culturally conscious congregation whose diverse members are in partnership. For congregations that are culturally conscious but do not include people from dancing cultures, young people are often excellent teachers of movement. With some contextual guidance from an enlivener, teenagers who have grown up dancing offer the possibility of teaching others how to be more comfortable with their bodies in worship. I am among those who feel vulnerable when I dance. I have found that becoming a student, laughing at myself, and giving it my best try reaches across cultural barriers. My teachers are not usually asking for perfection, but want to share with me the joy they find in worshiping while moving.

Identifying among a congregation those teachers who are naturally comfortable with their bodies is important. Possible teachers may be people from the two-thirds Christian world, young people and children, and even senior adults who enjoy dancing. I have found that moving while singing is an effective intergenerational experience. Children and young people are immediately captivated. In my experience as a leader of multicultural worship in a variety of denominations throughout the United States, I find that many senior adults—even those with walkers and wheelchairs—enjoy participating with their entire bodies to the best of their capabilities.

The enlivener who encourages movement will be aided by several techniques.

1. *Employ the choir (preferably an intergenerational group) as models for movement.* In addition to being part of a singing choir that helps the congregation discover its voice, they may be a moving choir that helps congregants discover their bodies. Choristers well prepared both as singers and movers will magnify the enlivener's leadership through their energy.

2. *Provide specific instructions about movements for the congregation.* In most cases, Euro–North American congregations will do much better when actual steps or movements are suggested. Movements may be as simple as shifting weight on the feet at a slow pace in time to the music. They may involve more specific steps at other times. In appendix E, Marcia McFee provides basic instructions for helping congregations move effectively.

3. *Create a safe space in which experimentation in movement may take place.* Gathering outside the worship space for events such as picnics, social occasions, retreats, and special-emphasis programs are excellent. Another solution is to teach a song and its movements before worship officially begins, incorporating both into worship later at an appropriate time. A brief five- to seven-minute gathering/teaching time has other benefits, including energizing the

beginning of a service in ways that permeate the entire worship experience.

4. *Sing songs that encourage moving.* Some congregational song structures allow for moving better than others. Generally, moving while singing is easier when hymnbooks or song sheets are not used. A short cyclic (repetitive) song or a memorized song works best. When teaching the movements it is sometimes helpful to sing on a neutral syllable (la, la, la) while practicing, adding the text later. Some song structures are easier to move to than others. Appropriate song structures are the subject of section 2.

5. *Give the people permission to choose either moving or singing.* While most will try both, those who feel frustrated or too vulnerable will relax if given an option. In some cases, the enlivener may request that the congregation sing, dance, and clap. Again, many will enjoy this. Suggesting that people may choose two out of three activities relaxes all.

6. *Adapt the space to accommodate movement.* It is ideal to move in a circle without chairs or other obstructions. Unfortunately, few sanctuaries offer this possibility. In many dancing cultures, circle dances are normative and help build community as people are able to see each other while dancing. Rectangular sanctuaries and fixed pews offer difficulties but not insurmountable problems. A congregation may encircle the pews standing in the outer aisles and facing each other across the sanctuary. Movements in line may take place only in the aisles. Even when people are moving at their seats in the pews, encouraging them to create more space by spreading out, overflowing into the aisles, often changes the atmosphere and gives permission to try something new.

7. *Encourage and compliment a dancing congregation.* Maintain a positive and playful atmosphere. Never criticize or ridicule a congregation that is learning to dance. The goal is not perfection, but building community.

8. *Dance in appropriate places throughout worship.* Just as songs need to be well chosen, dancing is most effective when integrated at the right moment into the fabric of cultural consciousness. Processionals are natural occasions to move. The choral ensemble may enter in procession to joyful songs in which the congregation joins, or the entire congregation may join the procession at the beginning

of worship. Other places for processionals include coming forward for communion. In African and African American communities, it is not uncommon for worshipers to walk toward the altar in procession to give their offerings. Simpler gestures may be incorporated during the prayers of intercession, petition, or blessing. Leading the congregation out of the sanctuary after the closing blessing and benediction may also be effective.

While my experience in enlivening congregations through movement has been overwhelmingly positive, some will resist or refuse to participate, just as some may choose not to sing. These worshipers must be respected and extended full hospitality. People may prefer not to sing or dance for any of a number of reasons. They may have been ridiculed for their singing or dancing as young children.[4] Someone may have a physical condition that does not make singing a pleasurable experience or allow dancing without discomfort or even pain. A worshiper may not be able to enter into a fully embodied expression of worship because of a specific emotional experience or trauma. Occasionally a few people object to specific songs or to movements of any kind. While this reaction may be the result of an ethnocentric prejudice, nothing will be gained by ridiculing or lecturing those who choose not to participate for any reason.

If some confront you, declaring that singing "world songs" or dancing is inappropriate during worship, try the following:

1. Keep the issue of hospitality in worship at the forefront of any conversation. Showing hospitality is natural. An invitation to mutual hospitality is more powerful than a mandate to conform to a set of multicultural expectations.
2. Remember that the enlivener's role is invitational, never coercive. Leave open the option to participate by watching.
3. Constantly reinforce the unity of singing and praying. Songs in corporate worship are not just a matter of personal taste and preference but have been chosen for specific liturgical reasons.
4. All songs may be prayed effectively. Perhaps some worshipers have not considered that many hymns in the Western tradition are sung prayers.

5. Remind the people that prayers in the world church may simply be spoken but that many people sing and move while praying. Prayer has many postures.

6. Teach new songs and movements incrementally. While feelings of inadequacy are normal, minimize these by a careful pedagogical process.

7. Be well prepared, and involve the choral ensemble and other appropriate teachers.

8. As an enlivener, avoid judging others by their apparent level of participation. Some individuals may not choose to engage actively with their bodies for any number of reasons. This response does not indicate that they are not engaged in spirit and mind.

9. Do not take criticism or even anger personally. Reaffirm your vocation as an enlivener; examine your principles, motives, and pedagogical process; and try again.

10. Develop a group of enliveners who mutually offer suggestions, help one another in the teaching process, share songs, and support each other in planning and prayer. Those in any vocation in the life of the church are strengthened when they meet regularly with others who share the same calling. Do not be a Lone Ranger, but develop a cadre of vocationally committed enliveners.

SONG STRUCTURES AND THE ENLIVENER

The enlivener has access to a wealth of songs from which to choose. Sources include those from the heritage of Christian faith (Western hymns), ecumenical sources since the Second Vatican Council, "Contemporary Christian Music" (CCM), African American gospel songs, music from intentional communities such as Taizé and Iona, and global songs from every corner of the earth. When selecting songs for worship, several factors come into play. *Musical diversity* focuses on the varieties of musical styles. *Thematic emphasis* centers on appropriate texts. *Pastoral concern* highlights congregational receptiveness and appropriate balance between the security of established ritual and the suspense of new rituals or modifications of long-held patterns of worship. The enlivener is an artist, skillfully crafting the worship mosaic each week. Enliveners should consider all of these as they select and integrate music into worship.

In addition to musical diversity, thematic emphasis, and pastoral concerns, I suggest that the enlivener of worship has an additional criterion for making musical decisions in culturally conscious congregations. *The musical structure or form of songs* offers guidance to the sensitive enlivener when choosing songs and weaving them appropriately into the fabric of worship.

Congregational song exists in an infinite possibility of structures. At one end of the spectrum are texts that are sequential in form. These texts consist of several stanzas that proceed in a linear fashion, progressing in concept from one stanza to the next. This is the structure of classic Western hymnody. At the other end of the spectrum are cyclic songs. This form usually includes fewer words and, according to the musical style and cultural context, usually involves textual and melodic repetition. Songs with refrains are somewhere between sequential and cyclic structures. This form includes the stanzas of sequential structures and a repeated section that takes on a cyclic function. A variety of musical styles may be used with each reference point on the spectrum of musical structures.

Between these major forms are numerous variations. A closer examination may reveal how each structure works and the potential each holds for enlivening worship. (A table in the notes for this chapter at the conclusion of the book provides sources for all songs cited in this chapter.[5]) Figure 10 illustrates the broad range of structures found in most congregational songs. You may wish to refer to this summary of congregational musical structures during the discussion that follows.

Sequential Song Structures

In sequential song structures, a train of thought is continued over several stanzas, and an idea is developed and brought to a high point or logical conclusion. The apex can be achieved in several ways. A hymn may be based on the Trinity with each of the first three stanzas devoted to a person of the Three-in-One, concluding with a doxological stanza of praise that lifts up the unity of the triune God. See "Come, thou almighty King" for a classic example.

Figure 10
Comparison between Sequential and
Cyclic Musical Structures

Refrain Forms
Response
Antiphon
Litany

Sequential Structures	Cyclic Structures
Strophic	Theme and Variation
Textual orientation	Movement orientation
Eye-oriented	Ear-oriented
Literate tradition	Oral tradition
Predictable performance time	Open-ended performance time
Linear in structure	Episodic in experience
Verbose	Concise
Comments on ritual activity	Participates in ritual activity
Content-oriented	Community-oriented
Moves toward climax in literary content	Moves toward total participation and integration of participants

Musical and Textual Considerations

The musical pulse (beat) may vary from stanza to stanza or within a stanza	Maintains a steady beat once the same music is repeated
Includes through-composed music and texts where there is no repetition of the music	Each repetition of a cycle needs some small variation
Includes minimal (if any) textual repetition	Texts are usually repetitive with a soloist (enlivener) singing a counter-melody in each cycle for variety
Monochronic (teleological or directional) sense of time	Polychronic sense of time (relational or community building)
Does not usually need a soloist	Improvisations by soloist are essential in most musical styles using a cyclic form
Usually accompanied by organ or piano	Often unaccompanied or accompanied by percussion and a wider range of musical instruments
May be sung seated or standing	May be sung seated or standing with movement
Harmonic and instrumental variations and descants may create musical differences from stanza to stanza	Variations are achieved through instrumental and vocal improvisations
Texts are fixed	Texts may be improvised to fit ritual context

A more recent trinitarian hymn is Jeffrey Rowthorn's "Creating God, your fingers trace." This hymn refers to the work of the members of the Trinity without mentioning the classic formula Father, Son, and Holy Spirit—"Creating God," "Sustaining God," "Redeeming God," "Indwelling God."

A hymn may follow the progression of a passage of scripture. In metrical psalmody, for example, psalms are arranged in the form of metered poetry. See the familiar setting of Psalm 23 from the Scottish Psalter, "The Lord's my shepherd," or for a New Testament example, "While shepherds watched their flocks by night," based on Luke 2. Both of these closely follow the narrative as presented in the King James Version. A more recent example is Timothy Dudley-Smith's paraphrase of Mary's Song (the Magnificat) in Luke 1, "Tell out, my soul, the glory of the Lord," derived in part from the translation found in the New Jerusalem Bible.

A sequential hymn may tell a story. Throughout the history of hymnody one can find hymns or carols that tell part, or all, of the story of the life of Christ as a musical ballad. The medieval hymn "O Love, how deep, how broad, how high" is a fine example. "O sons and daughters, let us sing" takes the singer through the passion, resurrection, and post-resurrection events of Christ's life. The stanzas of the African American spiritual "Were you there" focus on the progression of events during Christ's passion. Sydney Carter's "Lord of the Dance" is a more recent example of a hymn that tells the story of Christ's life in a ballad form around the metaphor of a dance.

Some hymns describe an attribute of God or praise God but conclude with a final stanza of petition. Petitions usually begin each line with an imperative verb. For example, note the petitions in the final stanza of Charles Wesley's famous hymn, "Love divine, all loves excelling." The imperative verbs are italicized:

> *Finish* then thy new creation;
> Pure and spotless *let us be.*
> *Let us find* thy great salvation
> Perfectly restored in thee.

A more recent example is the Japanese hymn "Here, O Lord, your servants gather" by Tokuo Yamaguchi, as translated by Everett Stowe. The first three stanzas elaborate on the theme of John 14:6,

"I am the way, the truth, and the life." The final stanza is a series of petitions with the imperative verbs "grant," "help," and "send." These petitions to God serve as a climactic conclusion to a sequential hymn.

Other hymns elaborate on a specific teaching of Christ and then bring the idea home by applying it to the lives of people today (a hermeneutic approach). The African American spiritual "When Israel was in Egypt's land" (Go Down, Moses) concludes with a hermeneutical stanza in some hymnals:

> O let us all from bondage flee (Let my people go)
> And let us all in Christ be free (Let my people go)

The classic Christmas hymn "Once in royal David's city," written for children by Cecil Frances Alexander, a children's educator and wife of an Anglican priest, has a strong hermeneutical bent:

> Jesus is our childhood's pattern,
> Day by day like us he grew;
> He was little, weak and helpless,
> Tears and smiles like us he knew;
> And he feels for all our sadness,
> And he shares in all our gladness.

Some hymns drive their point home with a final stanza or closing emphasis on heaven as the goal of Christians. This eschatological approach (referring to the last things) was a technique often applied by Charles Wesley. See, for example, the second half of the final stanza of "Love divine, all loves excelling":

> Changed from glory into glory,
> Till in heaven we take our place,
> Till we cast our crowns before thee,
> Lost in wonder, love, and praise.

In the 11th century, Bernard of Clairvaux closed his hymn with a reference to heaven, as translated from the Latin by 19th century poet Edward Caswall:

Jesus, our only joy be thou,
As thou our prize will be;
Jesus, be thou our glory now,
And through eternity.

Hymns on communion often use this technique, referring in the final stanza to the celestial banquet in which all Christians will share with Christ at the head of the table. Cesáreo Gabaráin's communion hymn "Sheaves of Summer" ("Una Espiga") captures this spirit beautifully in his final stanza:

En la mesa de Dios de sentarán.
(At God's table we will sit.)
Como hijos su pan compartirán.
(As God's children we will share the bread.)

Finally, the concluding stanzas of some hymns may call us to a commitment to Christ in response to what Christ has done for us. Isaac Watts's "When I survey the wondrous cross" is a classic example:

Were the whole realm of nature mine,
That were a present far too small;
Love so amazing, so divine,
Demands my soul, my life, my all.

John Bell's more recent hymn "The Summons" asks the question, "Will you come and follow me?" in the first four stanzas. The final stanza responds to Christ's summons:

Lord, your summons echoes true when you but call my name.
Let me turn and follow you and never be the same.[6]

Classic sequential hymns use endless variations. The list above is only illustrative. Questions to ask of sequential hymn texts include:

1. What theme is being developed?
2. How does the hymn writer develop this theme?

3. What is the biblical basis for the theme?
4. Is this essentially a hymn of praise or a hymn of petition?
5. How does the writer bring the hymn to a climax in the final stanza?

On the basis of answers to these questions, the enlivener may decide what musical resources may be used in creative ways to bring the hymn's theme and progression of ideas alive.

1. What instrument(s) should accompany this hymn? Organ, piano, guitar, melody instrument, percussion, or a combination?
2. Do the stanzas lend themselves to being sung by soloists, with the congregation and choir coming in later or on the last stanza?
3. Does the hymn have a parallel structure suggesting an alternation between choir and congregation?
4. Can the congregation sing all or a part of the hymn unaccompanied with the choral ensemble's support?
5. If the hymn should be sung with the organ, does the organist phrase and set registrations for each stanza according to the text?
6. How can the enlivener bring this hymn to life? Should a soloist sing the first two or three stanzas, especially if the hymn is unfamiliar? Would a brief note on the hymn's historical or cultural context printed in the worship folder or offered orally before the service help the people participate more fully? What scripture serves as the foundation for this hymn? Would it help the congregation to read the text aloud before singing it? What tempo communicates the text, serves the music, suits the accompaniment, and is attainable by the people?

Using the Organ in Worship

Sequential hymns may have an enervating effect on worship for many congregations if they are accompanied only on the organ without any sensitivity to text, progression of ideas, and textual/ musical climax. Variety in accompaniment is one of the keys to enlivening congregational singing. Unaccompanied or a cappella singing from time to time on appropriate selections also varies the hymn-singing experience. I hope that the organ will remain a normative instrument for congregational singing because of its vast potential and range of sounds. However, "normative" does not mean the only instrument, especially when songs of the world church are used. Furthermore, there are many parishes where a capable organist is not available and other instrumental solutions need to be devised. The organ should not become so common and uninteresting in its role in worship that the effect is one of musical wallpaper. Any single instrumental medium (piano, guitar, trap set) may have this effect, however, when used exclusively and unimaginatively. One goal for the enlivener might be to sing one congregational selection unaccompanied each service, even if it is a single stanza or short refrain. If prepared carefully and supported by the choir, unaccompanied singing will strengthen the congregation's sound, increase singers' confidence and add variety to the musical soundscape of worship.

Cyclic Structures

Cyclic forms also offer many possibilities for worship. They are usually more textually and musically compact. Unlike the literary approach of sequential structures, cyclic forms may be sung with little or no reference to printed text or music once the song has become familiar to the assembly. Their brevity and oral or aural means of transmission of song allow worshipers to move their bodies to the music without being encumbered by books, and to observe other ritual actions taking place in the liturgy as they sing. Congregations might sing, for example, while the offering is being taken, while communion is being shared, as families and sponsors come forward for baptism, or as the people welcome a newly baptized person. While these rituals may be observed in part while singing hymns from a book, I have noticed that the level of congregational participation rises when people participate in liturgical actions unencumbered by hymnals. A common ritual action is bringing forward the congregation's offering. Usually a short, familiar song accompanies this ritual. In some traditions, before the reading of the gospel, the Bible is held high, and the altar party moves in procession to the center of the people, as a symbol of the Word made flesh among us. These are excellent times for a brief cyclic song that can both gather the community around this important event and free them to watch and participate in the procession as singers at the same time.

One of the common misunderstandings about cyclic structures by those trained in Western classic hymn traditions is that they are repetitive. While this appears to be the case on the surface, I have observed that the enliveners of cyclic songs creatively vary nearly every cycle in some modest way. They may change the instrumentation slightly or sing some cycles unaccompanied. They may vary the text slightly, changing only a word or two. For example, "Father, I adore you" uses this approach with successive cycles, including the remaining persons of the Trinity. Varying the dynamic level from cycle to cycle is another way to add variety. The enlivener may improvise or sing separate parts over the congregation's ongoing cycle.

Many Taizé chants use this technique. Note the cantor's (enlivener's) parts for the familiar Taizé song "Bless the Lord, my soul," based on the first verse of Psalm 103. African songs in particular, though not exclusively, often use an additive approach to each cycle. A soloist may begin, followed by the choir, and finally all of the people. Through successive cycles the enlivener signals slight changes in the text or sings with increasing energy a separate part above the congregation's cycle.

Percussion instruments may be added or layered on little by little. Movement may begin minimally but increase in intensity as the musical experience "heats up." What could have been a boring experience of static repetition deepens by taking a theme-with-subtle-variations approach to each successive cycle. Variations may be planned to some degree, but groups that work together over time learn to vary cycles spontaneously. This observation applies to congregations as well as instrumental groups, including a West

African drum ensemble, a Taizé accompaniment group, or a praise team preparing "Contemporary Christian Music" (CCM). Cultural groups whose traditional music is cyclic seem to understand instinctively how these forms work. Others can learn to lead cyclic songs effectively, however, by becoming sensitive to the possibilities of the form.

The enlivener functions in a variety of ways to teach different musical styles that use cyclic structures. In guiding music from the Taizé Community, for example, the enlivener is usually out of sight, leading the people indirectly with the voice or instruments. African music, on the other hand, often requires a more active role. Since African music is usually danced, it requires visible leaders who lead with the movement of their bodies as well as their voices. "Freedom Is Coming," a well known South African freedom song, was sung on the move during apartheid days. Swaying or even stylized marching enhances the activity implied by the use of the present progressive tense, "Freedom is coming" and "Jesus is coming." Regardless of the musical style, enliveners should follow two principles:

1. Whenever possible, share leadership with others.
2. Prepare choirs to lend their voices and bodies to the shared experience of music making.

Refrain or Responsorial Structures

The third musical structure, the refrain form, combines aspects of both sequential and cyclic structures. The refrain reinforces the overall theme of a hymn. Recent hymns using refrains, many coming from Roman Catholic renewal music, have become popular. "I, the Lord of sea and sky" ("Here I Am, Lord") uses this form effectively. The stanzas speak from the perspective of God. The refrain offers the opportunity for the people to respond, "Here I am, Lord," borrowing from Isaiah 6:8. The text of the hymn suggests that a soloist or choir could sing the stanzas while the congregation responds on the refrain.

"Lord, you have come to the lakeshore" (*"Tu has venido"*) has a similar feel. The refrain, beginning with "O Lord, with your eyes you have searched me," establishes a strong first-person perspective, drawing the singer into the story as participant. Examine other refrain hymns to see if assigning stanzas to a soloist or choir might enhance the text.

Refrains may be helpful when teaching a congregation new hymns. Begin with the refrain when introducing the hymn, and use choir or soloists on the stanzas. This approach allows the congregation to participate quickly while learning parts of the song by listening. Brian Wren's "Woman in the Night" is an example of a hymn that may be taught effectively by this method. Each of the stanzas reflects the perspective of a different female biblical character. Using various women soloists on the stanzas not only personalizes the story, but also creates contrast when the people all enter on the refrain, "Come and join the song, women, children, men."

Closely related to refrains are call-response forms. African American spirituals often use this approach. Not only does a call-response add variety to the musical presentation; it is a more authentic way of singing spirituals, as this pattern was used by African Americans during slavery. Here are some examples:

"They crucified my Lord"
Call (Solo):   They crucified my Lord;
Response (All):   And he never said a mumbalin' word.

"When Israel was in Egypt's land"
Call (Solo):   When Israel was in Egypt's land;
Response (All):   Let my people go.
Call (Solo):   Oppressed so hard they could not stand;
Response (All):   Let my people go.

In many hymnals, the call-response patterns may not be indicated. The leader will need to decide how to achieve this effect after examining the song.

CHOOSING SONGS FOR WORSHIP BY STRUCTURE

A knowledge of underlying structures not only adds variety to the presentation of the music in worship but also may bring out the meaning of the text for the singers. Structural knowledge of congregational songs can be helpful when placing songs within the liturgy.

Three general principles emerge:

1. *Sequential structures communicate theological content in an ample and carefully worded manner.* Because of their literary form, sequential hymns often work well to provide theological commentary, reinforcing the theme of the day and anticipating or following ritual actions.

Sequential hymns are not generally effective during ritual activity in worship unless they are very familiar to the congregation—virtually memorized. If well known, sequential hymns may function in a cyclical manner. The selection of these hymns varies from congregation to congregation and by faith tradition. Even congregations that use sequential hymns for choir processionals usually sing only familiar songs for this purpose. Generally, ritual activity that demands the congregation's complete participation does not blend well with sequential hymn singing. In other words, a procession during communion is not the best time to introduce a new sequential hymn and expect full and active participation in singing by the congregation.

2. *Cyclic structures focus on community building and supporting ongoing ritual activity, especially since they may easily be sung without the aid of books.* The essentially oral character of cyclic forms (even though appearing in hymn books or other media) calls for a physical response. This necessity is obvious in African and African American cyclic music as well as in many "Contemporary Christian" songs with which an outward physical response is normative. The mantralike cyclic structures of the Taizé chants also have a profound physical effect on the one who sings or prays the song, relaxing the body and focusing the mind for centered prayer.

Congregations may benefit by having a variety of cyclic songs at their disposal, perhaps as many as 30 to 40 at any one time. The assembly may sing memorized cyclic songs in liturgy on short notice, giving the order of worship a sense of spontaneity. While a memorized sequential hymn may work spontaneously, the flow of the service may be lost if the people need to take time to look up a song in the hymnal.

3. *Refrain forms can be used in a variety of situations.* When soloists or choir sing the stanzas, leaving only the refrain for the congregation, the congregation may be able to participate in a ritual activity as they sing. An example of a ritual activity in which cyclic songs or refrain forms are effective is singing during communion, especially if the congregants go down and kneel at the altar to receive the communion elements. Cyclic songs such as "Eat this bread" or "Jesus, remember me" from the Taizé Community work well. Refrain hymns such as "One bread, one body," "You satisfy the hungry heart," and "Alleluia, Alleluia, give thanks to the risen Lord" are effective during this ritual activity as the choir or a soloist sings the stanzas.

SONGS AND THE FABRIC OF LITURGY

All congregational song structures have the potential for providing valid liturgical experiences. Community formation takes place and theological content is provided whenever a congregation sings. Using a variety of song structures at appropriate places in the liturgy recognizes the strength of each.

Enliveners will add energy to worship and integrate music more completely into the fabric of liturgy if they choose music not only for thematic emphasis or a particular musical style, but also for structural reinforcement of the rituals in the liturgy. A common misuse of cyclic structures takes place when congregations attempt to create so-called "blended worship" with both traditional and contemporary Western musical styles. Often congregations in this situation will substitute a string of two or three cyclic songs for one of the sequential hymns they usually sing. This approach is usually unsatisfying for both those who prefer cyclic structures and those who enjoy sequential hymns.

Blended worship is more than inserting cyclic songs where a sequential hymn usually appears. While worship can be enriched by using a variety of structures, each structure should be incorporated in ways that permeate the shape of the liturgy. According to the principles of valence, music does not draw undue attention to itself, but enhances scripture and deepens the rites and rituals of worship.

I am encouraging the use of a greater variety of musical song structures throughout worship, but with an understanding of the potential each brings to the fabric of liturgy.

The enlivener has a significant role in planning and participating in culturally conscious worship, especially because of the importance of music in Christian worship. The next section looks more closely at potential strategies for enabling multicultural worship.

PENTECOST RENEWED: 10 STRATEGIES FOR CULTIVATING COMMON PRAYER

Part I suggested ways to understand cultural differences. Part II presented case studies of four culturally diverse congregations at worship. Part III, section 1, explored musical leadership, congregational song structures, and the integration of music into liturgy. The writers of these pieces have made several assumptions:

1. Congregations seeking diversity come in many varieties, including predominantly Anglo, Latino, and African American churches.
2. The fact that a congregation has significant and effective ministries to the surrounding neighborhood does not guarantee that it worships in a way that spans cultural differences.
3. Congregations should consider worshiping in a manner that reflects the diversity of the community in which they reside.
4. Congregations that reside in more culturally uniform areas may also benefit from culturally diverse worship experiences as a means of broadening their vision of the universal church and expanding their witness to include others.
5. Worshiping together—establishing a space for common prayer—is hard work. Creating a culturally conscious worshiping community is potentially so difficult that many may decide that such an experience is neither practical nor perhaps even desirable.

Yet, the Spirit calls Christians to build a new community around Christ that follows the model presented in Galatians 3:27-29. Such a community does not show preference for cultural distinctions ("neither Jew nor Gentile"); does not show partiality according to social background ("neither slave nor free"); nor does it favor one gender over another ("neither male nor female").

While fraught with conflicting cross-currents, establishing a new community, one new humanity in Christ (Eph. 2:15) is a response to Christ's commandments to love one's neighbor as we love ourselves (John 13:34), and to love one another as God loves us (15:12). These commandments function as an ethical guide for our conduct in the world and in our worship. They guide our worship as we pray not only for those near and dear but also for those in need around the world. Questions emerge from these ethical imperatives. Might we deepen and broaden our prayers for the world by incorporating ritual actions, images, languages, songs, understandings of time, and senses of space from the regions for whose peoples we pray?

Can culturally diverse Christians pray together? How may people with disparate worldviews can gather around one table?

WORSHIP STRATEGIES FOR THE CULTURALLY CONSCIOUS

The following strategies are starting points for congregations that seek to become more culturally conscious. They are neither fail-safe recipes for success nor quick fixes. Employing these strategies will undoubtedly cause conflict. We are reminded from part I that conflict may be healthy, and that the lack of conflict may typify a declining congregation unwilling to confront the hard issues it faces. Those initiating these strategies need to possess an abundance of pastoral sensitivity. That gift is not limited to the pastor of the congregation. It is a defining characteristic of congregational members who try to think beyond their own biases (and perhaps prejudices) and see the perspective of others. Those with pastoral sensitivity do not avoid conflict but respect the experience and opinions of others by engaging people with a variety of views in the process for change.

Hallmarks of pastoral sensitivity include operating by consensus, preparing people for change, and making changes moderately while moving forward with all deliberate speed. Working by consensus rather than by parliamentary vote allows ample time for all voices to be heard and respects a diversity of views. Consensus may not work every time, but it should be the goal and normative decision-making process. It is not as efficient as some would like, but decisions born of consensus tend to ease the anxiety that change brings because the process does not rush to a quick conclusion, and all participants are encouraged to express their views.

Professional staff, clergy, and laity alike, are notorious for failing to prepare congregations for change. Ideas that arise in a small group may seem great at the moment of their conception, but they can cause significant destruction if they are put into practice without careful preparation. I recall a seminary intern and her pastor who instituted an "inclusive-language" version of the Lord's Prayer in worship one Sunday. Although the intern's intentions were noble, the decision to substitute the revised Lord's Prayer with no theological explanation or liturgical preparation proved disruptive. This congregation was not averse to innovation; it accepted the new version the first week. But after several weeks of use with no explanation, resentment smoldered as many parishioners began to feel betrayed. Would the traditional Lord's Prayer ever be used again? An eruption of rancor polarized many in the congregation. I was called in at this point to discuss inclusive language and worship. While I may have been of some assistance, how much more enjoyable my task might have been, had I been engaged with the congregation before the changes were made.

The art of change is to make small modifications that are appropriate to the congregation's history and tradition, while moving ahead thoughtfully and carefully. Incremental change, well timed, engenders trust and confidence in the leadership and prepares people for further successful change. The goal is not to be the first culturally conscious congregation on your block. The goal is to move steadily and faithfully in this direction, realizing that the journey toward inclusion and breaking down divisive barriers in the ways we worship will not end until all gather around Christ's table. Meanwhile we partake of a foretaste of the glory of culturally diverse worship on our journey together.

Strategy 1: Develop Committed and Informed Leadership

Both the study of the four congregations in Dallas and extensive research by Hartford Seminary sociologist Nancy Tatom Ammerman strongly suggest that committed leadership by the professional staff and lay leaders is essential for developing a culturally conscious congregation. Ammerman places this item at the top of her list for changing congregations: "Most visibly, congregations need people with leadership skills, especially effective clergy. They need people who can envision what should be done and motivate others to participate in doing it."[1]

Charles Foster, then professor of religion and education at Emory University's Candler School of Theology, offered helpful guidance for leaders of diverse congregations in his book *Embracing Diversity: Leadership in a Multicultural Community*,[2] including approaches for negotiating cultural differences and establishing congregational conversations.

Three aspects of leadership will be the focus here: vision for change, rationale for change, and inclusion of others. Specifically, Ammerman says that vision and rationale are the primary attributes needed by congregational leaders when churches undergo significant change. It is hard to underestimate the importance of establishing a broader vision of the church. A vision for change, combined with a mission to engage the diversity of the world and its needs, leads a congregation to broaden its vision. Ammerman notes in her study of hundreds of congregations, "Of those [congregations] currently experiencing serious declines in membership and resources, all have either actively resisted change or have continued with existing patterns, apparently unable to envision how things might be different."[3] Ammerman's research provides empirical proof that supports the axiom found in Proverbs, "Where there is no vision, the people perish"(29:18 KJV).

Part I of this book outlines some of the complex dynamics involved in envisioning a culturally diverse congregation. This approach counters the ideas put forward by some proponents of church growth, who build their congregations around cultural uniformity, targeting specific generations and socioeconomic strata. I envision a congregation that attempts to embody a new humanity in Christ—a diverse assembly finding community in praying together, welcoming strangers and aliens, enjoying and embracing diverse perspectives, and feeling themselves imbued with the Spirit of Pentecost, whose diverse voices were heard and understood.

Ammerman also notes that fundamental shifts in congregational perspective require "some conscious rationale for what [congregants] are doing."[4] A committed pastor may offer a theological rationale that inspires many in the congregation, but embodying that vision is the work of the people. A conscious rationale offers direction and purpose around which the people may gather. The case studies in this book are a witness to congregations that struggle to define their rationale for relating to the community. Charles Foster and Charles Brelsford of Emory University's Candler School of Theology offer additional case studies of inclusive pastoral visions in their book *We Are the Church Together: Cultural Diversity in Congregational Life.*[5] Though worship is not the focus of their book, the vision offered in *We Are the Church* extends to this arena of congregational life. Among the ideas explored in this book is a re-envisioning of tradition that includes the perspective of those who have often been relegated to the margins of society or the "underside of community life."[6] Examples from congregational case studies reinforce this vision.

Establishing a congregation that values culturally conscious worship is a mutual effort involving clergy and laity. This is not the place for Lone Rangers or go-it-alone zealots. Committed pastors are essential for this task. It will be difficult, if not impossible, for committed laity to move the congregation toward culturally conscious worship if the pastor resists. It will be equally difficult, however, to engage the congregation fully in culturally conscious worship if the minister's vision does not become a shared one, embodied by the church.

A process of discernment is paramount in building a shared vision. A practice that leads to culturally conscious worship is one that will encourage gradually widening circles of trust from staff and lay leaders to the entire congregation. A shared vision will lead also toward broadening the leadership base from those who have traditionally held positions of power to creating a more culturally diverse leadership cadre. The result is a new paradigm of community and common worship.

The discernment process, especially if it is consensus-based, will modify or supplant the original vision as more perspectives are brought into play. The use of discernment is the opposite of a product-driven mentality that uses clever advertising to persuade consumers that they need the item being sold. A process of discernment constantly evolves as the circle widens and the Holy Spirit imbues the congregation with the spirit of Pentecost.

Congregational leaders should be familiar with group strategies devised by Eric Law, referred to in part I. An annotated bibliography at the end of this book provides a summary of his four books to date. Of particular note is his "mutual invitation process" as a model for bringing diverse groups together. I believe that Law's process is an effective tool for staff and volunteers who plan worship together. The strength of the mutual invitation process is embedded in its name: It is *mutual*, allowing all to be heard without interruption and avoiding domination by any single person; highly *invitational*, avoiding coercion; and *orderly*, reducing the anxiety of being unsure how to proceed or wondering whether all voices will be heard—a discomfort that often accompanies meetings bringing together diverse cultural groups. Drawn from Law's first book, *The Wolf Shall Dwell with the Lamb*, Appendix F outlines this process.[7] Mutual invitation is not a panacea for negotiating all cross-cultural issues, but it does set the stage for frank and fruitful discussion. In other books, Law suggests processes for establishing deeper levels of trust and cooperation.[8]

Strategy 2: Select Worship Leaders Who Reflect Congregational and Neighborhood Diversity

This issue is crucial. Of the four congregations that participated in this study, two had leaders who worked deliberately to represent diversity in the leadership of worship each Sunday. All Nations Church balanced the presence of an African American female pastor with male leaders, both black and white, on most Sundays. The keyboard accompanist was an African American woman, but the pastor preferred to work with an Euro-American music director if at all possible. Diversity was most visible each week in the choir, whose membership was virtually half-and-half black and white. A Latina was often one of the greeters. An effort was made to spread the leadership of committees and councils among members of various ethnic backgrounds. When possible, the leadership should reflect generally the diversity of the congregation and neighborhood.

Diverse leadership on Sunday morning was also a high priority for Church of the Disciple. The co-pastors were an Anglo couple, but they worked diligently to bring ethnic diversity to the church's worship and committee leadership. An African American woman played keyboard and sang solos from time to time. Though moving more slowly than leaders at All Nations, both ministers at Church of the Disciple had a strong desire to incorporate ethnic diversity into their professional staffs and lay leadership.

While ethnic diversity is important, it is not the only kind of diversity. All four congregations in this study worked conscientiously to balance male and female leaders in worship.

Most of the congregations also worked hard to balance lay volunteers in worship leadership with professional staff leadership. In the case of Agape Church, lay leaders shared the role of presider each week with the pastor on a nearly equal basis, with the pastor leading the pastoral prayer and prayers of the people, and delivering the sermon, while the lay leader presided over almost every other part of the service. The ordained minister shared leadership with a layperson at the communion table as much as possible. At All Nations Church, a male church officer and an Anglo male seminarian assisted the female pastor each week throughout the service. It was not uncommon for committee chairs, both male and female, and of varied ethnicities, to bring progress reports during worship as a part of the "work of the people."

At Grace Church the professional staff made efforts to include gay and lesbian members in worship leadership along with

heterosexual members. The chair of the usher committee, a gay
man, took this aspect of his job especially seriously. Everyone was
welcome, but it was particularly important to Grace Church that
gay and lesbian members should feel welcome. In addition, minority members of various ethnic groups served as greeters and ushers.

Generational segregation is a problem for many congregations.
All four of the congregations in this study chose not to offer activities that separated children from the rest of the congregation
during worship. While this decision may in some cases have been
due to a lack of physical, human, or financial resources, the effect
was a congregational experience of intergenerational worship. *La
Familia* of Agape Church would not be complete if part of the
family were not in worship. At Agape, during the prayers of the
people, when worshipers were invited to kneel at the communion
rail, one could witness entire families coming forward. Young
people spoke out occasionally during the time for joys, concerns,
and announcements.

I would suggest that the inclusion of children and young people
as leaders in worship would be a worthy goal for congregations. The
weekly incorporation of children and youth into the leadership
fabric of worship is an excellent way to inspire future presiders and
enliveners. They may read scripture, lead prayers, serve as ushers,
play musical instruments, or sing brief responses. While all the
congregations in this study had a children's time (or children's
sermon), I would encourage worship planners in culturally conscious congregations to use young people in other worship roles.
People from most other parts of the world, as well as many minority groups, will be accustomed to an intergenerational worship
experience. Relegating children and young people to special days is
a form of liturgical segregation.

Leadership in the church should reflect the diversity (gender,
ethnicity, age, socioeconomic status, physical ability, regional
origin) of the congregation and its neighborhood in churches that
are developing culturally conscious worship. Congregations that
draw members from a broader area may also reflect the diversity
found in that region.

Strategy 3: Permeate the Worship Space and Worship Rituals with Inclusive Nonverbal Forms of Communication

Visual Images and Space

Preparing the worship space is one of the most crucial tasks for achieving culturally conscious worship. Is the space inviting to people from broader cultural perspectives, or does it support an underlying ethnocentric ethos? Let us consider the example of stained-glass windows for a moment. The Church of the Disciple had the advantage of building a sanctuary to fit the mission of the church. High above the congregation in the center of the chancel is a contemporary stained-glass window depicting the Lord's Supper. The window portrays Christ and the disciples in a stylized manner without distinct faces. Colored orbs represent each face seated around Christ. Each orb is of a different hue, indicating the diversity of those gathered at the table. Theologically, this representation of Christ with his disciples no longer refers only to the Last Supper; it also reflects a table around which the whole world sits. The design of this window was intentional. When it was delivered to the church during its construction, church members participated in placing it in the sanctuary, an event that captured the imagination of the entire congregation. As a young congregation that was able to build a new building, Church of the Disciple was given an opportunity to embody in the worship space itself the diverse congregation that members seek to become.

Grace Church also has beautiful stained-glass windows. Because the church is a registered historic site, the restoration of the windows was an important part of the revitalization of the Gothic Revival structure and was a point of pride for the congregation. With this restoration, however, come some stumbling blocks, as white representations of Christ and white seraphic and cherubic figures reflect the aesthetic sensibilities of the former residents of a neighborhood whose complexion has changed. Grace Church must work hard to counteract the ethnically uniform windows with other visual and nonverbal art works and symbols. The most important signs of diversity are the people who participate in the leadership of worship. Other means may include ethnically diverse art on the cover of the order of worship and larger pieces of such art displayed throughout the building. A variety of music will also help. As a designated landmark, Grace Church has restored its sanctuary to the specifications of its 1925 renovation. The restoration itself is a metaphor for a church renewed in spirit in a changing neighborhood. I believe that the congregation was correct in restoring the windows, but I also think that members will need to be creative in how they visually make manifest the diversity of the congregation they want to become.

Agape and All Nations have both had to adapt preexisting spaces. One of the noticeable ways they did so was through banners that reflect the mission and cultural heritage of each congregation. All Nations Church has moved from a movie theater to a building acquired from a Baptist congregation. The presence at the front of the sanctuary of the All Nations banner with a globe at the center is a constant reminder of the congregation's commitment to become a "United Nations" congregation. All Nations also has flexible seating in its new sanctuary. Compared to the theater seating in the earlier location, these upholstered wood-frame chairs designed for churches or chapels can be placed with more space between the rows. A higher percentage of this diverse congregation is African American, and gospel music plays an important role in the service. Congregational movement (swaying and clapping) is encouraged by the extra space between the rows of chairs.

In discussions with the pastor, the Rev. Dr. Clara Reed, I explored the possibility of reconfiguring the flexible seating. Rather than arranging all the chairs facing forward so that parishioners see only the backs of other worshipers' heads as they look toward the elevated chancel area, the sense of visible community might be enhanced by placing the chairs in a semi-circle. This curved arrangement would allow worshipers to see more of the body of Christ and not just the worship leaders. Stronger congregational singing usually emerges in a partial in-the-round configuration, because people sing toward each other rather than toward the front. I refer to a circular (or semi-circular) seating arrangement as a "community pattern" and the all-face-forward seating as a "cathedral pattern." Both have benefits and drawbacks, but for a congregation that is culturally conscious, the diversity of the gathered assembly is a nonverbal witness to the congregation's mission and to those who would participate in it. The community pattern also makes children and young people more visible to others, and the participation of the worshiping community is more visible to them. For example, seeing children sing the hymns makes people aware that children too are active members of a faith family. In many congregations, children may be seen only when they sing as a choir *for* the congregation, not as participants in worship *with* the congregation. If the prayers of the people (or, as some congregations may say, "joys and concerns") are voiced aloud, it is much easier for all to hear the softer voices of children and senior adults in the community pattern.

When Church of the Disciple designed its permanent structure in 1999, members decided to include two video projection screens. These visible yet unobtrusive screens have become an integral part of the liturgical landscape, displaying the words of songs and an outline of the pastor's sermon. I led a service of global song with this congregation during Advent 2000. During parts of the service the screens displayed images of Christ from around the world, capturing the global face of the Incarnate God. These images were never referred to aloud but were a nonverbal complement to the sung and spoken word. Because of the up-to-date technology included in this new building, the congregation occasionally sees and hears brief video clips that bring the witness of others into the liturgy. These clips often serve to connect this local congregation with the global church.

Sound and Space

One of the most important aspects of liturgical space is the degree to which it amplifies sound. Sound engineers often design systems to enhance only the sound that comes from the chancel area. This practice assumes that everything important happens up front. In culturally conscious worship, significant aspects of liturgy will be happening among the people—greeting, singing, moving to music, sharing petitions during the prayers of the people, and moving toward the table and baptismal area. While these are good liturgical practices for any congregation, they are essential for culturally conscious worship. The acoustical design of the sanctuary needs to enhance the sounds from the people, not deaden them.

I recently talked to a retired minister who served as an interim pastor for an aging congregation. The sanctuary had been refurbished not long before he assumed leadership. The decor included heavily padded pews, lush carpets, and ample sound-absorbent materials on the walls. The redesigned worship space also left a large empty area between the people and the elevated pulpit. The lighting was dim and included many recessed lights. After some exploration with church leaders, the pastor discovered that the space had been designed, literally, for the dead and not the living. The elderly congregation believed that the most significant experiences of worship in the future would be funerals and memorial services. The softer voices of senior adults did not stand a chance, surrounded by sound-absorbent materials. The added space at the front of the chancel, distancing the congregation from the leaders, was designed, after consultation with a local funeral director, to make more room for a coffin. Nonetheless, the senior adults proved to be lively singers in the fellowship hall, where the lighting was bright, the sound reverberated off hard surfaces, and they sat in a circle. By the design of its sanctuary, this congregation sent a nonverbal message of decay and dying that could become a self-fulfilling prophecy. While this congregation may be an extreme case, church architects and sound engineers need theological guidance indicating that much of what is done in worship will be happening not only *in front of* the people but also *among* the people.

Questions about Worship Space

Existing spaces may need careful examination. Some questions to ask include the following:

1. Can the people see each other as well as they can see the leaders?
2. Can the people hear each other as well as they can hear the leaders?

3. Is the choral ensemble in a position both to sing anthems on behalf of the congregation and to lead the congregation in its own song?
4. Are the aisles sufficiently wide and the space between rows adequate for congregational movement, both to music and in shared rituals that call for the worshipers to move out of their seats to pass the peace, greet each other, or come forward for communion or prayer?
5. Are there blank areas on walls or space for well-designed screens that encourage the use of images that enhance the spoken word while not obstructing important Christian symbols?
6. Does the space allow sound to reverberate and yet permit words to be clearly understood?

Strategy 4: Develop an Extensive and Inclusive Program of Hospitality that Integrates with Worship

Hospitality and Greeters

Those who prepare culturally conscious worship need greeters who reflect the diversity of the congregation in its fullness—ethnicity, gender, age, socioeconomic position, and marital status. Imagine a congregation that incorporates families of all kinds into its schedule of greeters! These may include single-parent families, couples without children, gay or lesbian couples, extended intergenerational families, or single friends who pair up to be greeters. Imagine children and teenagers with their families, greeting other children and teenagers as they enter. Imagine a biracial couple greeting others as they enter the sanctuary. Imagine a bilingual Latino family that greets visitors and members alike in both Spanish and English. If these families also serve as ushers, receivers of the offering, and communion servers, their presence has permeated the service in a manner that needs no spoken explanation.

Each of the four congregations in our study had given careful attention to greeters. Though Agape Church had designated greeters at the front door, other greeters seemed to emerge as one entered through the kitchen from the back parking lot. Grace Church had a more challenging physical arrangement, because many people did not use the "official" front entrance of church, but entered from the back parking lot, stopping by on the way to the sanctuary for coffee in an adjacent fellowship hall. Greeters were stationed between the parking lot and the sanctuary. Because of the church's openness to gay and lesbian members, greeters were well represented by this group. It was also common at Grace for Cambodians, African Americans, or Latinos as well as Anglos to be greeters.

All Nations Church often paired African American and Anglo greeters. When the congregation met in the movie theater, ample supplies of coffee, juice, and doughnuts were available in the theater lobby. An African American layman, a Latina, and an Anglo couple engaged worshipers as they entered. Church of the Disciple, incorporated an ample greeting area into its new building. It is open and bright. A table contains an attractive display of drawings, photos, and printed information about the church. A spiral staircase in the narthex leads to a small prayer-and-meditation space that is near the flow of traffic, yet private. Coffee, juice, and pastries abound. Besides offering warm greetings to those who enter, members are available to direct newcomers to the nearby nursery and Sunday school rooms.

As in other areas of church life, existing spaces may not gracefully accommodate the gathering of the community. Sometimes inadequate structures need to be creatively adapted. A pastor told me of an older building that had virtually no narthex and very little space adjacent to the sanctuary for gathering, and for greeting visitors and members. The sanctuary held 450, but the congregation had an average Sunday morning attendance of just over 100. After some discussion, the congregation decided to remove seven pews from the rear of the sanctuary to create a space for a welcoming display, and for coffee, juice, and doughnuts. An unexpected byproduct: several members accustomed to sitting in these pews, after reflecting on their displacement, moved to seats closer to the front. As a result the congregation started sitting closer together, enriching their sense of community. As the worshipers could now hear each other more easily, congregational singing improved. The pastor concluded that the congregants' ability to meet and greet one another, as well as visitors, seemed to be a contributing factor in the increased attendance and membership.

Hospitality and Gathering Rituals

Hospitality may be more welcoming when the greeting at the door blends imperceptibly with the beginning of corporate worship. During many worship experiences in Africa, I have found myself greeted not only at the door, but also by the sound of congregational singing that set the tone for the day. The congregation's song merges directly into the choir's sung processional and then into the rest of the service. Practical reasons account for this way of starting worship in sub-Saharan Africa. In the rural areas people often arrive by foot over a 30- to 40-minute time span. Being greeted by singing pulls together this gradually expanding intergenerational congregation into a unified body. I observed a similar pattern in a rural congregation in Taiwan, where a musical elder in the congregation (a true enlivener) led the people in informal singing between the close of Sunday school and the formal beginning of worship. In congregations around the United States, I often teach new songs during this liminal (in-between) time. I find that it relaxes the congregation, unites the individuals into a singing body, and focuses them on aspects of the worship that follows.

Participatory gathering music before worship blends into the worship experience itself, creating a seamless whole. Gathering rituals provide an important liminal threshold between entering the worship space and beginning worship.[9] Expanding the gathering portion of the service indicates that no clear break divides our work from our worship. And through an extended gathering, the people, rather than the pastors, begin worship. An example from Church of the Disciple: As people gather, moving from the spacious narthex into the sanctuary, the pastor walks among the people dressed in casual, comfortable street clothes (slacks and a pullover shirt). He greets and converses with individuals, embracing some, stopping to sit and chat more extensively with others, and, by example, encourages others to do the same. A praise team of five or six singers then engages the congregation in some informal singing for about 10 minutes; a greeting from the minister follows. He emerges from among the people with a stole over his casual clothing rather than wearing clergy vestments. This mode of dress signifies his role as pastor while signaling that he comes from among the people. Though this pattern might not be accepted in all congregations, it seems to work here and has the effect of creating a welcoming environment that blurs the boundaries between entering the church and beginning worship. (I am not sure that this level of informality would work as well at Agape Church, where some Latinos expect to relate to ministers from the standpoint of high-power distance.) When All Nations Church was meeting in a movie theater, a similar small group sang as people gathered. The ensemble has grown, but it continues a similar pattern of engaging the congregation in singing before the service.

Congregations with more Asian participants may prefer other ways of beginning worship. Many Asians enjoy periods of silence (though I am not prepared to make this statement a sweeping generality, especially when it comes to second- and third-generation Asian communities in the United States). A model similar to one practiced at the Taizé Community in southeastern France may be helpful. Taizé, an ecumenical Christian monastic setting, is a pilgrimage site for young people from all over Europe and beyond. Worship there takes the form of three meditative prayer services each day. Fifteen minutes before each service of daily prayer, the bells begin ringing, calling people to the Church of Reconciliation, where they are invited to enter in silence. Recorded orchestral or organ music is playing inside and complements the meditative display of candles, icons, and greenery. For 10 minutes or more, the sound of the bells outside the church mingles with the baroque or classical instrumental music (usually Bach or Mozart) inside the church. For me, this combination is an unspoken reminder that our witness outside the church (the bells) blends with our worship inside (instrumental music). After at least ten minutes, the bells stop, the recorded music fades, and a minute or two of silence ensues. It is out of this silence that the lone, unaccompanied voice of a cantor (enlivener) calls the assembly to prayer. Though the ethos of this gathering is totally different from that of an African congregation, it is no less effective. Both manage to blur the distinctions between work and worship. Both focus the people on worship.

In an unexplicable paradox of liturgical ritual, singing together and shared silence seem to work equally well in shaping fragmented individuals into a praying community.

Hospitality and Food

Sharing food is another way to blend fellowship into worship. At Agape Church coffee and *pan dulce* (sweet bread) or *postres* (desserts) greet those who enter the building from the back parking lot (usually the majority of members) before moving into worship. The choice of baked goods, fresh from a local *panidería* (bakery), provides an indication of the ethnic flavor of the congregation and complements the feeling of *familia* that is a strong part of Agape's identity. The availability of something to eat seems to encourage some to arrive early for fellowship, which bridges the gap between arrival at church and the beginning of worship. One Agape member testified that shared meals contributed to a merger between two congregations—one largely Anglo, the other Hispanic.

At Grace Church snacks, drinks, and small sandwiches are often available in the fellowship space adjacent to the sanctuary after the service. The presence of food serves several functions:

1. Visitors have a place to gather after worship to be greeted.
2. Some "street people" and regulars with fewer resources actually consume a light meal without feeling as if they were being given a handout.
3. The fellowship after worship seems to extend the community shaped during the service for 20 or 30 minutes longer, as many continue to share food together.

One barometer of a church's health may be related to the frequency with which members share meals. In my experience many Korean and Indian congregations, for example, enjoy gathering after church for full meals almost every Sunday. In many communities in the United States, an Asian congregation will draw people from a large area. Since many may have driven a considerable distance, worship followed by a full meal offers the possibility of continuing fellowship with others and allows churchgoers to maintain ties with people from their homeland. Children play together and relationships are renewed as members and visitors share a potluck meal that ties them to their country of origin.

Restoring the Agape Meal

A congregation that chooses to foster culturally conscious worship may consider a regular agape fellowship meal either after worship or during the week. The agape is a gathering with its origins in the early Christian church. This fellowship meal includes a brief table ritual. While it is similar in feeling to the Eucharist (and sometimes confused with this sacrament), a layperson may preside over an agape.[10] Mark W. Stamm, professor of worship at Perkins School of Theology, comments on the similarity between the institutional narratives (Matt. 26:26-29; Mark 14:22-25; Luke 22:14-23; 1 Cor. 11:23-26), around which the Lord's Supper is modeled, and the "wider meal ministry" of Jesus throughout the New Testament.[11] The multiplication stories (Matt. 14:13-21; Mark 6:30-44; Luke 9:10-17) "are obviously eucharistic in shape, portraying a Jesus who, when he fed the multitudes, took bread, blessed, and broke it, and gave it to them."[12] In other narratives, Jesus welcomes sinners and strangers and eats with them (Luke 15:2). The sharing of food has the potential to make a gathering into a community.

A culturally diverse congregation that extends its worship beyond Sundays with an agape meal at frequent intervals may meet several needs at once.

1. The sharing of food invites sharing experiences with each other.
2. The diverse culinary offerings that may result from such a tradition become a metaphor for the diversity of the church itself.
3. The agape itself may become an important ritual that establishes and sustains the identity of a multicultural congregation. As a Nigerian friend told me, "Once we have shared yam together, we are no longer strangers."
4. An established agape ritual offers a welcoming environment for inviting visitors ("strangers and aliens," according to Ephesians 2) into the life of a diverse community.
5. Sharing a meal and time together without an agenda is an important way for people who live primarily in monochronic

time (forward-moving and agenda-driven) to be with those
who come from cultures that place more value on polychronic time (guided more by relationships than agenda).

This is not a comprehensive guide to hospitality in multicultural
situations, but a starting place for a discussion. Each congregation
should decide on those rituals that will, as naturally and authenti-
cally as possible, foster hospitality and incorporate strangers and
aliens (anyone different from us).[13]

Strategy 5: Work Creatively within Normative Traditional Liturgical Patterns in Your Faith Heritage Rather Than Creating New Structures for Worship

Each of the four congregations that participated in this study had a
very different ethos in worship, yet each used a virtually identical
general worship structure. Each followed a modified traditional
fourfold worship pattern discussed in part I. Acolytes lit candles at
the beginning of each service. Choral ensembles entered, some in
procession down the aisle, and others directly into the choir loft.
Scriptures from the lectionary were read. Congregational hymns
and choral anthems were often supplemented by vocal and instrumental solos. Prayers were offered for the church and the world.
Sermons were usually based on the lectionary texts with applications to the community. The peace was passed weekly. Eucharist
was celebrated monthly, except at Grace Church, where an abbreviated communion service was celebrated on most Sundays. Offerings were taken, closing hymns sung, candles extinguished by child
acolytes, who then carried the remnant of light out into the world
(or at least out the rear of the church), and closing blessings offered.
Whereas the general uniformity of pattern may be attributable in
part to the single denominational tie shared by the four congregations and their location in the same urban area, this pattern has
deep historical and ecumenical roots.[14]

Variations within a Traditional Worship Pattern

The use of the classic *ordo* (the historic fourfold order of worship)
by each congregation and the incorporation of specific rituals into

this *ordo* reflect the identity of each congregation. The *ordo* and the specific ritual tell us something about the congregation's style and, therefore, about its underlying piety.[15] At Agape Church, for example, it was customary for people to be invited forward during the pastoral prayer and prayers of the people to kneel at the communion rail. I have observed this ritual practice in a number of Hispanic United Methodist congregations. Depending on the congregation, those coming forward may be thanking God for a celebration in their lives—for example, *aniversario* (wedding anniversary), *cumpleaños* (birthday), or *quinceañera*[16] (15th birthday celebration and rite of passage for a girl). Others come forward to offer specific petitions. In one Latino congregation, the laying on of hands as an act of healing was of primary importance during this time. Entire families may also come forward for prayer, offering support to the family member with special needs.

The participation each week by some members of the congregation in kneeling at the altar in prayer is a sign of this ritual's abiding significance in worship and of its importance as part of Agape's liturgical identity and worship style. I would suggest that coming forward weekly to kneel for prayer indicates both the congregation's belief in the efficacy of prayer and congregants' humility as they kneel before God. Though only those with special observances or needs come forward, the entire congregation surrounds them in prayer at this important time. God is with us throughout life's journey, in the joyful rites of passage and in times of need. Praying in the presence of *la familia* on a Sunday morning signifies the importance of journeying with others who celebrate with you at times of fiesta and walk with you in days of difficulty.

At All Nations Church, a distinctive ritual that shapes the identity of this congregation's worship is the passing of the peace. While it is an important part of worship for the other congregations in this study as well, passing the peace is an outward, joyful sign of All Nations members' commitment to worship together though diverse in ethnicity. The goal of becoming a "United Nations" congregation is celebrated weekly in the passing of the peace, a joyful and vital ritual that may last for a full five minutes as members move throughout the worship space embracing and greeting each other and welcoming visitors. The minister reminds the congregation of the church's name each week, keeping the vision of a community of all nations alive as members seek to become an increasingly diverse body of Christ that reflects the many faces of God. The spirit of celebration permeates the entire worship experience from the time of gathering to the moment of being sent into the world to serve. The congregants knows the vision that unites them; they celebrate each week the joy of gradually realizing the potential of their name, All Nations.

For Grace Church, the weekly celebration of communion seems to be the central ritual of its identity. It takes the form of an abbreviated rite on most Sundays, with a fuller celebration on the first Sunday of the month. I believe that the weekly celebration of Holy Communion indicates that this diverse congregation meets weekly to be fed and sustained. For Grace's gay and lesbian members, the sacrament is a sign that Christ accepts them at his table just as they are. For minority cultural groups and immigrants, communion is a sign that they have found a new home where a common meal is shared. For people off the street who may attend worship, it is a sign that the table is open to all and that social position is not a criterion for coming to the table prepared by Christ.

At Church of the Disciple the participation of the laity in worship leadership is a significant part of the congregation's identity and style. As I mentioned earlier, the pastor begins worship sitting with the people and emerges from among them to preside, dressed like the worshipers except for the clergy stole over his informal attire. The chancel is slightly elevated and easily accessible to the people. A seemingly constant flow of traffic moves from the congregation to the chancel to participate in the leadership of worship. This flow may include children coming forward for the children's time, members emerging from the people to lead a litany or read a scripture lesson, or musicians moving from their seats among the people to sing in a vocal ensemble, be part of the choir, or play instruments. The ministers often reciprocate this movement by the congregation toward the chancel by remaining seated with the people until they have a role to perform. At several points during the service, especially for the prayers of the people or the reading of scripture, the ministers walk among the people. This low-power-distance leadership is attractive to many in the community because it represents the accessibility of the church to the community and of God to the people. Furthermore, this style of worship indicates that what the people do is important in this congregation and that relationships with each other are an important part of relating to God. Church of the Disciple is the one congregation in this study that designed its own worship space to fit its vision. The flexibility of the seating, the accessibility of the chancel area to the congregation, the depiction of diversity in the stained-glass window, and the incorporation of high-tech video and video screens that fit the architecture are an asset for this congregation as it embodies its vision.

The congregations in this study all demonstrate a respect for the Christian liturgical tradition by using the fourfold pattern, but they have followed the guidance of the Holy Spirit to breathe new life into the potentially dry bones of traditional structures by employing specific rituals that embody their vision of worship. These rituals put flesh on the liturgical bones and reflect aspects of style that are keys to underlying piety and congregational values.

The examples cited above were not the only distinctive features that revealed the identity of each congregation, providing a basis for understanding the underlying piety of each. Agape Church has a strong tradition of hearing all lectionary readings, including the psalm for the day, a practice reflecting the importance of *la palabra de Dios* (the word of God) in Latino Protestant congregations. The pastor of All Nations Church maintains a smooth flow in the service, tying one element of worship to the next with brief explanatory statements. Since people in this church come from many ethnic contexts and faith traditions, establishing a common theology of worship is important in the formation of their identity and piety. Grace Church also takes time for a warm and welcoming passing of the peace each Sunday. Church of the Disciple effectively projects still photos and moving images on a video screen as a way to help worshipers visualize the Word as well as hear it. Each congregation embodies the *ordo* in fresh ways, according to its vision and cultural complexion.

The Christian Year and Cultural Diversity in Worship

Another tradition of the church is the larger structure of the Christian Year. Following the Christian Year allows a congregation to maintain a focus on the birth, ministry, death, resurrection, and ascension of Christ as well as the coming of the Holy Spirit. This is a natural framework that may unite diverse congregations around the central theme of the Christian faith. The Christian Year may be an ally in deepening a vision of unity among culturally diverse people. Some specific observances and seasons lend themselves to understanding God through many cultural traditions, with many faces. The following suggestions are not exhaustive, but may serve as natural entry points for congregations desiring more culturally conscious worship.

World Communion Sunday (first Sunday in October) is perhaps one of the most obvious possibilities for those from traditions that observe it. The table is central to the service, and local congregations are encouraged to consider global connections. Because of the nature of this celebration, congregations are open to visual symbols that reveal God manifested in many forms. Some examples might include a colorful tablecloth from Africa, a variety of communion breads from other parts of the world, indigenous dress worn by people of varied cultural contexts, banners of many nations, and various forms of dance.

The sounds in worship change as well. The scriptures may be read in several languages, a greater variety of musical instruments may be incorporated into worship, and the choir and congregation may sing a greater variety of global musical styles. Some congregations may explore new ways to perform traditional rituals based on customs from other cultures—for example, greetings, passing of the peace, reception of communion, blessings. At its best, World Communion Sunday is a glimpse of the future when all cultures will gather with Christ at the *Gran Fiesta.*[17]

Advent and Christmas, the seasons of Christ's incarnation, present possibilities for incorporating a variety of ethnic traditions. Cultures around the globe celebrate the Word made flesh, reflecting that the Incarnation, a unique occurrence in a specific place and time, is a cosmic event for all places and times. Congregations often express openness to other cultures and their traditions during Advent and Christmastide.

Christmas is also a time of generosity. Christian benevolence may be linked to the needs of a specific ethnic group in the church's neighborhood. Gifts for others should be accompanied by an increased cultural understanding of the people who will receive the church's gifts.[18] Children and young people enjoy learning Christmas traditions from other cultures, including songs, dances, and holiday rituals. The congregation may also decide to lift up for prayer a particular region in the world, especially one suffering political conflict, oppression, and war. The congregation might also incorporate litanies, prayers, songs, and ritual actions from a chosen culture into the worship life of the congregation. These experiences may be augmented by inviting speakers who may be able to shed light on the conflict in the chosen region to speak and evoke dialogue at a series of seminars outside of worship. Such learning opportunities put a face on the conflict and give congregations more insight for praying with the people in their time of need with songs and prayers from their culture. Local customs and material excesses of the Advent and Christmas seasons may be balanced to some degree by expressing global concerns for the church around the world and by linking traditional seasonal benevolence to worship.

The season of Epiphany focuses on the manifestations of Christ as the Son of God. Traditionally it is also a season when the church observes the work of missionaries. In past years, congregational interest in missions focused on the work of North American and European missionaries in other parts of the world. A culturally conscious congregation may consider looking at missions as a two-way street. What do Christians from other cultures have to contribute to our understanding of Christ's ministry? How do people of different cultures read the Bible?[19] How do the history and political contexts of various cultures affect people's faith? How do the political policies and media of the United States affect the lives of others? These are a few of the possibilities for an experience in "reverse missions" during Epiphany.

Some liturgical traditions in Latino cultures celebrate the journey of the magi. While many Anglos have already taken the Christmas tree down by Epiphany, many Latinos exchange gifts on Epiphany or the nearest Sunday as a ritual symbolic of the gifts of the magi. I arrived in Matanzas, Cuba, in 1993 with boxes of clothing and soup for our sister congregation. The effect of my arrival was magnified because I arrived "bearing gifts" on Epiphany.

As the magi returned home sharing the good news of the Christ child, congregations may use this season as an opportunity for sharing the good news and learning about Christ's witness in other cultures.

The additional obvious celebration of the Christian Year is one that has been central to this book from the outset—Pentecost. At the birthday of the church universal people spoke with understanding to each other in different languages. Pentecost is a time when congregations may be more open to fresh cultural winds of the Spirit within worship. Celebrating a global Eucharist, hearing the scriptures in different languages, singing songs that invoke the Holy Spirit from around the world, and celebrating a global agape meal are just some of the ways to embody the spirit of this season. Pentecost may be an excellent time to plan a multicultural liturgy with other congregations from various ethnic groups. Such a gathering could be a witness to a city torn by racial discord.

If seeds are planted during these theologically obvious seasons, it may be possible to continue some of the rituals, visual reminders of the global church, music, and prayers throughout the year, even if in reduced forms. The Christian Year is a tradition that has many windows into cultural awareness through worship.

Daily Prayer for the Culturally Conscious Church

Another form of historical liturgy is daily prayer. Compared to longer services using the fourfold pattern, daily prayer is a gathering that focuses on hearing the word read and sharing in common prayer. Its liturgical aims are modest and need not incorporate sacrament or sermon. Some daily prayer traditions are only spoken; others are rich in music.[20] If communion is not included in the rite, the service may be led by laypeople. The Taizé Community uses a form of daily corporate (versus private or devotional) prayer. In many urban areas, congregations work together, sharing in the preparations for and presentation of Taizé prayer.

Drawing on the historical practice of a service of daily prayer, a culturally conscious congregation may wish to consider daily or weekly common prayers. Practicing daily prayer has many advantages. The more modest form is less demanding to prepare and lead. Worship committees may try out rituals and songs in a less pressured environment and gain skills in planning and leading culturally conscious worship. Daily prayer may prove to be particularly helpful forum for enliveners who wish to sharpen their leadership skills with smaller groups. Aspects of daily prayer may enrich larger corporate liturgies. Daily prayers may be as brief as 15 minutes, allowing them to serve as gathering or concluding experiences in conjunction with other events such as committee meetings, meals, and church school classes.

Assuming that a congregation has some experience with multicultural prayers, it may be possible for several churches to use this structure to plan larger gatherings of weekly or monthly prayers just as some communities do for Taizé prayers. If these congregations include culturally diverse groups, community common prayers may establish a basis for trust among ethnic groups and a positive multicultural witness in the community. The Taizé model is a rich one, especially because of the ecumenical nature of the common prayer. A multicultural common prayer has additional possibilities of recognizing diversity within unity.

Strategy 6: Involve in Worship Planning a Group That Reflects the Congregation's Ethnic, Gender, and Generational Diversity

Those who plan culturally conscious worship should regularly seek input from a diverse, representative group from the congregation. Worship planning includes not only the various rites and rituals that shape the liturgy, but also the scriptural foundations that support liturgical themes each week. Creative cross-cultural worship planning should be based on a foundation of ongoing, interactive Bible study, especially around the lectionary or the scriptures that shape weekly corporate worship. The mutual invitation process referred to earlier in this chapter (see appendix F) may provide a helpful model for ensuring that each person has the opportunity to share his or her perspective on a given passage. Scriptural interpretation may be affected by a difference in cultural perspective, age, or gender. A diverse study group may discover new insights as group members listen to one another and reflect together on how a given scripture relates to their experience.[21] Culturally conscious congregations should avoid the trap of allowing a single cultural perspective to dominate scriptural interpretation. Through a process of ongoing cross-cultural Bible study around the scriptures used in worship, a mosaic of interpretations should evolve that provides a broader vision of the gospel seed planted in the diverse soil of a congregation. The pastor who participates regularly in a cross-cultural Bible study will develop sensitivities toward other perspectives as he or she engages the scripture each week. Ideally, the pastor should not lead or dominate this study, but should be a participant-observer seeking to broaden his or her worldview.

A base-community approach to Bible study is one example of this approach. Base communities were established in Central America as a way for smaller groups of poor, and sometime illiterate, people to participate in Bible study and contribute their perspective. While guided by a prepared teacher, the teaching style is interactive, allowing time for each person to weigh in on a passage of scripture explored verse by verse.[22]

It may prove unwieldy for a diverse worship committee to plan each week's liturgy. A representative, diverse group may be formed, however, to provide periodic guidance and evaluation. The committee should consider the following possibilities for a cross-cultural worship committee:

- Serve as a resource team of trained lay worship leaders who may participate on a regular basis by offering specific skills. These skills may include multilingual expertise for interpretation, singing songs in specific languages, or reading the scripture in various languages; specific artistic skills such as dance, drama, music, or visual arts that contribute to worship. The committee should establish contact with those in the community who may provide expertise in needed areas of the congregation's worship life.
- Serve as a member of a planning committee for specific recurring observances and rites of passage that may help the culturally diverse congregation worship together. Examples of observances include a bilingual or multilingual liturgy for World Communion Sunday, Epiphany, or Pentecost Sunday.

Rites of passage may include bilingual or multilingual baptisms, weddings, funerals, or memorial services according to the needs of the individual congregation. Thoughtfully prepared bilingual or multilingual liturgies should make it easier to incorporate friends and family beyond the congregation who would participate in these important rites of passage.

• Plan joint, bilingual liturgies where separate services now exist according to language or ethnicity.

• Serve on a representative evaluation group, meeting monthly to review corporate worship experiences for that month. Criteria for evaluation should include diversity of leaders, accessibility to the community, congregational participation, intergenerational effectiveness, and diversity of visual (nonverbal) symbols. The group should make recommendations to the worship leaders for improving the congregation's cultural consciousness in worship. Figure 11 offers guidelines for evaluating culturally conscious worship.

Strategy 7: Visit Congregations That Are Representative of the Ethnic Groups You Would Like to Reach, and Observe the Rituals That Shape the Worship of Each Group

Becoming culturally conscious requires one to become vulnerable and open to another's cultural perspective. If a predominantly Anglo congregation wishes to attract African Americans in the neighborhood, members should become participant-observers in African American worship settings. Some years ago, Grace Church experienced an influx of Cambodian refugees who attended the church. Grace members were confused by the response of the Cambodians to various aspects of the worship. Some Cambodians talked at what seemed to be inappropriate times. Others moved around the sanctuary with their children when the members of the congregation were still. In their attempt to understand the behavior of the Cambodian guests, several members of Grace visited an Asian Buddhist Temple in the city. After experiencing the level of

Figure 11
Evaluation Questions for Culturally Conscious Worship

The following questions pose some of the major issues in culturally conscious worship. Not all services will relate to every question.

1. Was one additional language beyond the congregation's primary language heard in each service? For example, a refrain of a hymn sung in Spanish, a scripture lesson read in Korean, or a prayer spoken in Yoruba?
2. Was at least one musical instrument included in addition to the primary instrument used to accompany congregational singing? For example, if the organ usually accompanies, were other instruments used such as congas, flute, djembes (West African drums), piano, or guitar, according to the style of the music?
3. Was the invitation extended to move (dance) during the service and appropriate music used to encourage movement?
4. Was time set aside at the beginning of the service to teach any unfamiliar songs or rituals that would be used in the service?
5. Were nonverbal symbols used (for example, art, ethnic cloth on the communion table, musical instruments from other cultures) and gestures supportive of the diversity manifest in the congregation?
6. Did children and young people serve as worship leaders? Did worship leaders include a balance of men and women, laity and clergy, people of difference ethnicities, and the like?
7. Did the choir help the congregation learn new music and movements and encourage them to sing and move more comfortably?
8. Was there a balance of sung and spoken words in the service? Though this balance will vary from church to church, generally churches of other cultures have more singing than many Anglo mainline churches do. In some cultures (African and African American), worship services have almost an equal distribution between sung and spoken words.
9. Did the congregation both sing and pray from the historical depth and current breadth of its faith heritage?
10. Was adequate space and time set aside for fellowship before and after the service?
11. Was a balance kept between polychronic (timeless) and monochromic (forward-moving) time in the service?

ambient noise (talking to one another) during the priest's prayers and the freedom of movement that took place during the Buddhist ritual, the members of Grace understood the cultural and religious context of the Cambodians and felt more comfortable entering into conversation with them and involving them in the worship at Grace. Attempts by Grace Church members to ask about Cambodian worship traditions before the visit were not successful. In many cultures people are not accustomed to articulating the distinctions between cultures or explaining why they do a particular ritual, especially if they are not fluent in English. According to Eric Law, some Asian cultures reflect this pattern.[23] By visiting a ritual where Cambodians were the majority present, members of Grace Church could better understand the differences from the perspective of their Cambodian guests, and a more fruitful discussion could take place. The Cambodians were pleased that Grace members showed significant interest in their cultural perspective. Appendix B, "Guide-lines for Cross-cultural Observations," offers suggestions for those who wish to observe worship in other cultural settings.

Strategy 8: Develop a Diverse Group of Musical Leaders (Enliveners) Focused on Enabling Congregational Singing, Choral Music, Dance, and Drama

This strategy was discussed in part III, section 1. I will lift two salient features from this discussion, however. Think of music holistically. Music is not so narrowly defined in many cultures as it is in Western musical traditions. Rather than focusing only on the study of music or playing an instrument or singing a song, African music making, for example, involves singing, dancing, and drum-ming—a complete integration of the body and the voice.

Many global cultures also use music in storytelling and drama. Western hymns have some examples of this kind of integration of song and story, such as Sydney Carter's "Lord of the Dance." Rather than using music only as a solo or an anthem, use music to add energy to a story. The salvation story is the greatest drama ever told. Use music to bring this story to life in your congregation.

Strategy 9: Develop an Approach to Worship in Which Approximately 60 Percent of the Liturgy Is Sung, Using a Variety of Musical Structures and Styles

Culturally conscious worship will be more saturated with music than many worship traditions represented by the dominant culture in the United States. Thomas Long, professor of homiletics at Emory University's Candler School of Theology, notes several significant characteristics in the "vital and faithful" worship of the congregations he observed:

> [V]ital congregations represent a trend toward the increased use of music in worship. But the shift is more than quantity. While some churches may see worship as a series of words punctuated occasionally by pieces of music—a hymn, a response, an interlude—in the vital congregations one has the sense of being carried along in the service by music, of music as the thread that ties the flow of the service together.[24]

Long also says that vital worship is "done to some degree by heart, as an expression of bodily wisdom and a deep memory of how we are to be in the presence of God."[25] Developing musical memory in a congregation is essential to its identity formation as a particular body of Christ. "What the group knows by heart becomes stamped on the members' hearts as well."[26]

My observations of congregations around the world correspond with Long's thesis. Music permeates vital worship. It reinforces themes, enables the flow between spoken rites and ritual action, and draws worshipers into the unfolding drama of salvation. I propose that enliveners develop a corpus of from 40 to 50 cyclic songs that may be sung by all and incorporated spontaneously throughout the liturgy as deemed appropriate by the enlivener and the presider. Some will not know specific songs. The advantage of cyclic structures is that the songs may be learned quickly, especially if the choral ensemble and many in the congregation have taken them to heart. These songs should not supplant sequential hymns that have been carefully chosen to elaborate on the theme of the day. Congregations that are totally book- and bulletin-bound, however, risk losing a "sense of a congregation worshiping in common."[27]

The Word—spoken and sung—was made flesh. Sung and spoken words have much more power to shape a community than written materials.[28] Worship planning in Anglo mainline Protestant congregations tends to focus on preparing a written order that those in the pew follow as worship unfolds. The result may be a primarily left-brain, monochronic (sequential) experience during which a worshiper never enters into the polychronic world that suspends clock time and heightens community awareness. Depending too much on written orders of worship, relegating music to brief interludes between spoken information, and focusing primarily on those who lead worship in front tend to produce a monochronic spectatorism. I am not calling for the elimination of printed orders of worship. I am suggesting that written orders reflect only one way of relating to rituals, and that oral tradition should be employed as well. Vital worship develops the ritual and musical memory of the people (pulling their heads out of books and bulletins as much as possible), brings spoken and sung words into closer parity throughout the liturgy, and engages the people of the assembly with one another as well as with the worship leaders.

Variety in musical styles is another aspect of Strategy 9. Thomas Long notes that "One of the most remarkable features of the music in the vital congregations is how varied it is in style and genre."[29] Section 1 of part III proposes using a range of diverse musical structures and styles. This approach calls upon the culturally conscious congregation to embrace diversity. Singing a variety of musical styles from the heritage of the church may result in some "rough edges," Long says. "Not everyone likes every form of music, and an ethic of tolerance and mutual participation is required. People need to be willing to sing music they do not necessarily like for the sake of the unity of the body."[30]

Exploring a variety of ways of gathering the congregation is one example of developing an ethic of tolerance in a culturally diverse congregation. While worshipers of some traditions prefer organ preludes, others enjoy singing together as they gather. During certain seasons of the Christian year, a congregation may even draw from the experience of the Society of Friends (Quakers), gathering in corporate silence. Consider the possibility of using all of these at some time in the Christian calendar as one way to tap into the spirit of the season. Advent might be a season of gathering through congregational singing. Learning a few new Advent hymns at the beginning of worship, and new Christmas carols as the congregation approaches Christmas Eve, might heighten the anticipation of this favorite season. While it is traditional not to sing Christmas carols until Christmas Eve (a practice I support in theory), congregations need opportunities to learn new carols in preparation for Christmas. I have found that teaching new carols on Christmas Eve or between Christmas and Epiphany works very well. The gathering-time music during Advent may offer an excellent opportunity to teach new carols, even though they may not appear formally in worship until Christmas Eve.

Epiphany may be a season to return to traditional organ voluntaries at the beginning of worship. Lent and Holy Week could be set off as a time to gather in corporate silence. It would be a new experience for most congregations. Gathering in corporate silence, perhaps with a printed meditation or prayer in the worship folder, could be cultivated as a spiritual discipline. Imagine the contrast on Easter Sunday when the people gather in high-spirited singing or to exuberant organ music. In traditions that observe the Easter Vigil, worshipers begin solemnly in the dark. The light then penetrates the darkness and culminates in a joyful singing of the *Gloria in excelsis* (Glory to God in the highest), a practice that was withheld during the long days of Lent. Vital Christian worship integrates a wide variety of musical styles and structures into its fabric and, by developing the congregation's liturgical memory, frees worshipers as much as possible from a printed worship bulletin or a liturgy read from the hymnal or prayer book.

Strategy 10: Consider Starting a New Pentecost Congregation in a Diverse Neighborhood—A Congregation That Has a Goal of Being Culturally Conscious about Its Worship and Ministries.

Developing culturally conscious worship is hard work. Two congregations I studied for this book had a long-standing presence in their respective communities. As the community constituency changed, the Agape and Grace churches developed effective ministries to reach out to the newcomers, but had varying degrees of success in adapting their liturgical traditions to incorporate these people into worship. The existing worship ethos, established over decades, still dominated the churches' approach to liturgy even though longtime members had either moved out of the neighborhood or came largely from other areas of the city.

The other two congregations I studied were relatively new. Church of the Disciple was six years old at the time of the study, and All Nations Church was in its first year as the study began. These congregations had the benefit of extensive demographic surveys, provided in part by their denominational body, and the motivation to develop a vision that reflected the diversity of their respective communities. The denomination appointed liturgically savvy ministers who had clear theological visions for growing culturally conscious congregations. As this book went to press, Church of the Disciple and All Nations were still evolving culturally conscious worship. Both had made great strides, but neither would claim to be a congregation that worships in cultural partnership, as described in the model proposed in part 1. They have had the benefit, however, of attracting people who have for the most part subscribed to the concept of an inclusive and diverse congregation. Congregational diversity has assumed a substantial part of the identity of these congregations.

Existing congregations may undergo a metamorphosis that takes them from cultural uniformity to cultural diversity. The experience of this study indicates that new Pentecost congregations have an important role for the future of the church. Pentecost congregations are born with an eschatological vision of what God's realm will ultimately be and the discernment to pursue that vision *now*. The petition "Thy kingdom come" is a theological imperative that motivates culturally conscious worship.

I believe that all congregations have the potential to become culturally aware and to reflect this awareness to varying degrees in their corporate worship life. Culturally conscious worship has the potential to enrich any congregation. To this end, it is my hope that this book may offer insight and suggest strategies that any willing congregation might employ.

MOVING TOWARD PENTECOST

As I conclude the final section of this book, I recall the words of the faithful layman in Nora Tubbs Tisdale's congregation quoted in the preface: "I chose this church because there were people like me here, music I liked, and a homogeneity that made me feel at home. Why now do I have to worry about how to make the church a welcoming place for all these other types? Don't they have their own churches?" Tubbs Tisdale responded that the answer to his question was "as complex as Pentecost itself." She continued by offering a vision of Pentecost that continues to ring in my ears after several months.

> For on Pentecost Day the Spirit of God blew upon all the locked doors and bolted windows in the room where those disciples huddled together with the inner circle, and revealed God's will to create a church that was bigger, broader, more inclusive, and more open than any in the room had ever imagined. Into that room blew new converts whose budding theologies must have surely shaken the status quo of those disciples—just as did Jesus' own unorthodox teachings. Into that room blew tongues that rested on people the disciples probably never—left purely to their own devices—would have imagined worthy of carrying on Jesus' ministry: women, children, slaves, and gentiles from all nations on earth. And into that room blew a mighty wind through which God announced boldly and powerfully: "You ain't seen nothing yet, disciples! And just look at the power I'm going to bestow upon ALL believers, so that the Gospel—MY glorious world-upending gospel—can be carried into the uttermost reaches of the earth."[31]

As difficult as it may be, as uncomfortable as we may feel, as unfamiliar as it may seem, the idea of a culturally diverse worshiping community still compels. Our discomfort and unease with those who are different from us may reflect, like the frightened disciples huddled together, the "locked doors and bolted windows" of our lives. In a world where ethnic stereotyping is on the rise, the refuge of gated communities is increasingly sought, and the balkanizing of nations is becoming commonplace, the church must claim the power of the Spirit to upend the structures of division and evil. The same Spirit that brought comprehension and community out of chaos at the birth of the church is able to unite us in our cultural differences when we worship as "one body" sharing "one bread."

NAIROBI STATEMENT ON WORSHIP AND CULTURE: CONTEMPORARY CHALLENGES AND OPPORTUNITIES (1996)

This statement is from the third international consultation of the Lutheran World Federation's Study Team on Worship and Culture, held in Nairobi, Kenya, in January 1996. The members of the Study Team represent five continents of the world and have worked together with enthusiasm for three years thus far. The initial consultation, in October 1993 in Cartigny, Switzerland, focused on the biblical and historical foundations of the relationship between Christian worship and culture, and resulted in the "Cartigny Statement on Worship and Culture: Biblical and Historical Foundations." (This Nairobi Statement builds upon the Cartigny Statement; in no sense does it replace it.) The second consultation, in March 1994 in Hong Kong, explored contemporary issues and questions of the relationships between the world's cultures and Christian liturgy, church music, and church architecture and art. The papers of the first two consultations were published as *Worship and Culture in Dialogue.*[1] The papers and statement from the Nairobi consultation were published as *Christian Worship: Unity in Cultural Diversity.*[2] In 1994–1995, the Study Team conducted regional research, and prepared reports on that research. Phase IV of the Study commenced in Nairobi and will continue with seminars and other means to implement the learnings of the study, as LWF member churches decide is helpful. The Study Team considers this project to be essential to the renewal and mission of the Church around the world.

1. INTRODUCTION

1.1. Worship is the heart and pulse of the Christian Church. In worship we celebrate together God's gracious gifts of creation and salvation, and are strengthened to live in response to God's grace. Worship always involves actions, not merely words. To consider worship is to consider music, art, and architecture, as well as liturgy and preaching.

1.2. The reality that Christian worship is always celebrated in a given local cultural setting draws our attention to the dynamics between worship and the world's many local cultures.

1.3. Christian worship relates dynamically to culture in at least four ways. First, it is transcultural, the same substance for everyone everywhere, beyond culture. Second, it is contextual, varying according to the local situation (both nature and culture). Third, it is countercultural, challenging what is contrary to the Gospel in a given culture. Fourth, it is cross-cultural, making possible sharing between different local cultures. In all four dynamics, there are helpful principles which can be identified.

2. WORSHIP AS TRANSCULTURAL

2.1. The resurrected Christ whom we worship, and through whom by the power of the Holy Spirit we know the grace of the Triune God, transcends and indeed is beyond all cultures. In the mystery of his resurrection is the source of the transcultural nature of Christian worship. Baptism and Eucharist, the sacraments of Christ's death and resurrection, were given by God for all the world. There is one Bible, translated into many tongues, and biblical preaching of Christ's death and resurrection has been sent into all the world. The fundamental shape of the principal Sunday act of Christian worship, the Eucharist or Holy Communion, is shared across cultures: the people gather, the Word of God is proclaimed, the people intercede for the needs of the Church and the world, the eucharistic meal is shared, and the people are sent out into the world for mission. The great narratives of Christ's birth, death, resurrection, and sending of the Spirit, and our Baptism into him, provide the central meanings of the transcultural times of the church's year: especially Lent/Easter/Pentecost, and, to a lesser extent, Advent/ Christmas/Epiphany. The ways in which the shapes of the Sunday Eucharist and the church year are expressed vary by culture, but their meanings and fundamental structure are shared around the globe. There is one Lord, one faith, one Baptism, one Eucharist.

2.2. Several specific elements of Christian liturgy are also transcultural, e.g., readings from the Bible (although of course the translations vary), the ecumenical creeds and the Our Father, and Baptism in water in the Triune Name.

2.3. The use of this shared core liturgical structure and these shared liturgical elements in local congregational worship—as well as the shared act of people assembling together, and the shared provision of diverse leadership in that assembly (although the space for the assembly and the manner of the leadership vary)—are expressions of Christian unity across time, space, culture, and confession. The recovery in each congregation of the clear centrality of these transcultural and ecumenical elements renews the sense of this Christian unity and gives all churches a solid basis for authentic contextualization.

3. WORSHIP AS CONTEXTUAL

3.1. Jesus whom we worship was born into a specific culture of the world. In the mystery of his incarnation are the model and the mandate for the contextualization of Christian worship. God can be and is encountered in the local cultures of our world. A given culture's values and patterns, insofar as they are consonant with the values of the Gospel, can be used to express the meaning and purpose of Christian worship. Contextualization is a necessary task for the Church's mission in the world, so that the Gospel can be ever more deeply rooted in diverse local cultures.

3.2. Among the various methods of contextualization, that of dynamic equivalence is particularly useful. It involves re-expressing components of Christian worship with something from a local culture that has an equal meaning, value, and function. Dynamic equivalence goes far beyond mere translation; it involves understanding the fundamental meanings both of elements of worship and of the local culture, and enabling the meanings and actions of worship to be "encoded" and re-expressed in the language of local culture.

3.3. In applying the method of dynamic equivalence, the following procedure may be followed. First, the liturgical ordo (basic shape) should be examined with regard to its theology, history, basic elements, and cultural backgrounds. Second, those elements of the ordo that can be subjected to dynamic equivalence without prejudice to their meaning should be determined. Third, those components of culture that are able to re-express the Gospel and the liturgical ordo in an adequate manner should be studied. Fourth, the spiritual and pastoral benefits our people will derive from the changes should be considered.

3.4. Local churches might also consider the method of creative assimilation. This consists of adding pertinent components of local culture to the liturgical ordo in order to enrich its original core. The baptismal ordo of "washing with water and the Word," for example, was gradually elaborated by the assimilation of such cultural practices as the giving of white vestments and lighted candles to the neophytes of ancient mystery religions. Unlike dynamic equivalence, creative assimilation enriches the liturgical ordo—not by culturally re-expressing its elements, but by adding to it new elements from local culture.

3.5. In contextualization the fundamental values and meanings of both Christianity and of local cultures must be respected.

3.6. An important criterion for dynamic equivalence and creative assimilation is that sound or accepted liturgical traditions are preserved in order to keep unity with the universal Church's tradition of worship, while progress inspired by pastoral needs is encouraged. On the side of culture, it is understood that not everything can be integrated with Christian worship, but only those elements that are connatural to (that is, of the same nature as) the liturgical ordo. Elements borrowed from local culture should always undergo critique and purification, which can be achieved through the use of biblical typology.

4. WORSHIP AS COUNTERCULTURAL

4.1. Jesus Christ came to transform all people and all cultures, and calls us not to conform to the world, but to be transformed with it (Romans 12:2). In the mystery of his passage from death to eternal life is the model for transformation, and thus for the counter-cultural nature of Christian worship. Some components of every culture in the world are sinful, dehumanizing, and contradictory to the values of the Gospel. From the perspective of the Gospel, they need critique and transformation. Contextualization of Christian faith and worship necessarily involves challenging of all types of oppression and social injustice wherever they exist in earthly cultures.

4.2. It also involves the transformation of cultural patterns which idolize the self or the local group at the expense of a wider human-ity, or which give central place to the acquisition of wealth at the expense of the care of the earth and its poor. The tools of the countercultural in Christian worship may also include the deliber-ate maintenance or recovery of patterns of action which differ intentionally from prevailing cultural models. These patterns may arise from a recovered sense of Christian history, or from the wisdom of other cultures.

5. WORSHIP AS CROSS-CULTURAL

5.1. Jesus came to be the Savior of all people. He welcomes the treasures of earthly cultures into the city of God. By virtue of Baptism, there is one Church; and one means of living in faithful response to Baptism is to manifest ever more deeply the unity of the Church. The sharing of hymns and art and other elements of worship across cultural barriers helps enrich the whole Church and strengthen the sense of the *communio* of the Church. This sharing can be ecumenical as well as cross-cultural, as a witness to the unity of the Church and the oneness of Baptism. Cross-cultural sharing is possible for every church, but is especially needed in multicultural congregations and member churches.

5.2. Care should be taken that the music, art, architecture, gestures and postures, and other elements of different cultures are under-stood and respected when they are used by churches elsewhere in the world. The criteria for contextualization (above, sections 3.5 and 3.6) should be observed.

6. CHALLENGE TO THE CHURCHES

6.1. We call on all member churches of the Lutheran World Federa-tion to undertake more efforts related to the transcultural, contex-tual, countercultural, and cross-cultural nature of Christian worship. We call on all member churches to recover the centrality of Bap-tism, Scripture with preaching, and the every-Sunday celebration of the Lord's Supper—the principal transcultural elements of Chris-tian worship and the signs of Christian unity—as the strong center of all congregational life and mission, and as the authentic basis for contextualization. We call on all churches to give serious attention to exploring the local or contextual elements of liturgy, language, posture and gesture, hymnody and other music and musical instru-ments, and art and architecture for Christian worship—so that their worship may be more truly rooted in the local culture. We call those churches now carrying out missionary efforts to encourage such contextual awareness among themselves and also among the partners and recipients of their ministries. We call on all member churches to give serious attention to the transcultural nature of worship and the possibilities for cross-cultural sharing. And we call on all churches to consider the training and ordination of ministers of Word and Sacrament, because each local community has the right to receive weekly the means of grace.
6.2. We call on the Lutheran World Federation to make an inten-tional and substantial effort to provide scholarships for persons from the developing world to study worship, church music, and church architecture, toward the eventual goal that enhanced theo-logical training in their churches can be led by local teachers.
6.3. Further, we call on the Lutheran World Federation to continue its efforts related to worship and culture into the next millennium. The tasks are not quickly accomplished; the work calls for ongoing

depth-level research and pastoral encouragement. The Worship and Culture Study, begun in 1992 and continuing in and past the 1997 LWF Assembly, is a significant and important beginning, but the task calls for unending efforts. Giving priority to this task is essential for evangelization of the world.

Notes

1. Geneva: Lutheran World Federation, 1994. Also published in French, German, and Spanish.
2. Geneva: Lutheran World Federation, 1996. Also published in German.

APPENDIX B

OBSERVING RITUALS IN CORPORATE WORSHIP IN NEW CULTURAL SITUATIONS: GUIDELINES FOR PARTICIPANT-OBSERVERS

C. Michael Hawn

Preparing for an observation:

1. To the degree that you are able, *avoid preconceptions* of how the ritual should be performed. If you have had no previous experience with this ritual or similar ones, it is likely that your preconceptions are stereotypical and unfounded.

2. You may experience *liturgical shock.* Expect some sense of disorientation or confusion, especially if you have had little or no experience with this ritual. If this is a cross-denominational or cross-cultural ritual, the confusion or uncertainty (when to stand, when to sing, what to say or sing, how to move, when to move), will likely increase proportionally to your lack of experience with this ritual.

3. *Read in preparation* of and/or following the ritual in sources that may provide some information about how to interpret the liturgical culture or this ritual.

During the observation:

4. Assume that this is an experience of *hospitality* analogous to being invited to someone's home to share a meal.

5. Function as a *participant observer* in ritual: i.e., you will learn something by attempting to say rites and move ritually rather than

observing only from the sidelines, even if you feel awkward or do not understand all that you are saying or doing. Participant observers must be willing to be self-conscious and culturally displaced. *The focus is on observation rather than on judgment, curiosity rather than critique.*

6. Focus equally on *verbal and nonverbal cues* (movement, dress, symbols, actions). Anglo cultures, for example, tend to place a high value on spoken comprehension, while many other cultures place nearly equal value on nonverbal communication.

7. The basic question is one of *identity, style, and piety:* What does the style (order, music, movements, rites, symbols, space, written order if used) say about the identity of this group—that is, how do they pray together? What styles of being together facilitate their corporate worship experience; that is, corporate prayer and identity? How does the style of worship reflect the piety of the people?

> Piety is the corporate inner life of the church, made visible in its worship, fellowship, and mission. Piety is a function of both reflective and "prereflective" assumptions and commitments about God's being and action, and about the proper shape of the Christian life. (Linda J. Clark, Joanne Swenson, and Mark Stamm, *How We Seek God Together: Exploring Worship Style* [Bethesda, Md.: Alban Institute, 2002], 17).

8. While there are usually technical aspects of any liturgy that may be improved, you may not be in a position yet to identify these if you do not fully understand the ritual. Focus on *understanding the piety and style of the group rather than on criticism of the ritual.*

After the observation:

9. *Record your impressions* (primarily descriptive) as soon as possible after the experience.

10. Conduct a *recall interview*, if possible, with someone for whom this ritual is a primary expression of piety. Ask questions that will clarify the underlying theology and piety of the experience that may not have been apparent to you.

11. On the basis of your experience of the ritual as a participant observer, your reading in related literature, and the recall interview,

pose some basic theological/spiritual possibilities for why this group prays the way it does (symbols, rites, songs, movements, actions, space).

12. After completing the process above, *consider the significance of this ritual to you personally.* Were you engaged? If so, when, where, why? Or why not?

13. Finally, *consider how your corporate worship style appears to someone* from a different culture or denomination, or to someone with a disability. Without giving up the identity of your ritual, how can you offer them hospitality?

Getting started:

Using the tribal metaphor of sociologist Desmond Morris may get you started. Think of this faith ritual as defining a tribe (in the anthropological sense).

1. What tribal insignia or badges do participants in this ritual use?—for example, special clothing, speech, initiation ceremony, or kind of music.

2. What shared rituals unite this tribe?—for example, displaying the tribe's existence, reinforcing the identity of the members, or use of synchronized movements.

3. How does this tribe display rank or status?—for example, increased height or size, color.

4. How does this tribe structure sacred space? Sacred space is usually highly defined—that is, it defines the roles of those present, the rules of the participants, and the relationship among those present.

INITIAL WORSHIP AUDIT FOR CULTURALLY CONSCIOUS CONGREGATIONS

C. Michael Hawn

1. Do a cultural neighborhood analysis. Taking a video camera, walk around the church within a five- or six-block radius. Take some footage of street signs before you shoot footage of the specific area so that those watching the video can note the location. Note the following:

- various kinds of housing in this radius,
- buildings devoted to religious activities (Christian or non-Christian),
- forms of public transportation available,
- schools and other public buildings,
- commercial establishments and activities,
- general level of traffic and pedestrian activity.

What does this analysis demonstrate about the generational, ethnic, and socioeconomic diversity present in the neighborhood?

Is this diversity present in the life of the congregation?

To what degree is the worship in your congregation representative of the predominant cultural tradition(s) evident in the neighborhood?

2. Visit the home page of the United States 2000 census site, *www.census.gov* for information on the constituency near the church.

3. What is the ethnic and socioeconomic history of the neighborhood in which the church is situated? How has it changed over the last 25, 50, 75, and 100 years?

4. Using figure 1 as a model, where does your congregation fit on this scale?

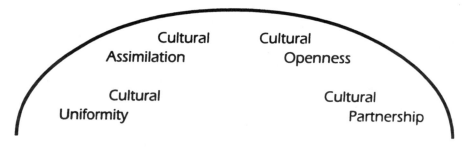

5. Eric H. F. Law's book *The Bush Was Blazing but Not Consumed* (St. Louis: Chalice Press, 1996) identifies seven ethnocentric perspectives that often arise in discussions about cultural difference (pages 46–60). They are:

- Difference does not exist.
- Difference is confined to broad categories.
- You are different; therefore you are bad.
- It's OK for you to be different, but I am better.
- I am different; therefore I am bad and you are good.
- If you don't include like I do, you are bad.
- I know there are differences, but they are not important.

To what degree can members of a group relate to these questions? How do they apply to worship planning?

6.   Using Appendix A, "The Nairobi Statement on Worship and Culture," evaluate with a diverse group those aspects of worship that are (1) transcultural, (2) contextual, (3) countercultural, (4) crosscultural.

7. Using Appendix B, assign teams of two or three to visit the worship of congregations whose primary constituencies reflect

minority groups in your congregation, ethnic groups in your neighborhood, or cultural groups with whom your congregation would like to develop a rapport as a culturally conscious congregation. Report back and discuss ways in which these experiences might affect your worship experiences. Include the visited congregation's

- sense of time,
- presence of nonverbal cues,
- written verses,
- oral traditions,
- issues of leadership and power (high- and low-power-distance cultures), and
- evidence of high- or low-context cultures.

TEN STEPS TOWARD A SINGING CONGREGATION

C. Michael Hawn

Singing is a natural act. Anthropologists tell us that virtually all cultures sing. It is also a natural part of corporate worship in the Christian tradition. Singing by the cantor and the people was part of synagogue life. Scholars suggest that even more of the service was sung in the early church than in Christian worship today. Christians continued this practice with their own modifications. The New Testament epistles suggest the use of at least three genres of Christian song—psalms, hymns, and spiritual songs (Eph. 5:18-20; Col. 3:16-17). At least two of these forms were congregational. Singing is a way to give thanks to God. Singing was also a metaphor in the writings of the early church fathers for the unity of the body of Christ gathered for worship.

Group singing is less common now than it once was. Many people have been told, some at a very young age, that they cannot sing. Teaching new songs under these circumstances can be difficult. Because many Americans do not think they can sing, the congregation must be encouraged to sing through direct invitations and complimented on its efforts. The suggestions that follow offer strategies for initiating singing with congregations and helping them become more comfortable with new songs.

LANGUAGE THAT INVITES PARTICIPATION

Step 1. Begin by inviting the congregation's participation as singers. Never command or coerce the congregation. Coercion will be futile because it is not a characteristic of worship. Demands are often met with walls of resistance. Any results that you achieve may be diluted by resentment. Give people permission to make mistakes. The purpose is to provide a medium through which the congregation may lift up its voice together, not to prepare a choral ensemble.

Step 2. The enlivener of the people's song needs to be thoroughly prepared to teach the song. (For a definition of "enlivener," see pp. 115–127.) Let me list the characteristics of thorough preparation:

- Memorize the selection to be taught, if at all possible.
- Use a lighter yet accurate vocal quality that invites the people to sing—that is, a voice that says, "Sing with me," rather than a voice that demands, "Listen to me."
- Teach songs voice-to-voice. If at all possible avoid teaching songs instrument-to-voice. Teaching a new song using one's voice is much more inviting than asking participants to respond to a melody played on an instrument.
- Teach one new song per service. In most congregations one will suffice.

Step 3. Create a "culture of singing" in your church. Find as many occasions as possible to teach songs. Grab as many opportunities as possible outside worship—social events, committee meetings, retreats, Sunday school classes, and even as gathering music in the minutes just before the service begins. It may be possible to teach a song during the liturgy, if it is brief and the choir or enlivener can introduce the melody without disrupting the flow of the liturgy. Point to examples of singing in the Bible such as the psalms, canticles, and early Christian hymns. Canticles include songs from both the Old and New Testaments.

Canticles and Hymns from the Bible

Selected Old Testament Canticles
- Song of Moses and Miriam (Exod. 15:1-18)
- Song of Moses (Deut. 32:1-43)
- Song of Hannah (1 Sam. 2:1-10)
- Songs of Isaiah (Isaiah 12 and 26)
- Song of Hezekiah (Isa. 38:10-20)
- Song of Habbakuk (Hab. 3:2-9)
- Song of Jonah (Jonah 2:2-9)

Selected New Testament Canticles
- Song of Zacharias (Luke 1:68-79) (*Benedictus*)
- Song of Mary (Luke 1:46-55) (*Magnificat*)
- Song of Simeon (Luke 2:29-32) (*Nunc dimittis*)
- Song of the Angels (Luke 2:14) (*Gloria in excelsis*)

Selected Early Christian Hymns
- *Kenosis* (self-emptying) *hymn* (Phil. 2:6-11)
- Selected hymns from the Book of Revelation (4:8; 4:11; 5:11; 7:12; 11:15-18; 15:3-4; 19:1b-2)

These examples as well as others may help the congregation understand that singing is integral to the biblical story and to Christian witness and, in doing so, encourage their singing.

Step 4. Relate a new song to the liturgy for the day. Tell the people why you have chosen this song. In a very few words, point out the most significant aspects of the song that they should watch for as they sing it. These aspects may include the relationship of the song to scripture, a season of the Christian year, a liturgical rite or ritual (intercessory prayer or offering, baptism or communion), or a theme of the service. In some congregations a new song may be introduced by adding a note in the worship folder.

Step 5. Prepare the choral ensemble to assist the enlivener in teaching a new song. In some congregations choral ensembles have discouraged congregational singing by implying through their negative attitudes about the "congregational choir" that carefully prepared choral music is more important. If a choral ensemble (including children's, youth, or adult choirs) establishes a rapport with the congregation by assisting in the teaching process, the congregation will feel truly welcomed to participate and less self-conscious about any real or imagined vocal inadequacies. The choral ensemble will improve the teaching process of any song, but an ensemble is essential in those places where the acoustics are dead and each member of the congregation feels as if he or she is singing a solo.

INSTRUCTIONS FOR SINGING

Step 6. The enlivener should sing the entire hymn or song through first, or ask the choir to sing the melody in unison. If the song has a refrain, then the refrain is usually a good place to begin. In many cases it may be best for the congregation to sing only the refrain during the first singing of the song, using a soloist or choral ensemble on the stanzas. If the song is in a language other than the congregation's primary language, this language may be sung during the initial presentation of the song, if a translation is available.

Step 7. Depending on the length and difficulty of the song, the enlivener may then ask the congregation to do one of two things: (1) echo-sing (call-and-response) after each phrase with the enlivener singing first, or (2) hum the melody as it is sung the second time by the enlivener or the choral ensemble. In most cases it will be advisable to echo-sing each phrase. The enlivener should avoid singing with the congregation. This method serves two purposes. The congregation will develop more independence and try harder, and the enlivener will be able to hear any phrases that need to be repeated. Always compliment the congregation on its progress and let worshipers know that you are sure they will not only appreciate this song but be able to sing it well in worship.

Step 8. Separate the words and the music. Explain any unusual words, or words that may be hard to pronounce. If the song is in a language unfamiliar to the congregation, it may be helpful to speak the text in shorter fragments without the music. If the melody moves quickly or is difficult for the congregation, it may be helpful initially to sing it on "la, la" without the words.

Step 9. In many musical styles around the world, singing and moving are unified. When a song can be sung securely by the congregation, teach movements that may accompany it. (See appendix E, "Ten Steps toward a Dancing Congregation" for specific guidance.) Separate the movements from the singing before incorporating them into the song.

Step 10. Sing the song through once (including the movements, if applicable) before inserting it into the liturgy. Give people permission to listen, watch, or sing. If a song is in a language foreign to the majority of the congregation, offer worshipers the choice of singing in their first language, singing the foreign language, or humming. If movements are also involved, give permission for people either to move or to sing. If the song has a separate melody for the enlivener, add this melody now. If the song has additional harmony, the choral ensemble may add the harmony now. Additional percussion or melodic instruments, if applicable, may also be incorporated into the song now. Repeat the new song in future services within a few weeks.

TEN STEPS TOWARD A DANCING CONGREGATION

Marcia McFee

The words in Hebrew and Aramaic (the language Jesus spoke) for "dance" are the same as the word for "rejoice." So to be a "dancing" congregation is to be one that rejoices with every ounce of its being. For many churches around the globe, congregants would never imagine their music separated from the expressions of rhythm and dance. These elements simply belong together as the embodiment of the joy and power of the people's faith.

Introducing global music with its inherent rhythms and movements can help many of us reclaim a more "full-bodied" faith—one that "moves" us, literally, toward our incarnation as the body of Christ alive and at work in the world. However, for many predominantly Euro–North American congregations, dancing does not happen spontaneously. There are many reasons for this situation, but suffice it to say that over the centuries, we have become more and more sedentary in our worship. These ten steps for becoming a dancing congregation will, therefore, involve more than simply teaching the steps. We need the language of invitation and permission (steps 1–5) as well as instruction (steps 6–10) from enliveners. (See pp. 115–126 for a discussion of this term.)

LANGUAGE THAT INVITES PARTICIPATION

Step 1. Take incremental steps toward being a dancing congregation. Even before introducing movement with a global song, begin
to focus on our bodies and our everyday movements as expressions
of God's creation. Here are some ideas:

- Breathe deeply together as a congregation and then sing a
  song that uses the metaphor of breath and the Spirit such as
  "Let it breathe on me" (text and music by Magnolia Lewis
  Butts, in *The United Methodist Hymnal,* 503).
- Emphasize the inherent rhythm of our bodies by calling
  attention to the heartbeat and the analogy of God as the
  "heartbeat of creation."
- Educate the congregation about the rich tradition of dance in
  the Bible, including Miriam worshiping at the Red Sea and
  David in front of the ark.
- Emphasize the inherent goodness of the body as the place
  where the "Word became flesh."
- Use the myriad metaphors of the "movement of the Spirit" in
  litanies and sermons.
- Incorporate more congregational movement throughout
  worship such as moving toward a baptismal font to touch the
  water, or facing one another across the aisle for a litany or
  creed. Whenever movement is incorporated, we become
  aware that we are three-dimensional living symbols.
- Finally, invite the congregation to use rhythm instruments
  (film canisters half full of popcorn are great for this) during
  spirited songs. There is no way to play a percussion
  instrument without moving your body. This is an excellent
  way to rediscover the natural rhythmic movements of our
  bodies. It is also easy to add simple instructions like "shake
  up high!" or "shake to this side . . . now the other side!"

Step 2. As you begin to teach a global song, put it in context with
information about the place of its origin, the people, and the spirit
of the movement of the song. This is an invitation to place our-

selves in another Christian's shoes. And those shoes (or bare feet) may be dancing ones! For instance, the people of Zimbabwe who sing "Jesu tawa pano" ("Jesus, we are here") step from one foot to the other as they sing, joyful that they have come together to worship despite difficult personal, economic, and political circumstances. We, too, can move our feet, walking in solidarity with Christian brothers and sisters who declare the good news in spite of difficulty. Could we walk the road they walk? Will we dance the good news that we are here as the Body of Christ together?

Step 3. Acknowledge the diversity of ability in the congregation. With the use of humor, encourage all to participate in some way. Offer them choices. Sometimes I will invite people to join in an easy rhythmic hand-clapping but will also say, "If you want to try this but you don't want anyone to know you're doing it, then toe-tapping is for you!" Laughter follows, and one can feel the relief that hesitant feelings have been recognized (and sometimes dispelled).

It is important to acknowledge that people can participate in many ways. Allowing a worshiper to find joy simply in watching others do the movement will raise the possibility that a reluctant participant will go ahead and try it. Also remember that not all congregants are physically comfortable reaching their arms high overhead and may not be able to keep up with faster rhythms. Always encourage individual adaptation to whatever is suggested. I never use negative put-downs ("Come on, you can do better than that!"), but rather use positive language at all times ("You are doing great!").

Step 4. As an enlivener, always demonstrate the movement and the energy. If the energy of your voice or body doesn't match what you are asking worshipers to do, they will follow your example rather than your instructions. The moment you stop, they will usually stop too. That reaction means that instrumentalists, whose primary task requires the use of their hands on keys or drumheads, cannot be the primary, or only, model of the movement. The enlivener will have to be hands-free to do what the congregation is doing while he or she continues to talk or sing. Obviously, a handheld microphone is a problem. An attractive combination for an example of energy is to invite children or youth who have learned the movement beforehand to assist the enlivener in demonstrating. They should exude a feeling of "This is easy!"

Step 5. Create an analogy to something from everyday life. If you are going to be swaying back and forth, talk about how the movement of rocking has been a part of our lives since we were babies. Or describe the movement like the swinging of a pendulum. If the pattern is based on walking, remind participants that "dancing" is not so different from walking down the street. A heavy accent with the foot can be connected to the way some of us stamp our feet during a hearty laugh, connecting the joy we feel in our everyday lives to the ways in which we might express our joy in the song and its dance.

INSTRUCTIONS FOR DANCING

Step 6. When teaching a specific pattern of movement, work incrementally. After learning the words and tune (see appendix D, "Ten Steps toward a Singing Congregation"), start with an invitation to a basic weight-shift alternation pattern. This helps folk feel the underlying motion before it gets more complicated. For instance, if the pattern involves going from one foot to the other, simply begin by shifting the weight from one foot to the other, side to side in rhythm to the music. Sing the song once just doing this. This action helps us feel the rush of adrenaline that comes with successfully matching our body movements to the music and whets our appetite for more.

Step 7. Add the basic footsteps. The shifting side to side now becomes a marching in place or a step-touch to one side and then the other. The walking motion may become two steps forward and two steps back, or two to one side and two to the other. It is helpful at this point to have a percussionist keeping time at a moderate sound level. When you feel that most people have it, add the humming of the song and then the singing of the words. Remember always to give permission for folk to take one incremental step back if it feels too complicated and simply let their dancing consist of the basic weight-shift pattern. The goal is "full-bodied" participation at whatever level.

Step 8. Add the basic arm pattern. By this time, you've done the foot pattern enough for people to keep doing it as you add another element. This is the moment at which hand claps or arm motions are layered onto the movement. For example, if folk are going to be dancing their offering forward, as is done in some African traditions, they will have learned the foot patterns and could now place their hand on the shoulder of the person in front of them.

Step 9. Add the final layers of movement. Sometimes a dance will involve something more complicated like stamping the foot and throwing the arms up in the air on the downbeat and then clapping the hands on the 2 and 3 beat of a song with a 3/4 time signature. You won't want to add everything at once. Again, use incremental steps to add one movement at a time, singing the song at each stage. Another good way to work incrementally is to add more complicated moves one Sunday at a time if the song is going to be used regularly during a particular season of the Christian year.

Step 10. Follow your instincts and follow the Spirit. "Read" the energy of the congregation to know when to slow the process, move to the next step, or combine movements for added interest. You may decide on the spur of the moment to ask half of the congregation to keep the dance going while the other half sings to them— and then switch. This variation can encourage better dancing and singing and a feeling of success and cooperation. You may decide to soften the volume and make the movements smaller for a while (you can do this simply by demonstrating it and by making sure that the instrumentalists are always "tuned in" to you), and then crescendo back up to a rousing ending. Finally, knowing when enough is enough is important for leaving the congregation hungry for more.

MUTUAL INVITATION

Eric H. F. Law

Objectives:	To facilitate sharing and discussion in a multicultural group.
Type of Group:	Any.
Size of Group:	4–15.
Setting:	Participants should sit in a circle.
Materials:	Newsprint and markers.
Time Required:	Depending on the size of the group. A good way to tell how much time will be required for each round of sharing is to multiply the number of participants by five minutes.

HOW TO PROCEED

A. Let participants know how much time is set aside for this process.

B. Introduce the topic to be discussed or information to be gathered or question(s) to be answered. Write this on newsprint and pull it up on a wall so everyone can see it.

C. Introduce the process by reading the following:

In order to ensure that everyone who wants to share has the opportunity to speak, we will proceed in the following way: The leader or a designated person will share first. After that person has spoken, he or she then invites another to share. Whom you invite does not need to be the person next to you. After the next person has spoken, that person is given the privilege to invite another to share. If you don't want to say anything, simply say "pass" and proceed to invite another to share. We will do this until everyone has been invited.

If this is the first time you use this with the group, it will be very awkward at first. The tendency is to give up on the process and go back to the whoever-wants-to-talk-can-talk way. If you are persistent in using this process every time you facilitate the gathering, the group will eventually get used to it and will have great fun with it. A good way to ensure the process goes well the first time is to make sure there are a couple of people in the group who have done this before and, as you begin the process, invite them first.

PROBLEMS TO ANTICIPATE

This process addresses differences in the perception of personal power among the participants. Some people will be eager for their turn, while others will be reluctant to speak when they are invited. If a person speaks very briefly and then does not remember to invite the next person, do not invite for him or her. Simple point out that this person has the privilege to invite the next person to speak. This is especially important if a person "passes." By ensuring that this person still has a privilege to invite, you affirm and value that person independent of that person's verbal ability.

From Eric H. F. Law, *The Wolf Shall Dwell with the Lamb: A Spirituality for Leadership in a Multicultural Community* (St. Louis: Chalice Press, 1993), 113–114. Used by permission.

NOTES

Preface

1. Nora Tubbs Tisdale, sermon, Westminster Conference on Worship and Music, July 8, 2002.
2. Justo González, "Hispanic Creed" in Raquel Mora Martínez, ed., *Mil Voces Para Celebrar: Himnario Metodista* (Nashville: United Methodist Publishing House, 1996), 70.
3. See Nancy T. Ammerman, Jackson W. Carroll, Carl S. Dudley, and William McKinney, eds., *Studying Congregations: A New Handbook* (Nashville: Abingdon, 1998).
4. Kathy Black, *Culturally-Conscious Worship* (St. Louis: Chalice Press, 2000). See also Kathy Black, *Worship Across Cultures: A Handbook* (Nashville: Abingdon, 1998), for a summary of ethnic worship traditions in United Methodist congregations.

Part I

1. To find out about the ethnic/racial population of your area, visit the home page of the United States 2000 census site, <*www.census.gov*>. A careful search will reveal not only the population of your area, but the economic spread, the racial/ethnic constituency, and future population projections for ethnic groups.
2. One of the more articulate cautions against a multicultural perspective in society at large is Arthur M. Schlesinger, Jr., *The Disuniting of America: Reflections on a Multicultural Society*, rev. and enl. (New York: W. W. Norton, 1998). In contrast to Schlesinger's proposal, the church should offer a more visionary and countercultural perspective in society.
3. Karen Ward, "What is culturally-specific worship?" in Gordon Lathrop, ed., *What Does "Multicultural" Worship Look Like?* (Minneapolis: Augsburg Fortress, 1996), 21, explores this distinction.

4. In 1989 Walbert Bühlmann noted that Christians in the "two-thirds" world would outnumber those in the northern world (United States, Canada, Western Europe) 60 percent to 40 percent by the year 2000. See Bühlmann, *With Eyes to See: Church and World in the Third Millennium* (Maryknoll, N.Y.: Orbis, 1990), 7.

5. Quoted in Paul-Gordon Chandler, *God's Global Mosaic: What We Can Learn from Christians Around the World* (Downers Grove, Ill.: InterVarsity Press, 1997), 16.

6. For a description of faithful and vital worship, I refer the reader to the criteria established by Thomas G. Long, *Beyond the Worship Wars: Building Vital and Faithful Community* (Bethesda, Md.: Alban Institute, 2001). Long's criteria relate integrally to the views taken in this book.

7. It may be human nature to associate community with uniformity, whether it be theological, political, racial, or social. The church may be a contributor to cultural fragmentation by sustaining the practice of worshiping in homogeneous interest groups. The drive toward individuality in some segments of society in the United States may also foster a kind of worship for people who want a sense of being with others in church without having to sacrifice their individuality. This practice leads to what Mark Searle calls "shared celebrations rather than common prayer." See Mark Searle, "Private Religion, Individualistic Society, Common Worship," in Eleanor Bernstein, C.S.J., ed., *Liturgy and Spirituality in Context: Perspectives on Prayer and Culture* (Collegeville, Minn.: Liturgical Press, 1990), 37. Francis Mannion is on the same track when he speaks of the "intimization of society" or "the process by which social complexity is eschewed in favor of a model of human coexistence that puts ultimate value on bonds of intimacy, personal closeness, and radical familiarity." M. Francis Mannion, "Liturgy and the Present Crisis of Culture," in *Liturgy and Spirituality in Context: Perspectives on Prayer and Culture*, Eleanor Bernstein, C.S.J., ed. (Collegeville, Minn.: Liturgical Press, 1990), 9.

8. My colleague Mark Stamm reminds me that there may be ecclesial limitations to openness. He poses the possibility that an Anglican may have difficulty being totally open to a believer from the Pentecostal tradition. Both desire a specific ethos in worship that makes it unrealistic for one to worship effectively with the other. The Anglican appreciates the security, structure, and carefully crafted texts of the prayer book, while the Pentecostal seeks a spontaneous communication with the Holy Spirit unfettered by prescribed rites and set liturgies. While I believe Stamm is correct, there are in fact charismatic Christians within the Episcopal Church in the United States; and a new denomination, the Charismatic Episcopal Church, attempts to bridge this gap. It uses *The Book of Common Prayer* but allows for charismatic expressions of piety throughout the liturgy.

9. Let me suggest that you begin with Gordon Lathrop's *Holy People* (Minneapolis: Fortress Press, 1999), and Don Saliers's *Foretaste of Glory Divine* (Nashville: Abingdon, 1994).

10. I prefer the term "co-cultures" to "subcultures" in accordance with Larry A. Samovar, Richard E. Porter, and Lisa A Stefani, *Communicating Between Cultures*, third ed. (Belmont, Calif.: Wadsworth, 1998), 10ff.

11. This description of culture is from a classic definition by Clifford Geertz, *The Interpretation of Cultures* (New York: Basic Books, 1975), 89.

12. Eric H. F. Law, *Inclusion: Making Room for Grace* (St. Louis: Chalice Press, 2000), 42.

13. This useful term comes from Kathy Black, *Culturally-Conscious Worship* (St. Louis: Chalice Press, 2000). Black expresses gratitude to the Rev. Dr. Mary Kraus for the term (p. 11).

14. The "Nairobi Statement on Worship and Culture: Contemporary Challenges and Opportunities" can also be found in S. Anita Stauffer, ed., *Christian Worship: Unity in Cultural Diversity* (Geneva, Switzerland: Lutheran World Federation, 1996), 25–28. This book also places the statement in a fuller context. An earlier book edited by Stauffer, *Worship and Culture in Dialogue* (Geneva, Switzerland: Lutheran World Federation, 1994), provides helpful background for the discussions leading to the Nairobi Statement.

15. "Nairobi Statement on Worship and Culture," *Christian Worship*, 24.

16. "Nairobi Statement." Numbers are added for clarity of *ordo* structure.

17. A description of early Christian worship from the Apologies of Justin (c. 150 C.E.), chapter 67, "Weekly Worship of the Christians," outlines this pattern:

> And on the day called Sunday, all who live in cities or in the country gather together to one place, and the memoirs of the apostles or the writings of the prophets are read, as long as time permits; then, when the reader has ceased, the president verbally instructs, and exhorts to the imitation of these good things. Then we all rise together and pray, and, as we before said, when our prayer is ended, bread and wine and water are brought, and the president in like manner offers prayers and thanksgivings, according to his ability, and the people assent, saying Amen; and there is a distribution to each, and a participation of that over which thanks has been given, and to those who are well to do, and is sent by the deacons. And they who are well to do, and willing, give what each thinks fit; and what is collected is deposited with the president, who succours the orphans and widows, and those who, through sickness or any other cause, are in want, and those who are in bonds, and the strangers sojourning among us, and in a word takes care of all who are in need.

18. Linda J. Clark, Joanne Swenson, and Mark Stamm, *How We Seek God Together: Exploring Worship Style* (Bethesda, Md.: Alban Institute, 2002), 17.

19. Edward T. Hall, *Understanding Cultural Differences* (Yarmouth, Maine: Intercultural Press, 1990), 43–50.

20. Hall, *Understanding Cultural Differences.*

21. Jack Goody, *The Power of Written Tradition* (Washington, D.C.: Smithsonian Institution Press, 2000), 24.

22. For a fuller understanding of this topic, see Geert Hofstede, *Culture's Consequences—International Differences in Work-Related Values,* abridged ed. (New York: Sage Publications, 1987), 65–109.

23. Eric H. F. Law, *The Wolf Shall Dwell with the Lamb: A Spirituality for Leadership in a Multicultural Community* (St. Louis: Chalice Press, 1993), 23–24. See pages 19–27 for Law's complete analysis of Hofstede's concepts of high- and low-power-distance cultures.

24. This information comes from Edward T. Hall, *Beyond Culture* (New York: Anchor/Doubleday, 1976), 85–104. Eric H. F. Law augments Hall's analysis in *The Bush Was Blazing but Not Consumed: Developing a Multicultural Community through Dialogue and Liturgy* (St. Louis: Chalice Press, 1996), 100–111.

25. Law, *The Bush Was Blazing,* 103.

26. Law, *The Bush Was Blazing,* 106.

27. Nancy Tatom Ammerman, *Congregation and Community* (New Brunswick, N.J.: Rutgers University Press, 1997), 335. Ammerman notes that a peaceful congregation is often a declining congregation, whereas a congregation responding to a changing community will naturally have conflict. Constructive conflict is a natural part of congregational change and broadening visions.

28. Black, *Culturally-Conscious Worship,* 67.

29. Black, *Culturally-Conscious Worship,* 36–37.

30. Long, *Beyond the Worship Wars.*

31. In personal correspondence between Thomas Long and the author on Feb. 21, 2002, Long noted that "to say that [the congregations I observed] were culturally diverse embraces a fairly wide range of realities. I think it is fair to say that for all but one of [the congregations in my book], diversity meant that they were mainly composed of a single racial group with a sprinkling of other groups (one was largely Hispanic, two largely African American, the rest mainly white). Only one of the churches was a true United Nations of diversity. But even the mildly diverse ones were more diverse culturally and racially than the average American congregation."

Part II Introduction

1. Charles R. Foster and Theodore Brelsford, *We Are Church Together: Cultural Diversity in Congregational Life* (Valley Forge, Pa.: Trinity Press International, 1996), 17.

Case Study 1

1. *Saving Grace*, publication of Grace United Methodist Church, 1991.
2. *Saving Grace.*

Case Study 2

1. As is the custom in articles written by many Hispanics, "Hispanic" and "Latino"/"Latina" will be used interchangeably in this book.
2. Correspondence with Minerva Carcaño, Sept. 2, 2002.
3. David Maldonado, "Protestantes: An Introduction," in David Maldonado, ed., *Protestantes/Protestants: Hispanic Christianity within Mainline Traditions* (Nashville: Abingdon, 1999), 14.
4. Justo L. González, "Hispanic Worship: An Introduction," in Justo González, ed., *¡Alabadle! Hispanic Christian Worship* (Nashville: Abingdon, 1996), 16.
5. Rubén P. Armendárez, "The Protestant Hispanic Congregation: Identity," in Maldonado, ed., *Protestantes/Protestants*, 241.
6. Armendárez, "Protestant Hispanic."
7. Armendárez, "Protestant Hispanic."
8. Armendárez, "Protestant Hispanic," 244.
9. González, "Hispanic Worship," 10–11.
10. Armendárez, "Protestant Hispanic," 247–248.
11. These themes form the chapters of González's book, *Santa Biblia: The Bible through Hispanic Eyes* (Nashville: Abingdon, 1996).
12. Armendárez, "Protestant Hispanic," 250.
13. Carcaño, correspondence with the author, Sept. 2, 2002.
14. Armendárez, "Protestant Hispanic," 250–251. Carcaño notes, "Inadequacy comes more from the church's institutional racism, which is of course reflected in under-representation and lack of institutional investment in ethnic ministries, as well as the institutional church's lack of openness to the way non-majority cultures approach decision making, worship, community life, etc."
15. Armendárez, "Protestant Hispanic."
16. González, *¡Alabadle!*, 11.

17. Maria Luisa Santillán Baert, "Worship in the Hispanic United Methodist Church," in Justo González, ed., ¡Alabadle!, 59.
18. Santillán Baert, "Worship in the Hispanic."
19. Santillán Baert, "Worship in the Hispanic," 60.
20. Roberto L. Gómez, cited by Santillán Baert, "Worship in the Hispanic," 61.
21. Gómez, cited by Santillán Baert, "Worship in the Hispanic," 62.

Case Study 3

1. See Nancy L. Eiesland, *A Particular Place: Urban Restructuring and Religious Ecology in a Southern Exurb* (New Brunswick, N.J.: Rutgers University Press, 1999), 5.
2. City of Plano, *Demographic Comparison, 1980, 1990 and 2000 Census* (Planning and Information Division, June 18, 2001).
3. Michael O. Emerson, Karen Chai, George Yancey, and Curtiss Paul DeYoung, The Congregations Project, *www.congregations.info/facts.html.* The following is an introduction to the Web site:

> The Congregations Project seeks to better understand America's congregations. We are studying multiracial churches all over the country, the first ever study of its kind. Our aim is to learn what works in such congregations, the joys and struggles, and the similarities with and differences from other congregations. We seek to do this by listening to the voices of those involved in such congregations—by conducting telephone interviews with members, collecting surveys from about 1,000 churches, and making site visits to churches in four diverse cities.
>
> This [Web site] is just one part of our project. On it, we have put the names of churches which identified themselves to us as multiracial. We hope that you will use this site to find churches in your area that are interesting to you.

4. Jeffrey Weiss, "Diverse by Design," *The Dallas Morning News*, Dec. 14, 2002, p. 1G.
5. On niche congregations, see Nancy Tatom Ammerman, *Congregation and Community* (New Brunswick, N.J.: Rutgers University Press, 1997), 36, 130–131.
6. Jeffrey Weiss, "Diverse by Design," p. 1G.
7. The Hispanic Creed may be found in English and Spanish in Raquel Mora Martínez, ed., *Mil Voces Para Celebrar: Himnario Metodista* (Nashville: United Methodist Publishing House, 1996), 69–70.

8. W. E. B. DuBois, *The Souls of Black Folk* (Chicago: A. C. McClurg, 1903 [original ed.]; New York: Bantam Books, 1903, 1989 [republished ed.]), 10.

Part III, Section 1

1. I also find the term used by the World Council of Churches for the musical leaders at its international assemblies, "*animateur,*" to be very attractive. An *animateur* gives life or breath to a gathered body. Unfortunately, the use of a French designation in most parts of North America may put most people off, because the closest English equivalent, "animator," is associated with animated movie features.
2. Michael Warren, *Faith, Culture, and the Worshiping Community: Shaping the Practice of the Local Church,* rev. ed. (Washington, D.C.: Pastoral Press, 1993), 39.
3. Swedish musician Anders Nyberg collected South African freedom songs during the apartheid era in the early 1980s and published them in 1984. He taught young people in Sweden to sing these songs, and they spread throughout Europe, helping to galvanize Europeans in the antiapartheid movement. See the collection edited by Anders Nyberg, *Freedom Is Coming* (Fort Lauderdale, Fla.: Walton Music Corporation, 1984).
4. John Bell, the chief enlivener of the Iona Community in Scotland, explores many reasons why people do not sing in his helpful book *The Singing Thing: A Case for Congregational Song* (Glasgow: Wild Goose Publications, 2000). This small volume is available in the United States through GIA Publications (Chicago).
5. Table of songs cited in part III, section 1.

    Key to hymnals:
    BOP: *Book of Praise* (Presbyterian, Canadian), 1997.
    CH: *Chalice Hymnal* (Christian Church [Disciples of Christ], U.S.), 1995.
    FWS: *The Faith We Sing* (United Methodist hymnal supplement, U.S.), 2000.
    H82: *The Hymnal 1982* (Episcopal Church, U.S.), 1985.
    NCH: *New Century Hymnal* (United Church of Christ, U.S.), 1995
    PH: *Presbyterian Hymnal* (Presbyterian Church [USA]), 1990.
    UMH: *The United Methodist Hymnal* (U.S.), 1989.
    WOV: *With One Voice* (Evangelical Lutheran Church in America hymnal supplement, U.S.), 1995.
    VU: *Voices United* (United Church of Canada), 1996.

    See table of songs on next page.

Song	BOP	CH	FWS	H82	NCH	PH	UMH	WOV	VU
Alleluia, alleluia, give thanks	260			178		106	162	671	
Bless the Lord, my soul (Taizé)		27	2013						
Come, thou almighty King	293	335		365	275	139	61	757	314
Creating God, your fingers trace				394,395	462	134	109		265
Eat this bread (Taizé)	527	414					628	709	466
Father, I adore you	725		2038						
Freedom is coming			2192						
Here, O Lord, your servants gather	250	278			72	465	552		362
I danced in the morning (Lord of the Dance)	592					302	261		352
I, the Lord of sea and sky (Here I Am Lord)	206	452				525	593	752	509
Jesus, remember me (Taizé)	367	569				599	488	740	148
Jesus, the very thought of thee		102		642	507	310	175		
Lord, you have come to the lakeshore (Tú has venido)		342			173	377	344		
Love divine, all loves excelling	371	517		657	43	376	384	784	333
Now thank we all our God	457	715		396,397	419	555	102		236
O Love, how deep	205	220		448,449	209	83	267		348
O sons and daughters				206	244	116,117	317		170
Once in royal David's city	166	165		102	145	49	250		62
One bread, one body	540	393					620	710	467
Sheaves of Summer (Una espiga)		396			338	518	637	708	
Siyahamba (We are marching)	639	442	2235		526			650	646
Tell out, my soul				437,438			200		
The Lord's my shepherd	11	78				170	136		747
The Summons (Will you come and follow me)	634		2130						567
They crucified my Lord							291		141
Were you there	233	198		172	229	102	288		144
When I survey the wondrous cross	231	195		474	224	100,101	298,299	670	149
When Israel was in Egypt's land	708	663		648	572	334	448		
While shepherds watched their flocks	138	154		94,95		58,59	236		
Woman in the night	657	188					274		75
You satisfy the hungry heart	538	429				521	629	711	478

6. John Bell and Graham Maule, "The Summons" in *Heaven Shall Not Wait* (Chicago: GIA Publications, 1987), 102.

Part III, Section 2

1. Nancy Tatom Ammerman, *Congregation and Community* (New Brunswick, N.J.: Rutgers University Press, 1997), 49.
2. Charles Foster, *Embracing Diversity: Leadership in a Multicultural Community* (Bethesda, Md.: Alban Institute, 1997).
3. Ammerman, *Congregation and Community*, 322–323.
4. Ammerman, *Congregation and Community*, 227–228.
5. See specifically the three case studies of Cedar Grove United Methodist Church, Oakhurst Presbyterian Church, and Northwoods United Methodist Church in Charles Foster and Thomas Brelsford, *We Are the Church Together: Cultural Diversity in Congregational Life* (Valley Forge, Pa.: Trinity Press International, 1996).
6. Foster and Brelsford, *We Are the Church Together*, 142.
7. Eric F. H. Law, *The Wolf Shall Dwell with the Lamb* (St. Louis: Chalice Press, 1993), 113–114.
8. For example, see Eric Law, *The Bush Was Blazing but Not Consumed* (St. Louis: Chalice Press, 1996), in which he offers a "Five-Session Intercultural Dialogue Program" and "A Dialogue Process: Focusing on Differences in Communication Styles." While not about worship directly, these processes may establish the kind of base from which multicultural worship planning may take place.
9. See "Liminality" in Nigel Rapport and Joanna Overing, *Social and Cultural Anthropology*, 229–236, for an excellent, concise summary of this term, including reference to rites of passage and anthropologist Victor Turner's original use of the term.
10. *The United Methodist Book of Worship* (Nashville: The United Methodist Publishing House, 1992) provides a sample format for a Love Feast (agape fellowship meal) along with a historical background of this practice in the Moravian Church. I would encourage congregations to examine this pattern and supplement it with rituals that support their unique identity.
11. Mark W. Stamm, "Open Communion as a United Methodist Exception," *Quarterly Review* 22:3 (Fall 2002), 268.
12. Stamm, "Open Communion," 267.
13. See Patrick Kiefert, *Welcoming the Stranger: A Public Theology of Worship and Evangelism* (Minneapolis: Fortress Press, 1992), for more insight into the theological ramifications of this area.
14. Thomas G. Long found that "Vital and faithful congregations have a relatively stable order of service...." See *Beyond the Worship Wars:*

Building Vital and Faithful Worship (Bethesda, Md.: Alban Institute, 2001), 86.

15. This is a reference to part I and Linda J. Clark, Joanne Swenson, and Mark Stamm, *How We Seek God Together: Exploring Worship Style* (Bethesda, Md.: Alban Institute, 2002), 17.

16. C. Gilbert Romero discusses the *quinceañera* in detail in *Hispanic Devotional Piety: Tracing the Biblical Roots* (Maryknoll, N.Y.: Orbis, 1991), 71–82.

17. Thomas Long notes that "vital and faithful congregations move to a joyous festival experience toward the end of their worship services" (*Beyond the Worship Wars*, 95). What better way to achieve this state than through the experience of a joyful Eucharist at the conclusion of each service?

18. Long, *Beyond the Worship Wars*, 78. Long notes that "Vital and faithful congregations have a strong connection between worship and local mission, and this connection is expressed in every aspect of worship."

19. For example, see Justo González, *Santa Biblia: The Bible Through Hispanic Eyes* (Nashville: Abingdon, 1996), for a Hispanic perspective on scripture.

20. Examples of daily prayer structures may be found in several denominational books of worship and are usually very ecumenical regardless of source. See *The United Methodist Book of Worship*, 568–580; *Chalice Worship* (St. Louis: Chalice Press, 1997), 15–22; *Book of Common Worship* (Louisville: Westminster John Knox, 1993), 491–595; *The Book of Common Prayer* (New York: Seabury Press, 1979), 37–146. *A New Zealand Prayer Book: He Karakia Mihinare o Aotearoa* (Auckland: Collins Liturgical Publications, 1989), 27–191, contains particularly effective services of daily prayer.

21. See John R. Levison and Priscilla Pope-Levison, eds., *Return to Babel: Global Perspectives on the Bible* (Louisville: Westminster John Knox, 1999).

22. See Ernesto Cardenal, *The Gospel in Solentiname*, vol. 1 (Maryknoll, N.Y.: Orbis, 1975, 1982), as an example of biblical study with a base community.

23. Law discusses the difficulty that Asians have with speaking in Anglo groups in the United States in *The Wolf Shall Dwell with the Lamb*, chapter 1.

24. Long, *Beyond the Worship Wars*, 61.

25. Long, *Beyond the Worship Wars*, 86.

26. Long, *Beyond the Worship Wars*.

27. Long, *Beyond the Worship Wars*, 93.

28. Jesuit scholar Walter Ong discusses the power of spoken words to shape community. The printed word isolates, while the spoken word builds a

common experience. See especially chapter 3, "Some Psychodynamics of Orality," *Orality and Literacy: The Technologizing of the Word* (New York: Routledge, 1982, 1988).

29. Long, *Beyond the Worship Wars*, 63.
30. Long, *Beyond the Worship Wars*, 64.
31. Nora Tubbs Tisdale, sermon, Westminster Conference on Worship and Music, July 8, 2002.

SELECTED BIBLIOGRAPHY

The following sources explore a wide range of topics and cultural contexts. Culturally conscious congregations should choose those most relevant to their situation. Besides giving a brief description of the focus of the book, I have suggested what group in the church might most benefit from using it.

General Studies

Chandler, Paul-Gordon. *God's Mosaic: What We Can Learn from Christians Around the World*. Downers Grove, Ill.: InterVarsity Press, 2000. This book provides an introductory exposure to various religions of the world, reflecting the author's travels in Christian work and exploring broad themes from selected cultural areas: Eastern Europe, the Middle East, Latin America, the Indian Subcontinent, Africa, East Asia. Good for a Sunday school class or a group at entry level on this topic.

Foster, Charles. *Embracing Diversity: Leadership in Multicultural Congregations*. Bethesda, Md.: Alban Institute, 1997. This book is a practical study guide for learning to lead in diverse congregational settings. Designed for church lay leaders and staff members.

Foster, Charles R., and Theodore Brelsford. *We Are the Church Together: Cultural Diversity in Congregational Life*. Valley Forge, Pa.: Trinity Press International, 1996. This book includes case studies of three congregations that have explored cultural diversity in church life. The text is a realistic look at the challenges and opportunities, with strategies for cross-cultural congregations that would be helpful for planning groups and church leaders.

Gittins, Anthony J. *Gifts and Strangers: Meeting the Challenge of Inculturation*. New York: Paulist Press, 1989. A more theological and theoretical text designed for missionaries, but it may also be helpful as background reading on working with those of differing belief and value systems. It presents

216 Selected Bibliography

important issues for people working in cross-cultural contexts. Helpful for
clergy and lay leaders.

Keifert, Patrick R. *Welcoming the Stranger: A Public Theology of Worship and
Evangelism*. Minneapolis: Fortress Press, 1992. Encourages a hospitable and
welcoming evangelism within liturgical situations. Provides strategies for
welcoming strangers in the context of corporate worship. A theological text
that would benefit church staff and worship committees.

Law, Eric H. F. *Inclusion: Making Room for Grace*. St. Louis: Chalice Press, 2000;
Sacred Acts, Holy Change: Faithful Diversity and Practical Transformation. St.
Louis: Chalice Press, 2002; *The Bush Was Blazing but Not Consumed*. St.
Louis: Chalice Press, 1996; *The Wolf Shall Dwell with the Lamb: A
Spirituality of Leadership in a Multicultural Community*. St. Louis: Chalice
Press, 1993. These four books by Eric Law are helpful in providing a general
perspective on multicultural interactions and group processes. The
theology of each book is biblically based and draws from the author's
extensive experience as a facilitator in multicultural situations. While not
exclusively about worship, each book has direct applications to inclusive
worship. Law comes from the perspective of an Asian American (Hong
Kong) Episcopalian. Essential for ministers and lay leaders planning
multiethnic events in the church.

Levison, John R., and Priscilla Pope-Levison, eds. *Return to Babel: Global
Perspectives on the Bible*. Louisville: Westminster John Knox, 1999. The
editors have brought together African, Asian, and Latin American insights
on 12 biblical passages (six from each of the testaments). Each passage
is examined by writers from each of the three broad ethnic perspectives.
An excellent source for a Sunday school class, pastor, or worship
committee.

Storti, Craig. *The Art of Crossing Cultures*. Yarmouth, Maine: Intercultural Press,
Inc., 1990. Written by a former Peace Corps volunteer and trainer, this brief
text explores general issues in cross-cultural relationships. While not
written from the perspective of the church, it is relevant and accessible as an
introductory resource for study groups in the church and community.

Hispanic/Latino/Latina Studies

González, Justo L. *Mañana: Christian Theology from a Hispanic Perspective*.
Nashville: Abingdon, 1990. An introduction to major theological themes
and how Hispanics experience them. Also serves as a helpful initiation into
the world and history of Hispanics in the United States. Especially helpful
for ministers and advanced theology classes in the church.

González, Justo L. *Santa Biblia: The Bible Through Hispanic Eyes*. Nashville:
Abingdon, 1996. An excellent introduction to the ways biblical narratives
and themes are interpreted from the experience of Hispanics. Explores the

themes of marginality, poverty, mestizaje and mulatez, exiles and aliens, and solidarity. Helpful for laity and clergy.

Maldonado, David, Jr., ed. *Protestantes/Protestants: Hispanic Christianity within Mainline Traditions.* Nashville: Abingdon, 1999. A collection of articles around four themes: historical roots and development, theological perspectives, sociological and contextual dynamics, ministry and congregational realities. Essays are scholarly and drawn from a wide range of Protestant denominational perspectives. An advanced book for ministers and church leaders.

African Studies

Paris, Peter J. *The Spirituality of African Peoples: The Search for a Common Moral Discourse.* Minneapolis: Fortress Press, 1995. An introduction to ethics from a pan-African perspective. The author relates an African worldview to African American realities. An excellent resource for ministers and advanced theological study groups in the church.

Asian Studies

Sugirtharajah, R. S., ed. *Asian Faces of Jesus.* Maryknoll, N.Y.: Orbis, 1993. This book's two parts discuss "Jesus Amid Other Asian Ways, Truths, and Lights," and "Newly Emerging Profiles of Jesus Amid Asia's Poverty and Religious Plurality." An excellent source for understanding how Jesus may be viewed from the diverse cultures and religious pluralism of Asia. A book for ministers and advanced study groups.

Takenaka, Masao, and Ron O'Grady. *The Bible Through Asian Eyes.* Auckland, New Zealand: Pace Publishing and Asian Christian Art Association, 1991. A book of beautiful color illustrations and background information featuring contemporary artists from various parts of Asia. This book would be especially helpful for worship committees that want to have visual representations of biblical narratives that reflect Asian culture.

Worship and Culture: General Studies

Black, Kathy. *Culturally-Conscious Worship.* St. Louis: Chalice Press, 2000. An introduction to worship from a multicultural perspective. The author stresses "kin-dom" (rather than "kingdom") values for the culturally conscious church. A required book for ministers, church musicians, and worship committees exploring cross-cultural worship.

Black, Kathy. *Worship Across Cultures: A Handbook.* Nashville: Abingdon, 1998. A practical resource for worship planners. The author provides sketches from 21 cultural contexts prevalent in United Methodist churches. Chapters follow a similar format for each cultural group, including service of the word, sacramental practices, and rituals of passage (weddings and funerals). While many major ethnic groups in the United States are included, the book is especially strong in Asian and South Pacific cultures.

Blount, Brian K., and Leonora Tubbs Tisdale, eds. *Making Room at the Table: An Invitation to Multicultural Worship*. Lousiville: Westminster John Knox, 2001. A scholarly work that includes sections on biblical foundations for multicultural worship, theological foundations for multicultural worship, and toward multicultural worship today. This is a provocative and informative advanced text for pastors and study groups.

Brink, Emily, ed. *Authentic Worship in a Changing Culture*. Grand Rapids, Mich.: CRC Publications, 1997. This book raises basic issues of culture and worship. Its three parts deal with contemporary forces affecting worship; theological reflections; and questions and answers. The format is designed for general study groups. Though written from a Reformed perspective, it is usable by a broader group.

Clark, Linda J., Joanne Swenson, and Mark Stamm. *How We Seek God Together: Exploring Worship Style*. Bethesda, Md.: Alban Institute, 2002. This book focuses on the nature of worship style and the relationship between style and corporate worship piety. An accompanying video of three New England churches (African American, suburban, and urban) illustrates effectively the authors' thesis. Designed as an accessible resource for worship committees and staff.

Doran, Carol, and Thomas Troeger. *Trouble at the Table: Gathering the Tribes for Worship*. Nashville: Abingdon, 1992. This oft-quoted book by a church musician/seminary professor and a minister/seminary professor provides a well written introduction to the liturgical issues that arise among differing "tribes" in the congregation. An excellent resource for church staff and worship committees.

Francis, Mark R. *Liturgy in a Multicultural Community*. Collegeville, Minn.: Liturgical Press, 1991. This small book is written from a Roman Catholic perspective.

Long, Thomas G. *Beyond the Worship Wars: Building Vital And Faithful Worship*. Bethesda, Md.: Alban Institute, 2001. The author's 10 characteristics of vital and faithful congregations are relevant to culturally conscious congregations. Multicultural examples are used in the book. An excellent source for church staff and worship committees.

Maynard-Reid, Pedrito U. *Diverse Worship: African American, Caribbean, and Hispanic Perspectives*. Downers Grove, Ill.: InterVarsity Press, 2000. The author approaches each of the cultural groups similarly, with a general introduction to each culture's context, music, and ways of expressing the Word. While all cultures are introduced well, the Caribbean section is particularly valuable, as fewer resources are available on this section of the world. A book for parish pastors and musicians.

Schattauer, Thomas, Karen Ward, and Mark Bangert. "What does 'multicultural' worship look like?" in Gordon Lathrop, ed., *Open Questions in Worship*, vol. 7. Minneapolis: Augsburg Fortress, 1996. A small collection of three articles from a Lutheran perspective. Each chapter answers a specific question: How does worship relate to the cultures of North America? What is culturally specific worship? How does one go about multicultural worship? An excellent introductory resource for church staff and worship committees.

African American Worship

Costen, Melva Wilson. *African American Christian Worship*. Nashville: Abingdon, 1993. This has become a classic text on African American worship history and themes. Its strong theological thrust makes it even more helpful in understanding the traditions and cultural forces that have shaped African American worship. A book for church staff and worship committees.

Kirk-Duggan, Cheryl A. *African American Special Days: 15 Complete Worship Services*. Nashville: Abingdon, 1996. A handbook for the church staff and worship committees on special days in the African American tradition, including Children's and Youth Days, Graduation and Promotion Days, Father's and Mother's Days, Pastor's Day, Black History celebrations, and more.

Hispanic/Latino/Latina Worship

Elizondo, Virgilio P., and Timothy M. Matovina. *Mestizo Worship: A Pastoral Approach to Liturgical Ministry*. Collegeville, Minn.: Liturgical Press, 1998. A theological and liturgical resource on *religiosidad popular* (popular religion) among Catholic Hispanics. Explains in a Catholic context, among other topics, the significance of Ash Wednesday, Posada, and Pastorela, and the importance of Our Lady of Guadalupe.

González, Justo L., ed. *¡Alabadle! Hispanic Christian Worship*. Nashville: Abingdon, 1996. This collection of essays covers Hispanic Catholic, Pentecostal, United Methodist, and Baptist worship. It also has an introduction to Hispanic hymnody. A readable source for ministers, musicians, and worship committee members who want to understand the range of Hispanic worship experiences.

Romero, C. Gilbert. *Hispanic Devotional Piety: Tracing the Biblical Roots*. Maryknoll, N.Y.: Orbis, 1991. The author provides biblical foundations for some of the most common manifestations of *religiosidad popular* or devotional piety outside established Catholic rituals. These include Ash Wednesday, the Quinceañera, the home altar, and the Penitentes, a penitential tradition especially strong in New Mexico. Helpful for ministers working in Latino communities.

Music and Culture: General Studies

Bangert, Mark P. "Liturgical Music, Culturally Tuned." In *Liturgy and Music: Lifetime Learning,* edited by Robin A. Leaver and Joyce Ann Zimmerman, 360–383. Collegeville, Minn.: Liturgical Press, 1998. The author provides a synopsis of African, African American, Latino/Hispanic, and Asian musical styles. He calls into question some of the basic western musical assumptions about music making and encourages readers to retune their ears for a broader understanding of music and its possibilities. An article for church musicians.

Corbitt, J. Nathan. *The Sound of the Harvest: Music's Mission in Church and Culture.* Grand Rapids, Mich.: Baker Books, 1998. The author's experiences as an ethnomusicologist and a missionary come together as he examines the various roles that music plays within culture in the service of evangelism. These include music as priest, prophet, proclaimer, healer, preacher, and teacher. This book provides a blueprint for church musicians who want to reconceive their ministry in cultural and evangelistic terms.

Farlee, Robert Buckley, ed. *Leading the Church's Song.* Minneapolis: Augsburg Fortress, 1998. A practical book on musical styles with examples on CD, this book focuses on helping the church musician perform various musical styles in an authentic manner. Includes western and nonwestern musical examples.

Hawn, C. Michael. *Gather into One: Praying and Singing Globally.* Grand Rapids, Mich.: Wm. B. Eerdmans, 2003. This book takes an in-depth look at five church musicians from around the world who have had an influence on hymnals and congregational song in the United States since 1990: John Bell (Scotland), David Dargie (South Africa), Patrick Matsikenyiri (Zimbabwe), I-to Loh (Taiwan), and Pablo Sosa (Argentina). The author also suggests the skills needed by musical leaders to enliven global congregational song in the 21st century. A book for the church musician.

Reck, David. *Music of the Whole Earth.* New York: Da Capo Press, 1997. A comprehensive book (545 pages) on global musical cultures and musical instruments. While valuable to the musician who wants to understand more about the music from specific areas of the world, it is written so that the musical layperson may also benefit from it. Full of graphics and pictures, it is everything that the novice would want to know about world (earth) music.

African American Music

Abbington, James. *Let Mt. Zion Rejoice! Music in the African American Church.* Valley Forge, Pa.: Judson Press, 2001. A guide for church musicians functioning in African American contexts. In addition to many practical considerations, chapters are included on "The Current State of Music in the African American Church," "Hymnody in the Church," "Anthems in the Church," "The Spiritual as Congregational Music," and "The African American Christian Year."

Boyer, Horace Clarence. *How Sweet the Sound: The Golden Age of Gospel.* Washington, D.C.: Ellliott & Clark Publishers, 1995. A comprehensive and readable guide to African American music since the middle of the 18th century to the late 20th century. The majority of the book focuses on gospel music between 1945 and 1965.

McClain, William B. *Come Sunday: The Liturgy of Zion. A Companion to Songs of Zion.* Nashville: Abingdon, 1990. A standard work on the role of music in the African American church. This book accompanies the ground-breaking African American hymnal, *Songs of Zion* (1981). It provides helpful information on the meaning behind African american spirituals.

Reagon, Bernice Johnson, ed. *We'll Understand It Better By and By: Pioneering African American Gospel Composers.* Washington, D.C.: Smithsonian Institution Press, 1992. This book contains the text of a series of videos aired on PBS. One of the most informative sources on gospel music in the 20th century.

Walker, Wyatt Tee. *"Somebody's Calling My Name": Black Sacred Song and Social Change.* Valley Forge, Pa.: Judson Press, 1979. A classic, comprehensive history of African American sacred music and its role in political movements.

CONTRIBUTORS

C. Michael Hawn has been on the faculty of Perkins School of Theology, Southern Methodist University, since 1992 in the areas of church music and worship. He previously taught at two Baptist seminaries and served as a church musician in congregations throughout the South. He has published over 80 articles and two collections of congregational songs.

Justo L. González, a United Methodist minister born in Cuba, is a retired member of the Río Grande Conference of the United Methodist Church. After his basic college and seminary education in Cuba, he came to study at Yale University, where he obtained the S.T.M., M.A., Ph.D. degrees. In 1969 he moved to Atlanta, where he now resides, to teach at Candler School of Theology (Emory University). He has published over 70 books, as well as hundreds of articles, both at the academic and at the popular level. His has also long promoted the theological education of Latinas and Latinos and has been involved in numerous organizations that support those efforts.

Edwin David Aponte is assistant professor of Hispanic Christianity and culture at Perkins School of Theology, Southern Methodist University, Dallas. He is an ordained minister of the Presbyterian Church (PCUSA).

Evelyn Parker is assistant professor of Christian education at Perkins School of Theology, Southern Methodist University, Dallas. A member of the Christian Methodist Episcopal Church (CME), she has conducted research on the spiritual formation of African American girls.

Susan Knipe and Robin Stevens are students in the master of divinity program at Perkins School of Theology, Southern Methodist University, Dallas. Both women are preparing for ordination in the United Methodist Church.

Marcia McFee combines experience in the arts, performance, and liturgical studies in her work of training worship leaders. She has taught workshops across the U.S., Europe and Asia, and has worked professionally with theater and dance companies. Author of *The Worship Workshop* (Abingdon, 2002), McFee earned a master of theological studies at Saint Paul School of Theology, Kansas City, Missouri.